For Frank Luther Mott (1886 - 1964)

America's Greatest Magazine Historian
with Gratitude and Respect

Very Special Acknowlegement to Suze Bienaimee

Copyright 2014, Steven Lomazow, M.D.

Foreword

Over the years, I have written four short, profusely illustrated books and created one lecture about various topics in magazine history using images from periodicals acquired over forty years of intensive collecting. They appear on my blog (magazinehistory.blogspot.com) and website (thegreatamericanmagazine.com). Many of the magazines are quite rare and each has its own story of acquisition at a book, ephemera or pulp fiction fair, online marketplace, auction, or the dusty shelves of long extinct antiquarian bookshops in countless corners of America.

The books have over fifty-thousand combined downloads and page views. Now the time is ripe to publish them in a permanent volume for those who still derive pleasure from the rapidly disappearing pastime of reading from actual pieces of paper.

Periodically yours,

Steven Lomazow, M.D.
West Orange, New Jersey
2014

Table of Contents

Eighteenth Century 9

Literature 33

Movies... 103

Radio and Television 133

America at War 155

THE GREAT AMERICAN MAGAZINE

The Eighteenth Century

Steven Lomazow, M.D.

THE GREAT AMERICAN MAGAZINE

The Eighteenth Century

by
Steven Lomazow, M.D.
Montclair, New Jersey

2005

Since the very beginning of things truly American, magazines have been the most comprehensive documentation. No aspect of the broad spectrum of American popular culture has escaped their uniquely comprehensive, textual and visual eye. As America grew, so did the scope of its magazines. In the 18th Century, about 80 magazines were published, with few lasting more than a handful of issues. From 1800 to 1809 there were 136 in 40 cities and in the next decade there were 282 in eighteen states.

Initially, the distinction between magazines and newspapers was not clear. Newspapers were generally issued weekly and magazines were mostly monthlies, but there were many exceptions. Newspapers often included literary content and magazines frequently paid considerable attention to current events.

This little volume is intended as both an overview and a visually tantalizing supplement to the study of the early American periodicals. For more comprehensive information, the following references are suggested:

Evans, Charles, <u>American Bibliography</u>. Privately printed, Chicago, 1903-1955.
The masterwork for all American printing prior to 1800.

Lewis, Benjamin M. <u>A Guide to Engravings in American Magazines</u>. 1741-1810. New York, New York Public Library, 1959.

Mott, Frank Luther. <u>A History of American Magazines</u>. Cambridge, Harvard University Press. 5 Volumes. Issued irregularly, 1930-1955.
Any study of American periodicals begins here.

Richardson, Lyon N. <u>A History of Early American Magazines, 1741-1789</u>. New York, Thomas Nelson and Sons, 1931.
By far, the most comprehensive and informative treatise on this topic.

Thomas, Isaiah. <u>The History of Printing in America</u>. Various editions, first published in 1810.

Zinman, Michael. <u>18th Century Engravings From American Magazines</u>. Ardsley, N.Y. Privately printed, 1994.

All illustrations are from the personal collection of the author. Additional titles are anticipated as part of a comprehensive American Periodical Series. Copies of
American Periodicals. A Collector's Manual and Reference Guide, 1996
are available for purchase for on my website, thegreatamericanmagazine.com.
Dr. Lomazow can be contacted at
drlomazow@gmail.com
(973) 751-5643

With this issue of his *New York Weekly Journal*, John Peter Zenger initiated the debate over freedom of the press in America. His controversial writings brought about his trial and imprisonment by the colonial government and laid the groundwork for a basic tenet of democracy, later codified in the First Amendment to the Constitution.

The idea for the first magazine to be published in America was conceived by Benjamin Franklin. Andrew Bradford's *American Magazine, or, Monthly View of the Political State of the British Colonies* beat him to press by three days in January, 1741, and stole the credit.

The first use of the word "magazine" in the context of a "storehouse" of information, was in *Gentleman's Magazine*, first published in London in 1731.

The Great American Magazine: Eighteenth Century

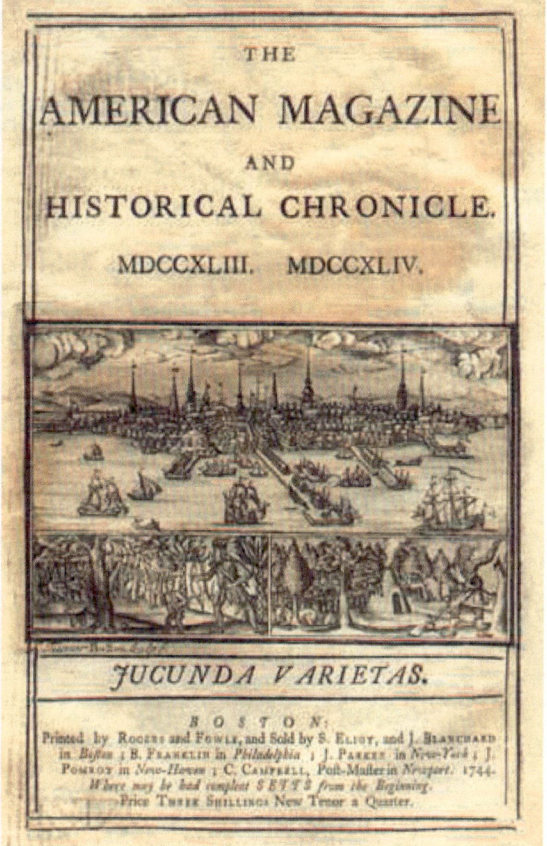

The first magazine in America to last more than one year was *The American Magazine and Historical Chronicle*, published in Boston between 1743 and 1746. It is most collected for its early, rare and valuable engravings.

The issue on the upper left also features the first map published in an American magazine, a plan of the Battle of Louisbourg. Note that the magazine was distributed in Philadelphia by none other than Benjamin Franklin!

America's fifth magazine and the first devoted to religious matters, *The Christian History*, was started by Jonathan Edwards in 1743 to report "Accounts of the Propagation and Revival of Religion".

15   The Great American Magazine: Eighteenth Century

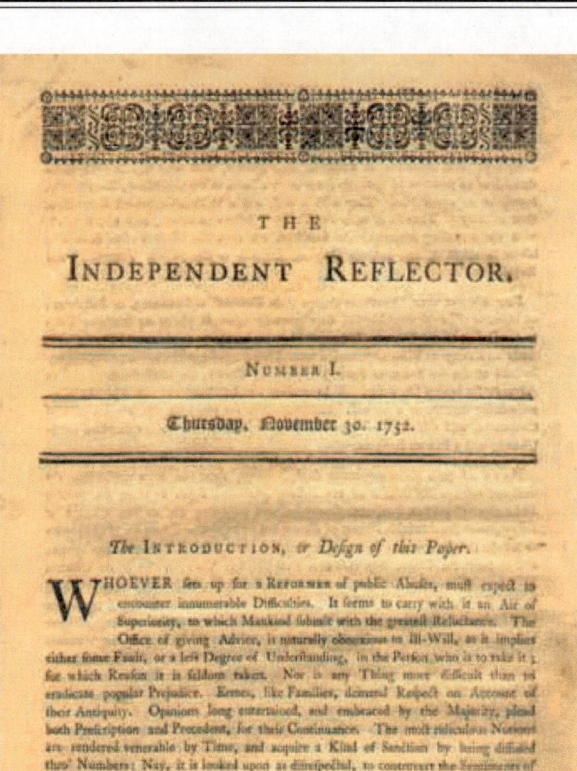

The first magazine published in New York was *The Independent Reflector*, in 1752, edited by William Livingston, subtitled "Weekly Essays on Sundry Important Subjects More Particularly Adapted to the Province of New York". Apparently, these essays were not to the liking of the local government, which banned it. Livingston eventually moved across the river to New Jersey and became its first Governor and a signer of the Declaration of Independence.

New Jersey's first magazine, *The New American Magazine*, appeared in 1758.

The Great American Magazine: Eighteenth Century

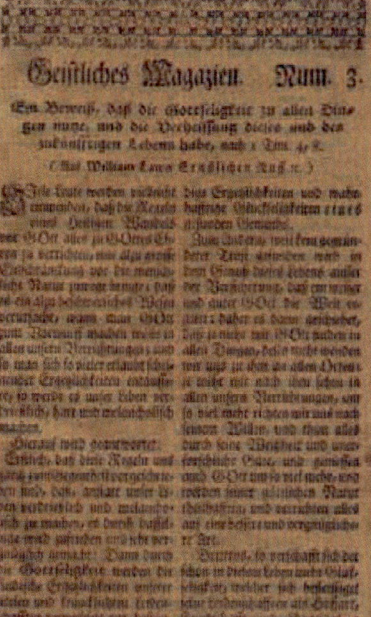

Geistliches Magazien appeared in 1764 for the Pennsylvania Germans. It was printed with the first German type cast in America.

The American Magazine, and Monthly Chronicle for the British Colonies, was published during the French and Indian War. Its title page contains perhaps the first American political cartoon.

The Bee, published in 1765, is considered the first American periodical of politcal satire. The local government didn't get the joke and banned it after three issues!

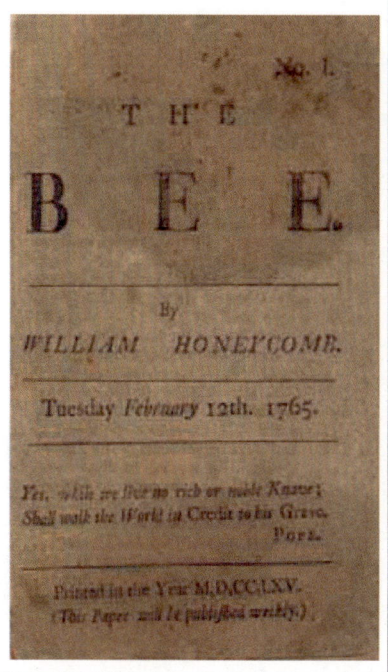

17 The Great American Magazine: Eighteenth Century

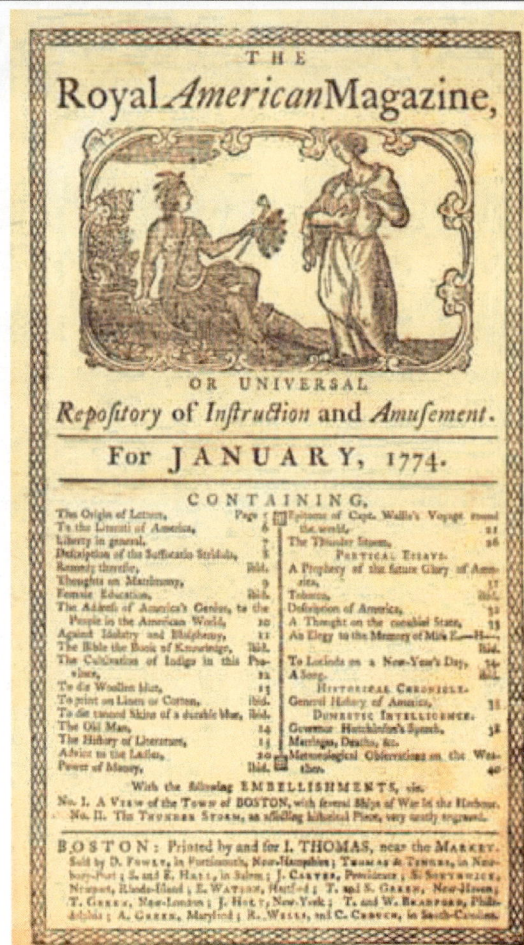

The Royal American Magazine,

initially edited by Isaiah Thomas, was the only American magazine being published just prior to the start of the Revolution. Its pro-colonies stance helped fuel the fires of independence, in large part due to the provocative illustrations engraved by Paul Revere. Like other magazines of this era, it was issued in decorative wrappers, usually containing advertising, which were rarely preserved during binding.

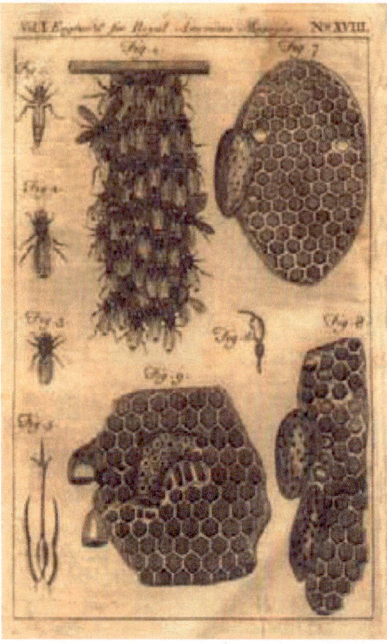

December 1774.
The earliest American reference to Bees, engraved by Revere.

The Great American Magazine: Eighteenth Century

"The Able Doctor" (June 1775) was adapted by Revere from a British cartoon. John Hancock (March 1775) and Samuel Adams (April 1775) were of obvious importance to the cause of liberty.

The Great American Magazine: Eighteenth Century

Pennsylvania Magazine, edited by Thomas Paine, was the only magazine published during the Revolutionary War. A true and consistent advocate of independence, It featured engravings of battles, important original maps and the slave Phillis Wheatley's "Ode to George Washington", the first literary contribution by an African-American published in America. The last issue (July 1776) features the only contemporary magazine printing of the Declaration of Independence.

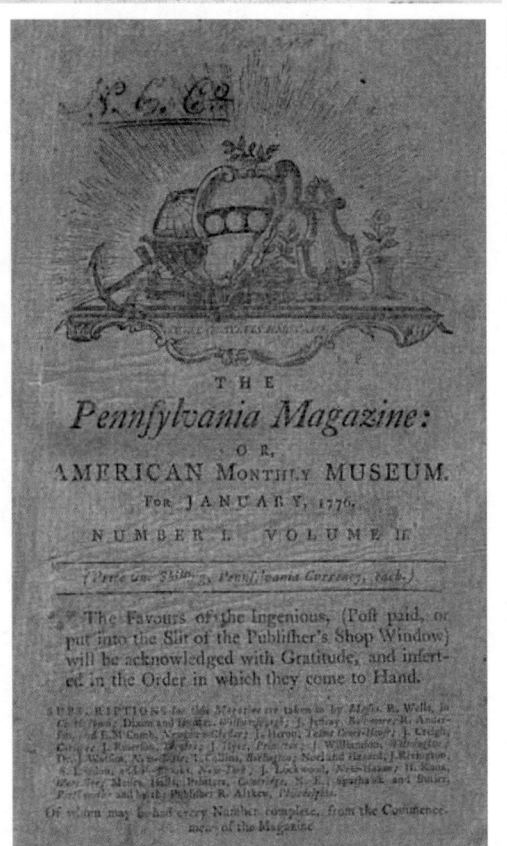

The Great American Magazine: Eighteenth Century

The Battle of Bunker Hill,
published September, 1775

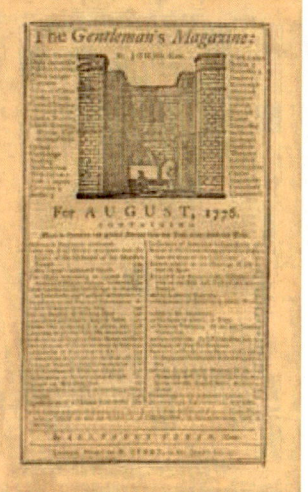

The British learned about the American rebellion one month later, with a slightly different editorial slant!

This is the first American map of Virginia, published in April 1776, and one of very few prior to the establishment of the national capital.

21 The Great American Magazine: Eighteenth Century

Images of George Washington appeared in American magazines nine times during his lifetime. Since newspapers did not contain illustrations, this was the only easily accessible way for the public to see what their hero and president actually looked like! The often regal poses reflected the esteem and respect he was held in and, undoubtedly, enhanced them as well.

Columbian Magazine
January 1787

Philadelphia Monthly Magazine
January 1798

Monthly Military Repository
1796

American Museum was sparsely illustrated compared to *Columbian*.
The few engravings that were published were highly important, including Benjamin Franklin's map of the Gulf Stream and this graphic and disturbing image published in 1789 in conjunction with
"Remarks on the Slave Trade".

The Great American Magazine: Eighteenth Century

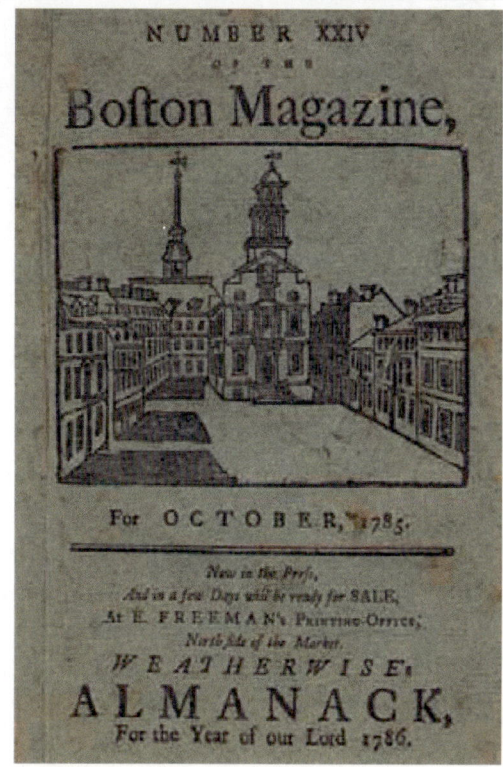

Boston Magazine was the first to be published after the Revolutionary War. Its illustrations included portraits of Franklin and the first successful balloon flight.

January 1784

February 1784

The American Eagle provides a handsome wrapper illustration for the rare *Gentlemen and Ladies' Town and Country Magazine*.

23   The Great American Magazine: Eighteenth Century

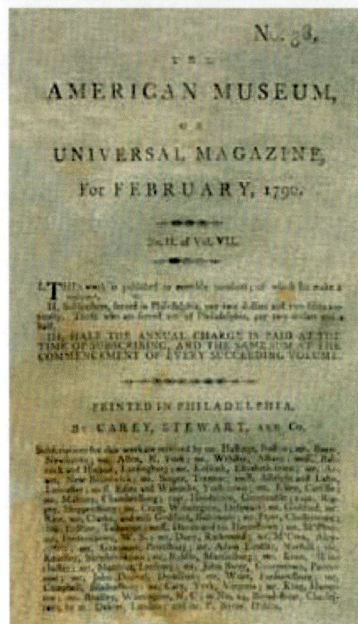 

The four most widely circulated magazines in America in the eighteenth century were Matthew Carey's *American Museum*, which proudly listed George Washington among its subscribers (the issue shown here contains the only magazine appearance of the Bill of Rights), *Columbian Magazine*, which published a wide variety of articles illustrated with many notable engravings (this issue contains one of the four contemporary magazine printings of the United States Constitution), Isaiah Thomas' *Massachusetts Magazine* and *New York Magazine,* both of which provided miscellaneous content, good illustration and lasted nearly a decade.

One of the last illustrations published in *Columbian Magazine* was the first printing of L'Enfant's plan of the City of Washington in 1792, engraved by Thackara and Vallance.

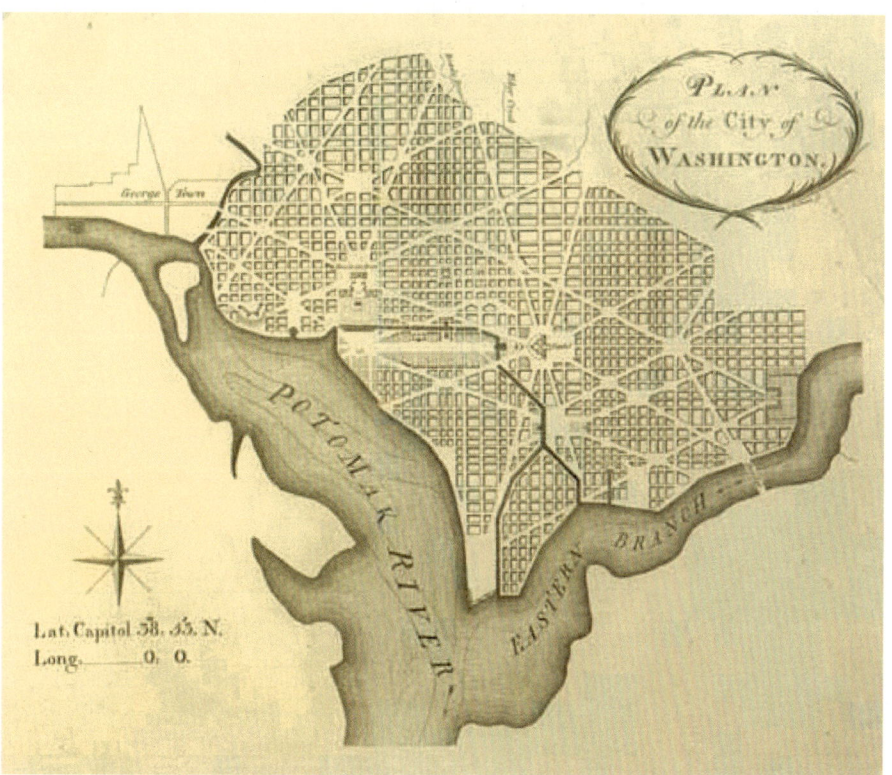

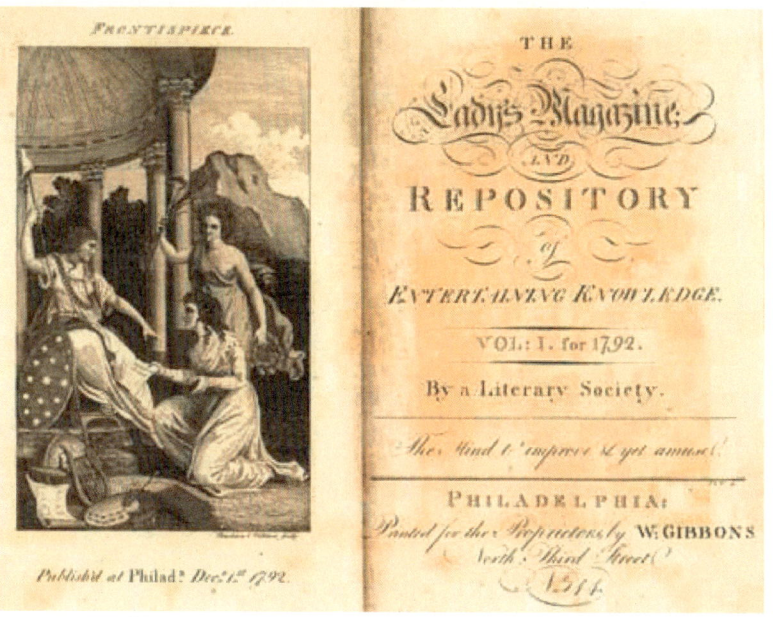

The first magazine published exclusively for ladies appeared in 1792.

25 The Great American Magazine: Eighteenth Century

The New Haven Gazette and Connecticut Magazine was an amalgum of a newspaper and a magazine. The news of the week of this issue is the United States Constitution, which is featured prominently on the front page.

Worcester Magazine is really a newspaper printed to look like a magazine. Editor Isaiah Thomas changed his newspaper *The Massachusetts Spy* to this title and format in protest of an increase in postal rates for newspapers. This issue also contains one of four contemporary magazine printings of the Constitution.

These 1787 views of Gray's Ferry, Pennsylvania and Christ's Church are fine examples of the dozens of well-accomplished engravings published in *The Columbian Magazine*.

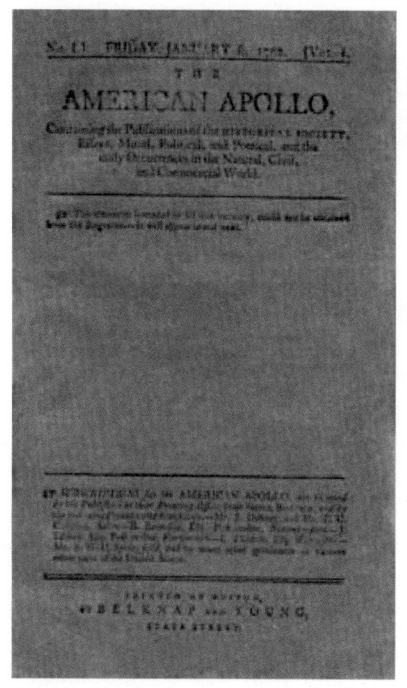

The publisher's of American Apollo, a general interest magazine, were so anxious to put out their first issue that they weren't able to include the cover engraving! As promised, it appeared on the second issue.

27 The Great American Magazine: Eighteenth Century

This is probably America's first commercial periodical

The Congressional Register is still the official record of the proceedings of the federal legislature.

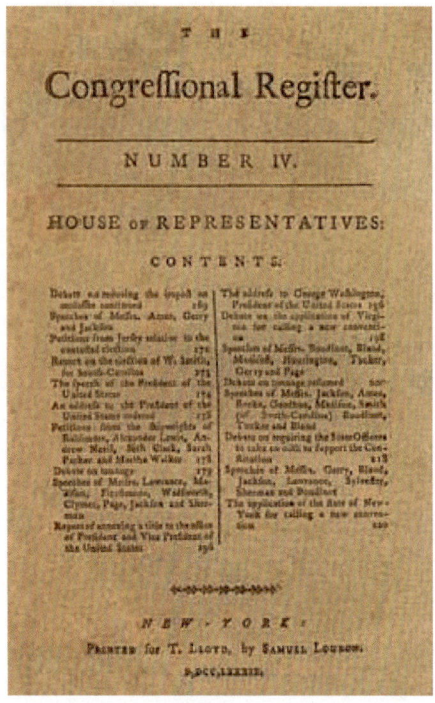

The Farmer's Almanac first appeared in 1793. It's still around, in pretty much the same form, 212 years later!

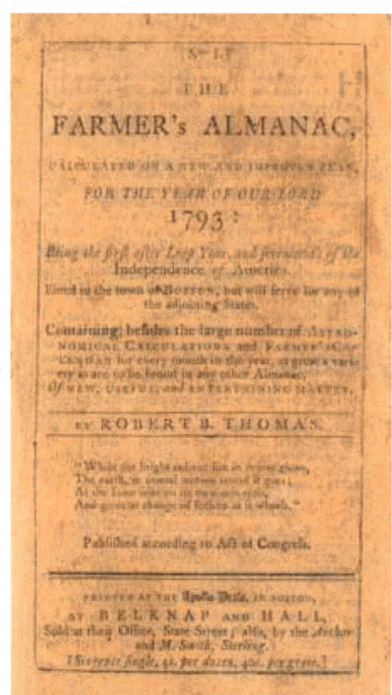

National Magazine, the first magazine published in Virginia, was brought about largely in response to the imprisonment of editor James Lyon's brother under the Alien and Sedition Acts. *Medical Repository* was America's first medical journal.

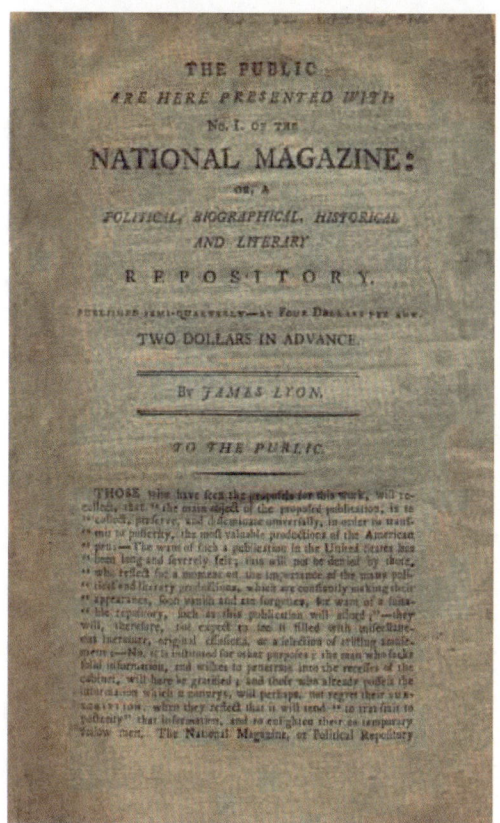

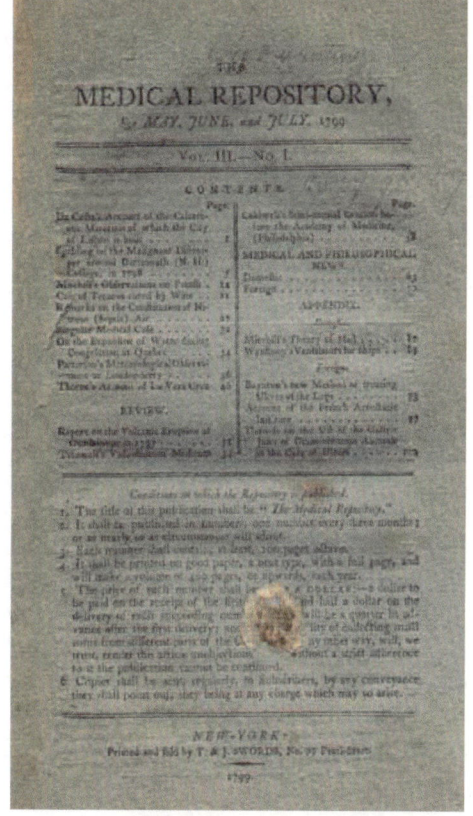

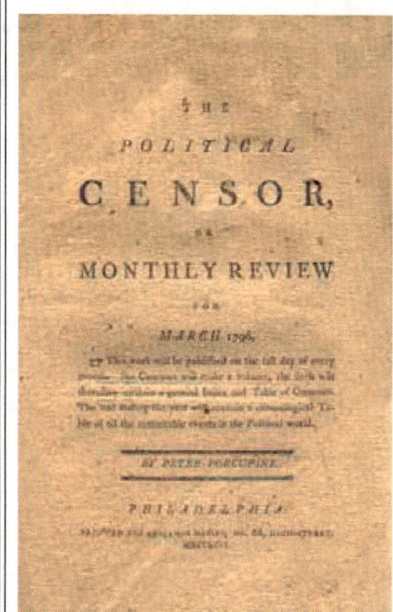

Political Censor, the first magazine devoted to politics, was one of a number of periodicals edited by British expatriate William Cobbett under the pseudonym Peter Porcupine.

Weekly Magazine, primarily literary in content, was edited by America's first man of letters, Charles Brockden Brown, and published his novels in serial form.

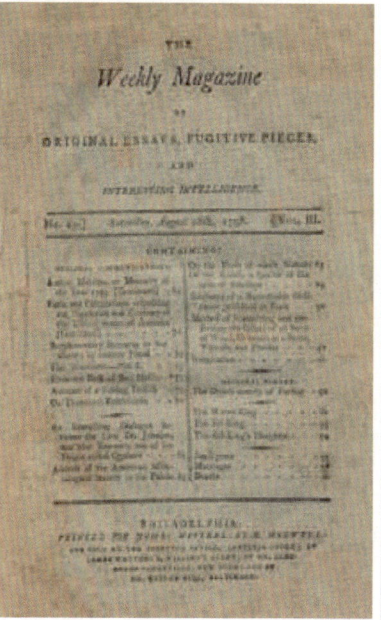

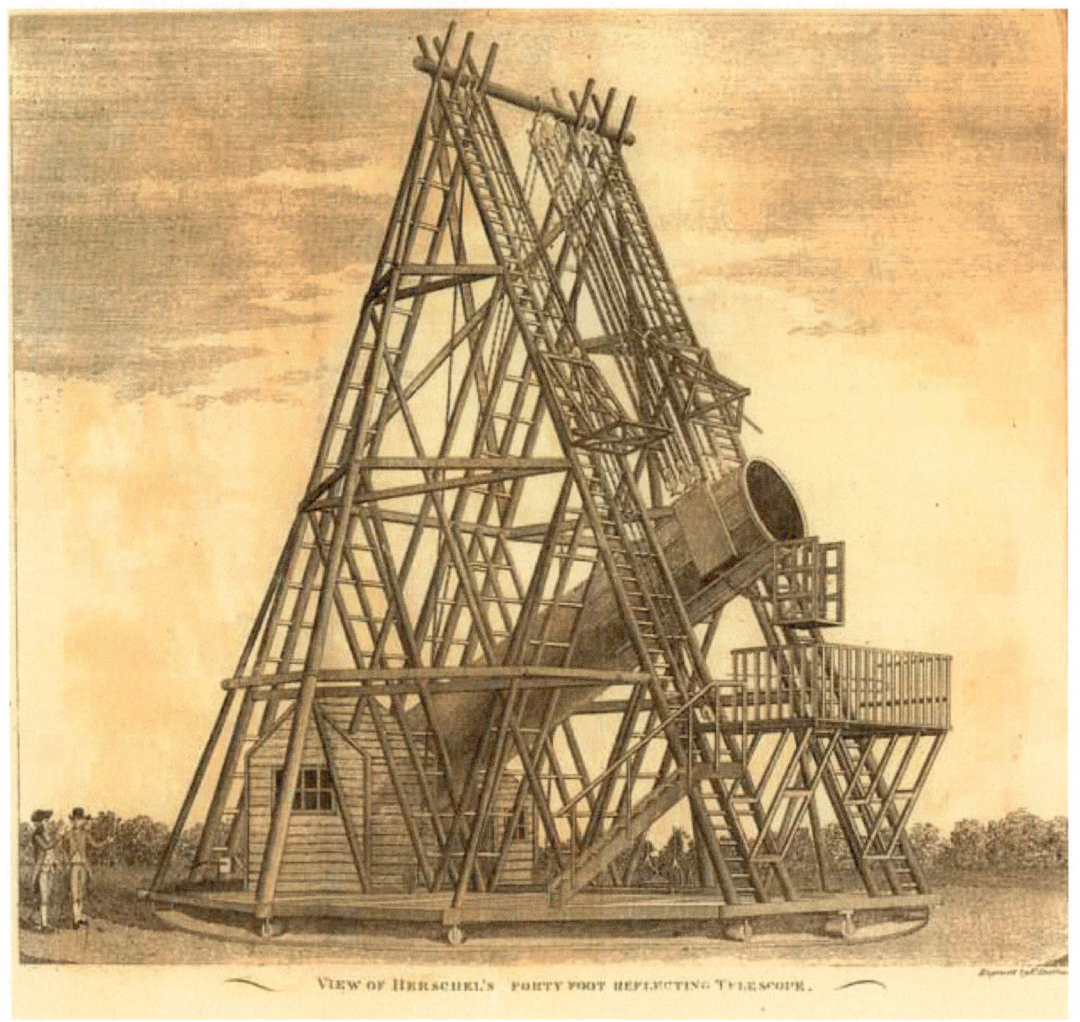

This large and skillfully produced engraving of Herschel's telescope adorned the first issue of *Literary Museum*, published in West Chester, Pennsylvania in 1797.

THE ANALECTIC MAGAZINE:
THE SELECT REVIEWS
SPIRIT OF FOREIGN MAGAZINES
NEW MASSES
The Lark
THE YELLOW KID
NORTH-AMERICAN REVIEW
MISCELLANEOUS JOURNAL.
HARVARDIANA.
VOLUME IV.—NO. VI.
CAMBRIDGE:
PUBLISHED BY JOHN OWEN.
The American Magazine
by Brother Jonathan
Steven Lomazow, M.D.
THE NEW YORKER
The Saturday Review of Literature
THE RED BOOK
ILLUSTRATED
MAY 1903
THE GREAT TEN PENNY SHORT STORY MAGAZINE
THE RED BOOK CORPORATION
THE DIAL
THE LITTLE REVIEW
A MAGAZINE OF THE ARTS
POKER CHIPS
A MONTHLY MAGAZINE
5 CENTS
AMERICAN
Literary
MAGAZINE
THE ALL-STORY
Tarzan of the Apes
PLAYBOY

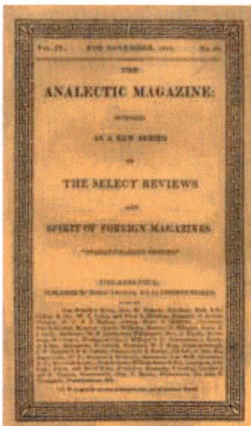

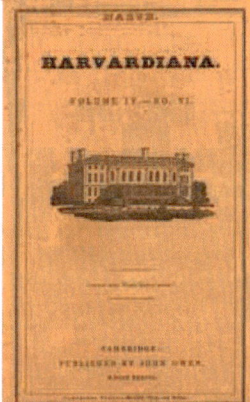

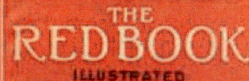

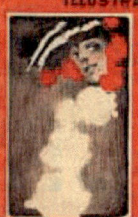

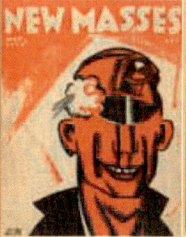

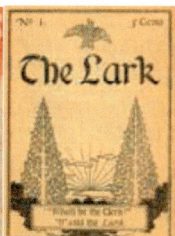

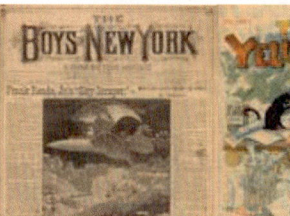

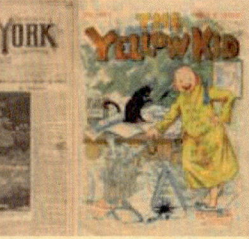

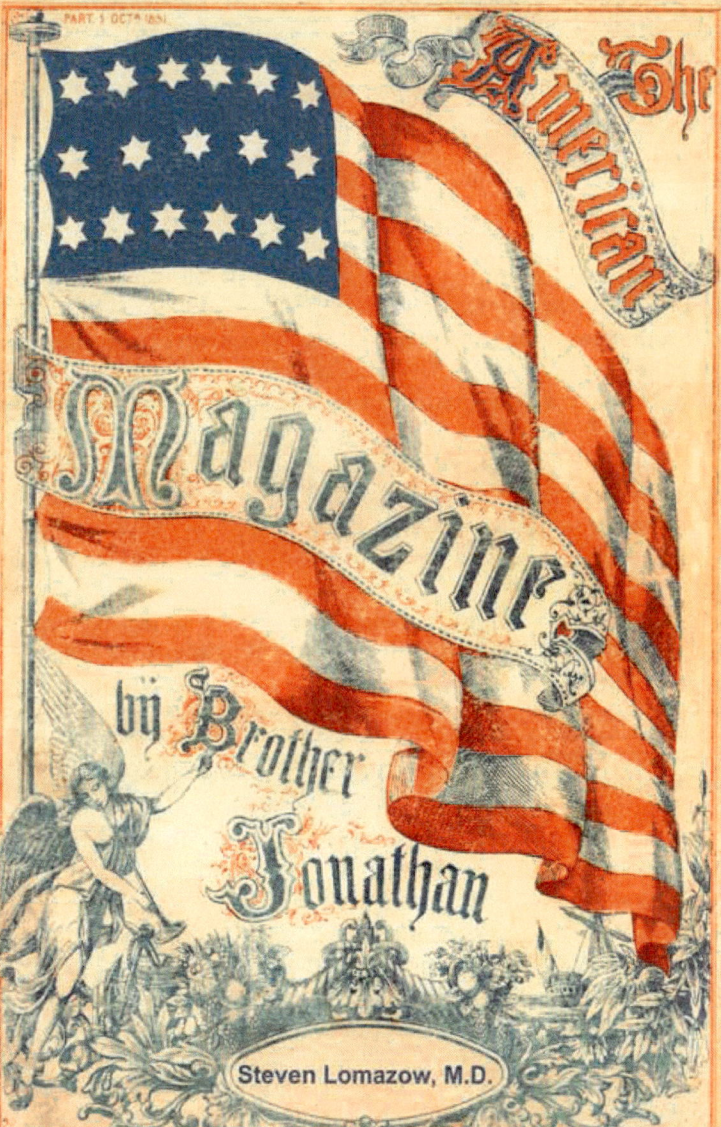

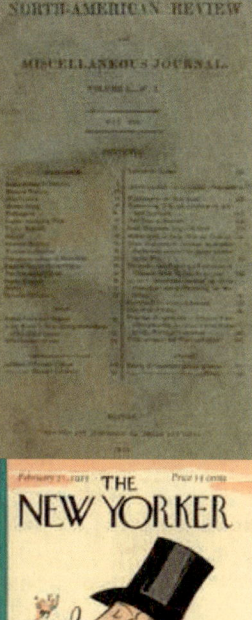

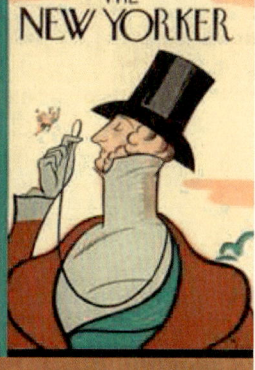

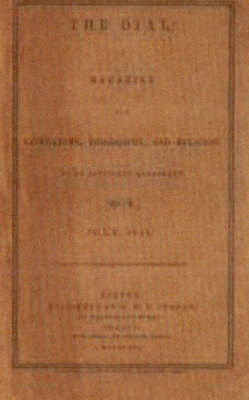

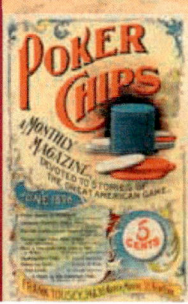

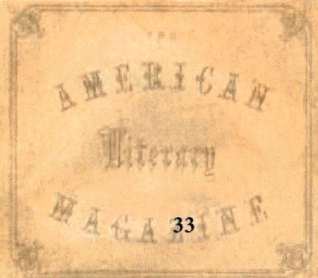

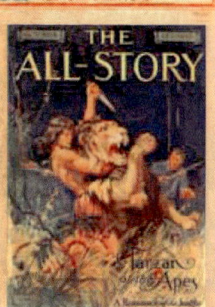

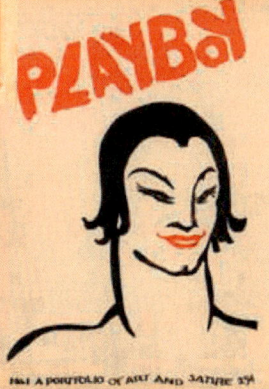

Foreword

Since the very beginning of American literature, magazines have been an important vehicle, giving opportunities for young authors and poets to put their works into the public forum and as a medium for the established writers as well. At one time or another, every important literary figure has been a contributor. Some have had fleeting associations yet many of the major American literary icons, such as Edgar Allan Poe, Mark Twain, Walt Whitman and Ernest Hemingway, were intimately associated with periodicals throughout their careers. American magazines often gave the first opportunities for American expatriates and foreign masters like Ezra Pound and James Joyce to display their talents as well.

Not infrequently, as with "Ulysses" which was banned prior to completion, a work was first serialized in a magazine prior to book publication. The first appearance of parts of "Uncle Tom's Cabin" "Walden" "Moby Dick" "Tom Sawyer" "Huckleberry Finn" and "Leaves of Grass", to mention a few, all were in magazines. Oscar Wilde's "Picture of Dorian Gray", Sir Arthur Conan Doyle's "The Sign of Four", Edgar Rice Burrough's "Tarzan of the Apes", Dashiell Hammett's "The Thin Man", John Hersey's "Hiroshima" and Ernest Hemingway's "The Old Man and the Sea" were all published in their entirety in a single issue of a magazine prior to the book form.

In this authors opinion, antiquarian book dealers and collectors have yet to appreciate the rarity and importance of periodicals. Only "Tarzan" carries a monetary value close to the later first book edition. A first book edition of "Ulysses" is many times more expensive than the far rarer and more fragile magazine first appearance four years earlier.

For those interested in American culture, magazines are invaluable. The way Americans think, the preferences they have and the beliefs they hold are often determined though the literature they read. For example, the ephemeral yet highly circulated story paper and dime novels of the second half of the nineteenth century are largely responsible for the present day American zeal for sensationalism, crime and western fiction. Relatively unknown figures such as Robert Bonner, Ned Buntline and Richard K. Fox have made a profound effect on how Americans think today. This fact is only now starting to be appreciated, largely through the study of the periodical literature.

While writing this work, the author continually found himself using the term "rare" or "extremely scarce" in describing the material displayed, often wondering if he was overusing the term. In fact, many of these items are encountered only once or a few times in an avid book collectors lifetime and many of even the finest collections and institutions do not have representations. Much more than books, magazines are ephemera, and are indeed rare. This work is the denouement of twenty-five years of voracious collecting. New information and insight into the scope and importance of the American literary periodical is ongoing.

Steven Lomazow, M.D.
Montclair. New Jersey
2005

In the 18th Century, some fiction, primarily of British authorship, was included in the miscellaneous magazines of the day. The first principally literary effort was *American Monthly Review, or, Literary Journal*, published in Philadelphia in 1795.

America's first man of letters was Charles Brockden Brown. His novel, "Arthur Mervyn", first appeared serially in *The Weekly Magazine* of Philadelphia. Brown edited a series of unsuccessful magazines that published his writing along with those of other contemporary authors. The first was *Monthly Magazine and American Review*, started in 1799.

The Weekly Magazine ceased publication when its editor, James Watters, died in the plague of 1798.

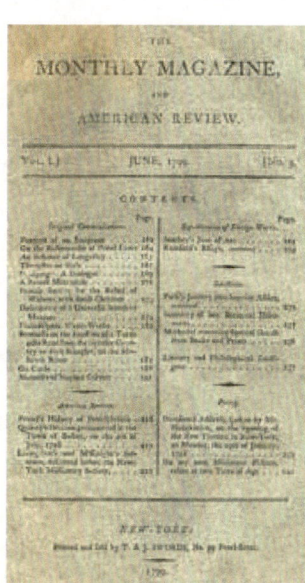

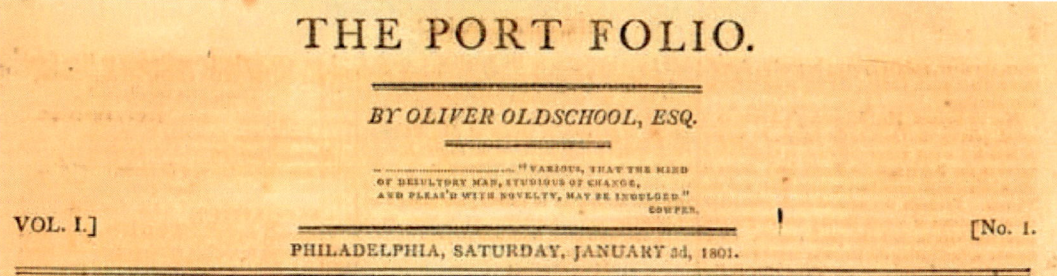

The most important American magazine of the first decade of the nineteenth century was *The Portfolio*.

It was edited by Joseph Dennie, "The Lay Preacher", under the pseudonym Oliver Oldschool. The opening article "A Journal of a Tour Through Silesia" was the work of John Quincy Adams.

Dennie's diatribes against Thomas Jefferson in *The Portfolio* precipitated his arrest and trial for sedition. He was acquitted.

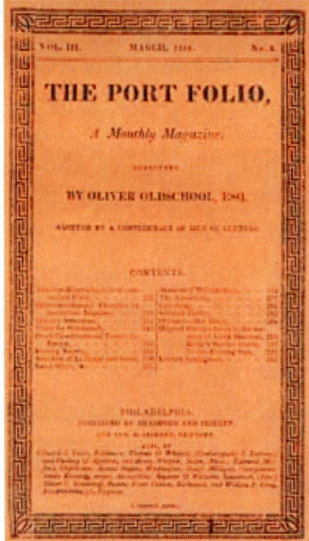
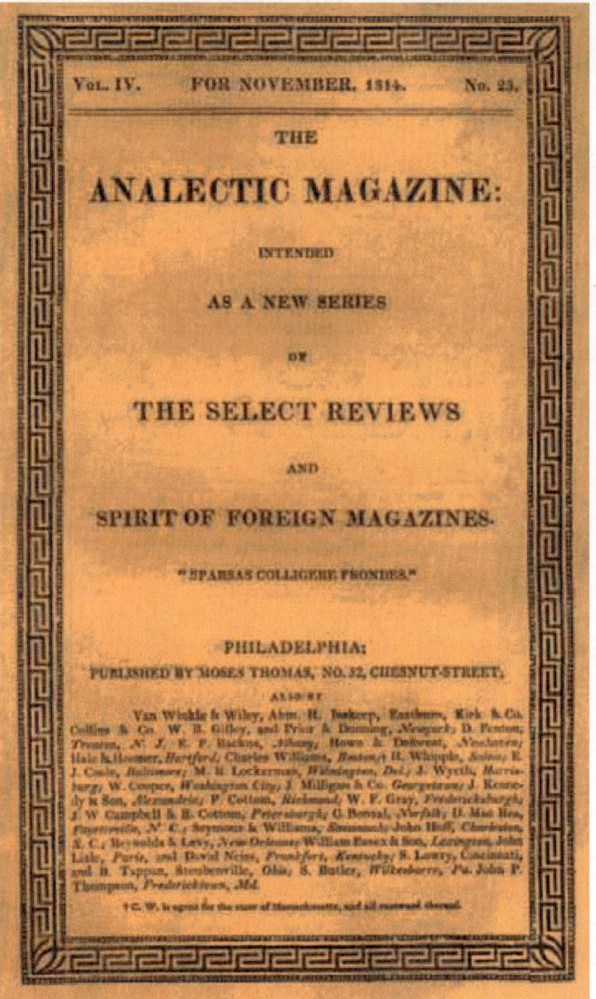

After Dennie's death in 1812, *Portfolio* continued publication and was joined in prominence in the second decade by *The Analectic Magazine*, initially edited by Washington Irving. In its November 1814 issue, *Analectic* published an unattributed poem, "Defence of Fort McHenry", which had previously appeared only in a few local newspapers. As its popularity grew, Francis Scott Key's epic verse, designed to be sung to an old English drinking song, was adopted as our national anthem "The Star Spangled Banner"

DEFENCE OF FORT M'HENRY.

[These lines have been already published in several of our newspapers; they may still, however, be new to many of our readers. Besides, we think that their merit entitles them to preservation in some more permanent form than the columns of a daily paper. The annexed song was composed under the following circumstances.—A gentleman had left Baltimore, in a flag of truce for the purpose of getting released from the British fleet a friend of his who had been captured at Marlborough. He went as far as the mouth of the Patuxent, and was not permitted to return lest the intended attack on Baltimore should be disclosed. He was, therefore, brought up the bay to the mouth of the Patapsco, where the flag vessel was kept under the guns of a frigate, and he was compelled to witness the bombardment of Fort M'Henry, which the Admiral had boasted that he would carry in a few hours, and that the city must fall. He watched the flag at the fort through the whole day with an anxiety that can be better felt than described, until the night prevented him from seeing it. In the night he watched the bombshells, and at early dawn his eye was again greeted by the proudly-waving flag of his country.]

The Great American Magazine: Literature

Literary magazines flourished throughout the country in the second decade. A similarity of wrapper design is evident. Wrappers were usually discarded at binding and are important for their unique bibliographic information and advertising.

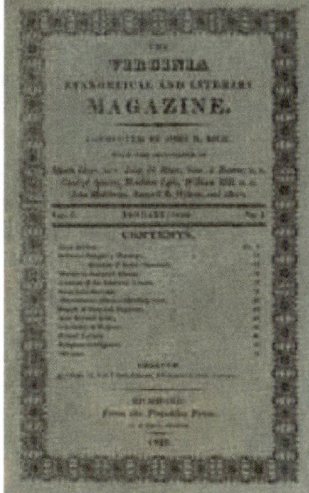
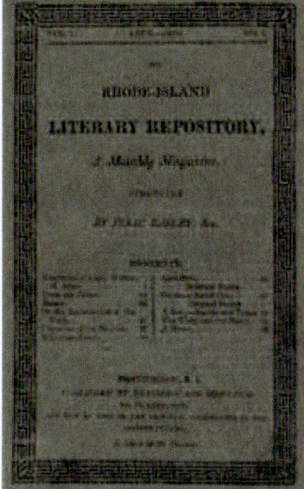

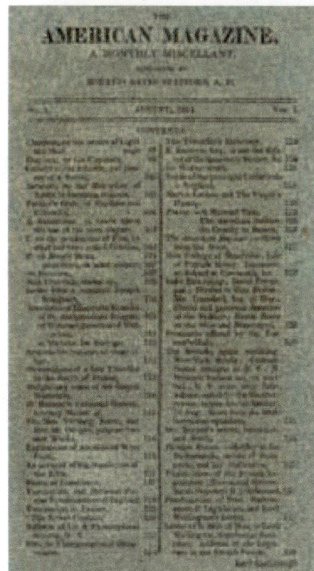

American Magazine and Critical Review is particularly interesting for the engraving of the site of publication on the front wrapper.

The Portico, published in Baltimore and conducted by "two men of Padua" (Tobias Watkins and Stephen Simpson) was important as a pioneer of the movement for native American literature.

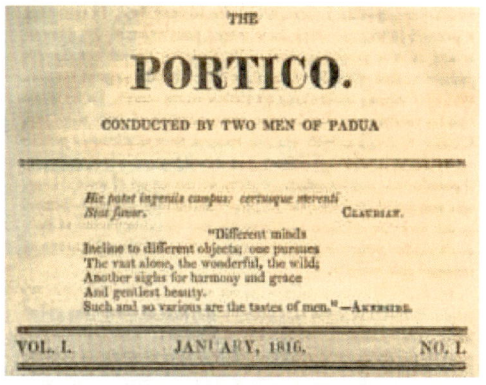

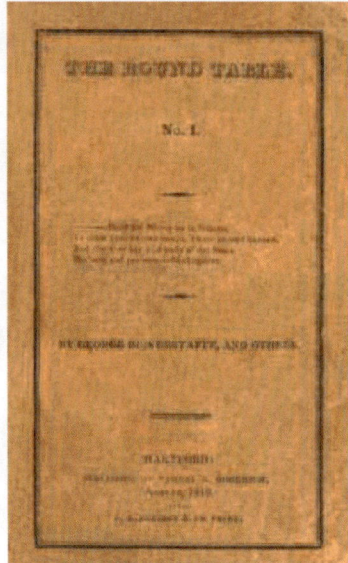 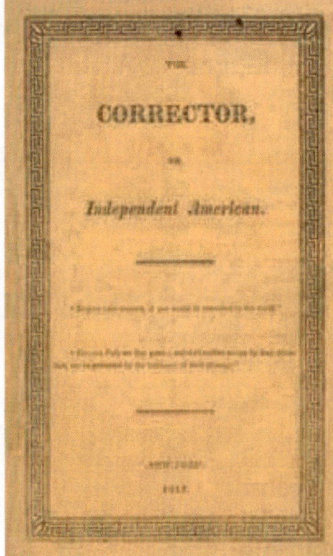 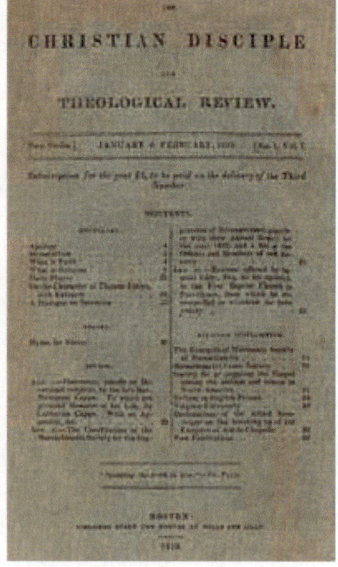

The Round Table was the first of a number of magazines published by literary clubs. *The Corrector* was a satirical review of caustic essays about contemporary literature. *Christian Disciple*, while primarily religious in content, published the first appearance of Ralph Waldo Emerson in 1824.

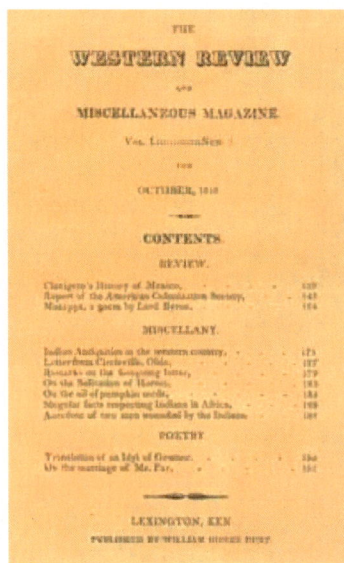

The Western Review, published in 1819, is a very early Kentucky imprint.

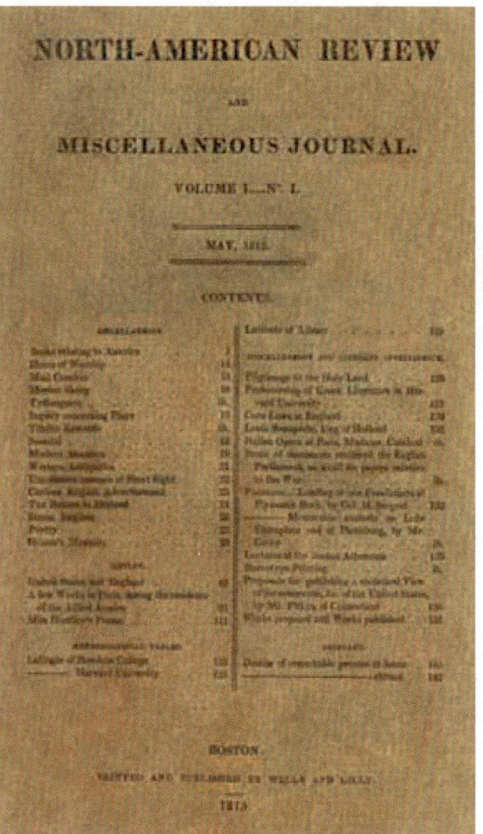

The very important *North American Review* enjoyed a long run. According to Neal Edgar, "during its life, it became the single most important American magazine dealing with American letters". It published the first great American poem, William Cullen Bryant's "Thanatopsis", in 1817.

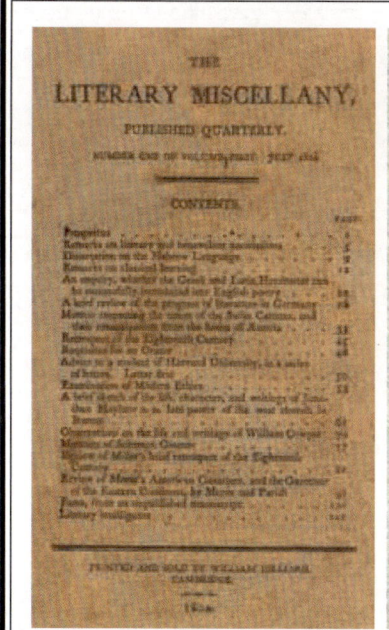

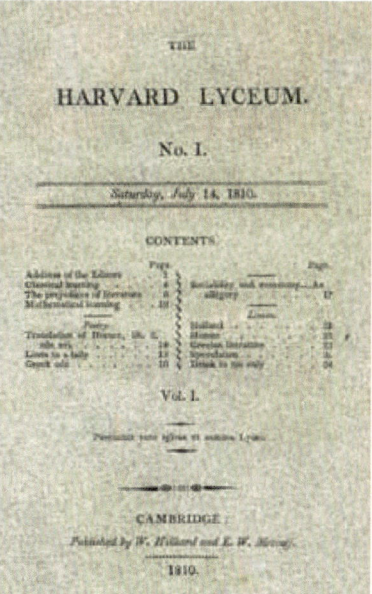

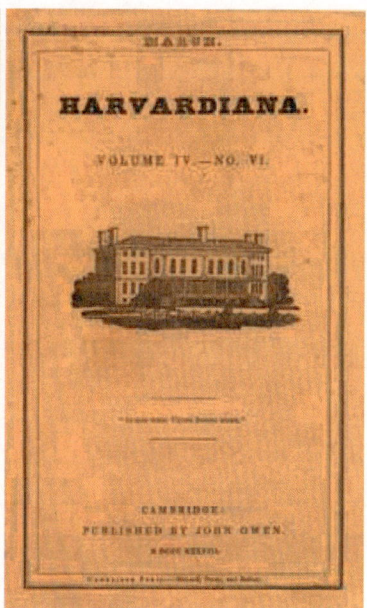

Mott cites *The Yale Banner*, started in 1806, as the first college literary magazine, but *Literary Miscellany*, published by the Harvard Phi Beta Kappa Society, clearly precedes it. *Harvard Lyceum* followed shortly afterwards. James Russell Lowell briefly served as editor of *Harvardiana*.

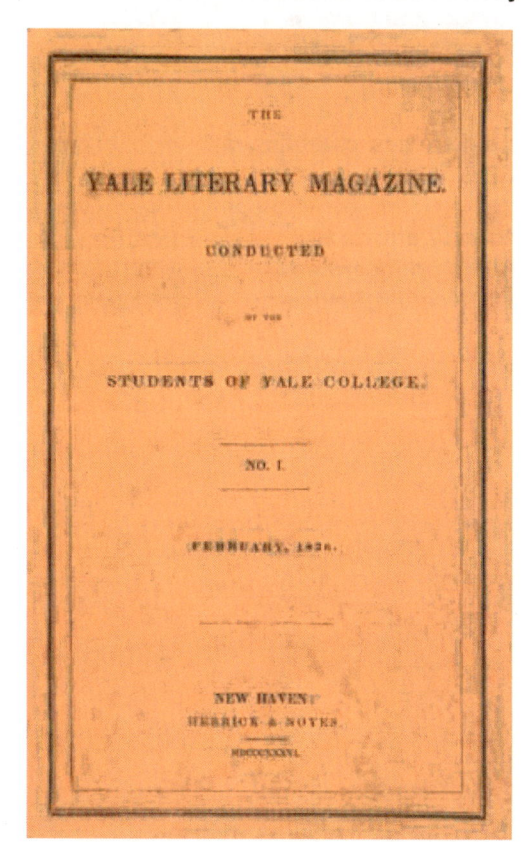

Yale Literary Magazine was the most important college literary periodical. *The Student's Companion* was a product of the Yale literary club.

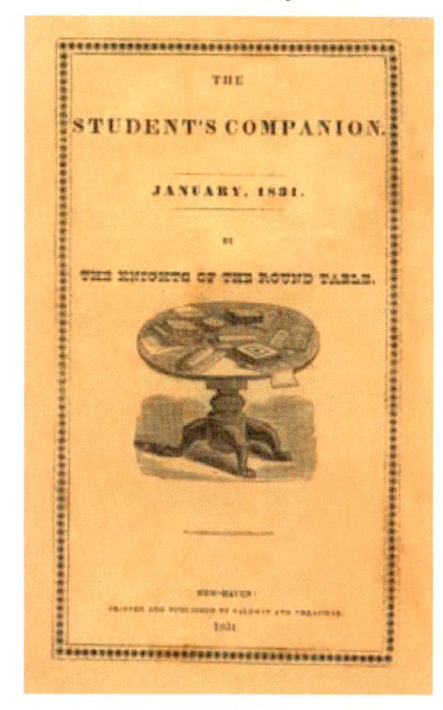

The Great American Magazine: Literature

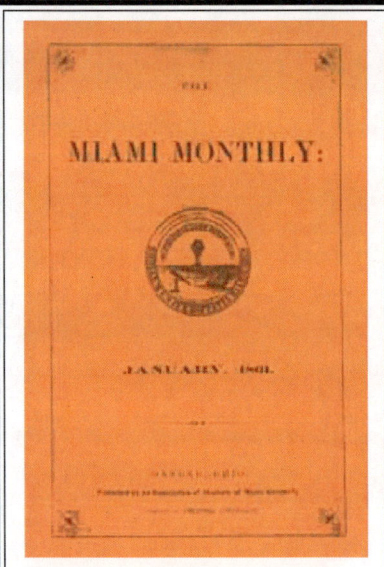

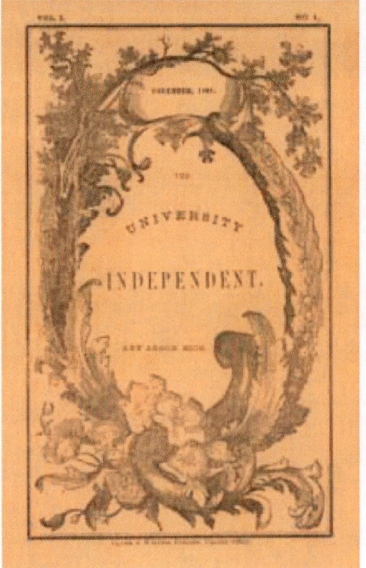

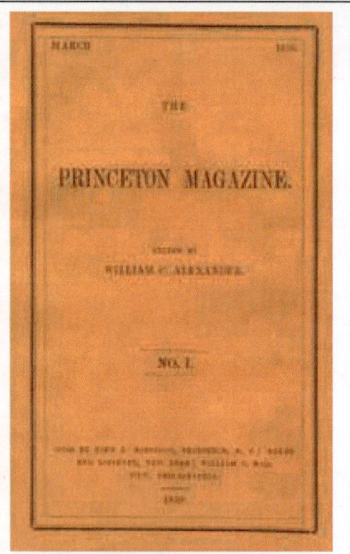

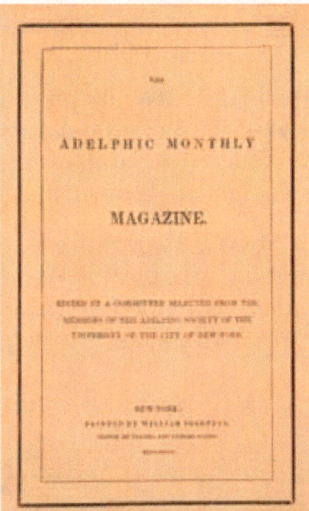

While the greatest amount of literary magazines came from Harvard and Yale, many other colleges had their own. Many are very scarce and unrecorded such as *University Independent*, published at Ann Arbor, Michigan in 1861. These magazines established the groundwork for later highly regarded student and college literary efforts like *Hound and Horn* and *The Kenyon Review*.

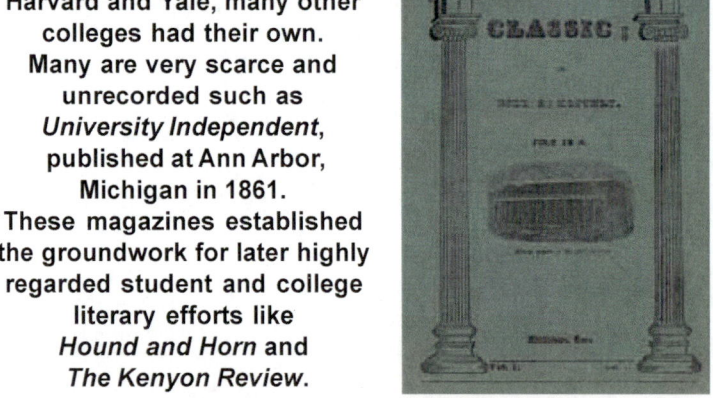

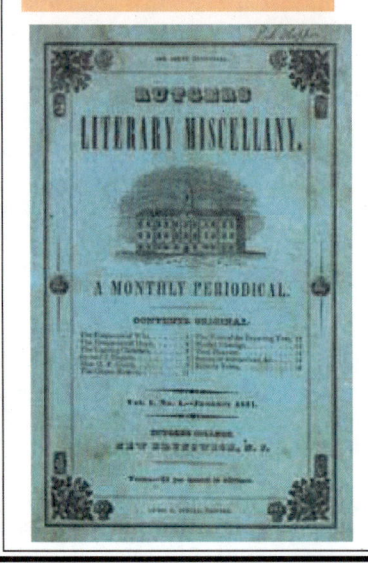

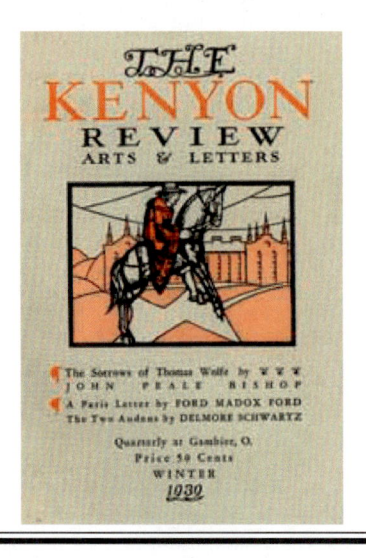

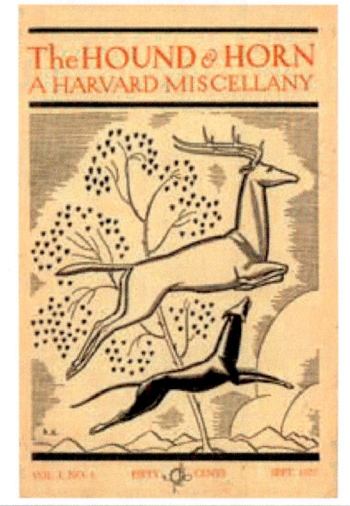

The Great American Magazine: Literature

Samuel Atkinson, a prolific publisher, began his famous weekly, *Saturday Evening Post*, in 1821 (despite the popular myth, there is no relationship to Benjamin Franklin). By the middle of the decade, he took the best material from the newspaper format *Post* and published it in a monthly octavo-sized magazine, *The Casket*. A very rare 16mo quarterly edition briefly preceded the monthly. *The Casket*, obviously having a different connotation then, was an important and widely circulated miscellany. Literature was a prominent feature, including the virtually unrecorded and unattributed 1826 first magazine printing of "A Visit From St. Nicholas", 11 years prior to its appearance in book form.

The June 1824 issue was 16mo in size in printed boards. Issue number 12 of the octavo *monthly* is the first with printed wrappers. *The Casket* eventually merged with William Burton's *Gentleman's Magazine* in 1840 to form the most widely circulated literary periodical of the 1840's, *Graham's Magazine*.

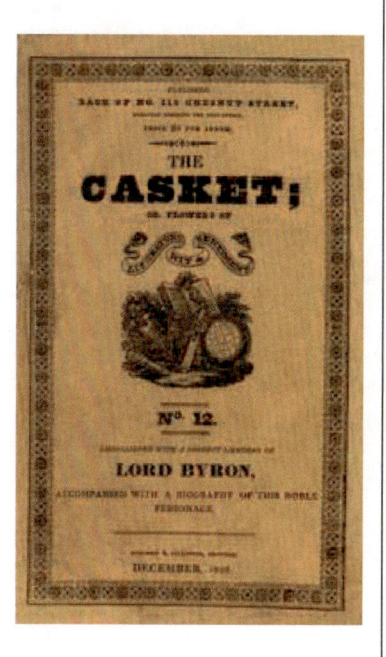

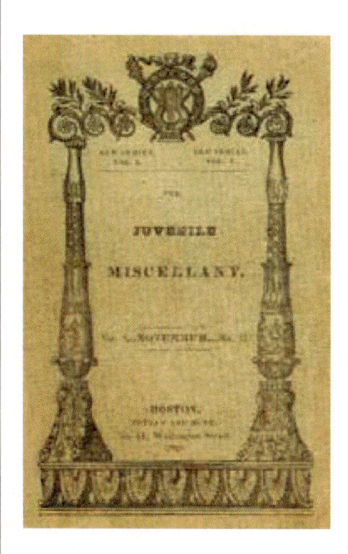

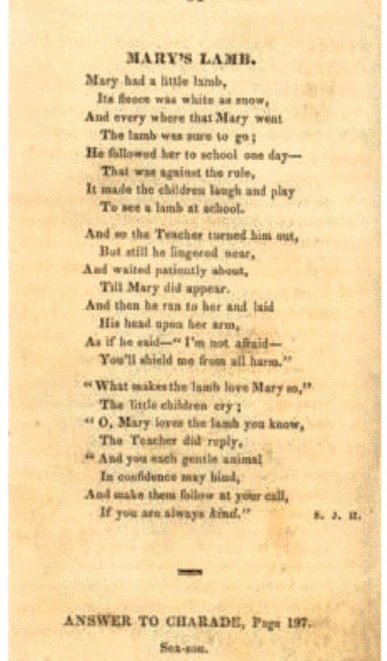

The American juvenile classic, "Mary's Lamb", written by Sarah Josepha Hale, first appeared in *Juvenile Miscellany* in 1830. One of America's pre-eminent female literary figures, Hale is best remembered as the long-standing editor of *Godey's Magazine*.

41   The Great American Magazine: Literature

The eighteen-thirties saw a wide variety of popular and successful literary magazines. The most important included William Gaylord Clark's *Knickerbocker,* which published the great American authors and poets of the day, including Longfellow, Bryant, Hawthorne and Oliver Wendell Holmes. Perhaps the most interesting appearance was "Mocha Dick, or The White Whale" by J.N. Reynolds, widely accepted to be Herman Melville's inspiration for "Moby Dick". Thomas W. White's *Southern Literary Messenger* was undoubtedly the south's leading literary periodical. Joseph Buckingham's *New-England Magazine* is especially notable for its association with Nathaniel Hawthorne. There were three magazines entitled *American Monthly Magazine*. Snowden's *Ladies' Companion* was widely circulated.

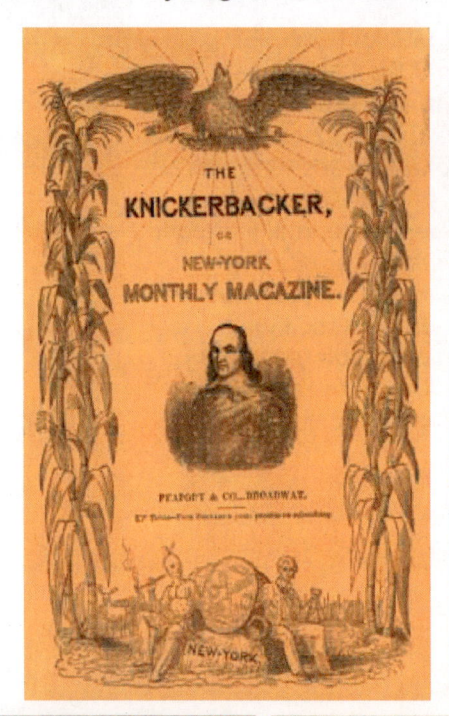

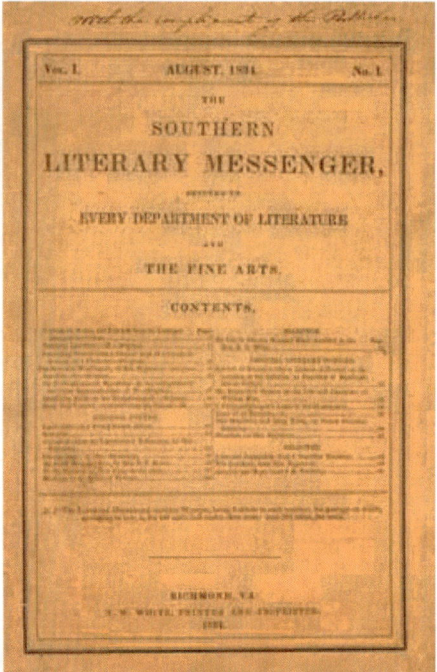

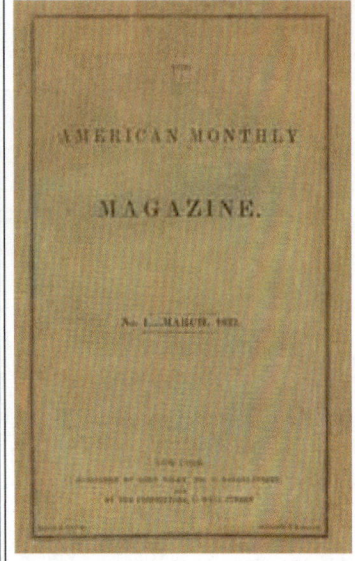

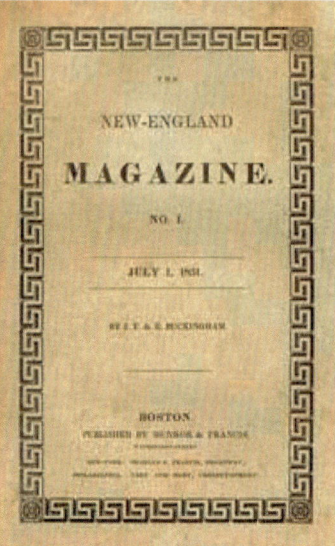

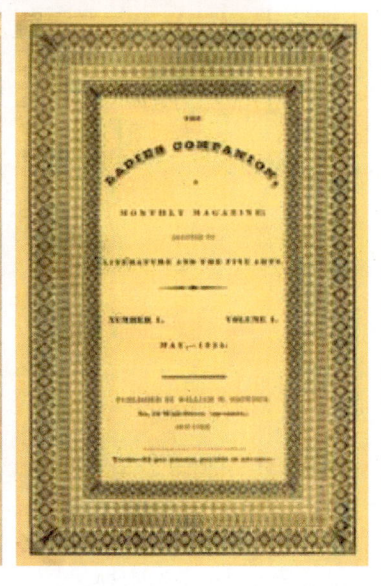

The Great American Magazine: Literature

There were about 1000 different American magazines prior to 1850 with literary content. Many were original, many reprinted works from other sources. All are reflective of the marvelous heritage of truly American literature.

The United States Literary Gazette
brought its readers the early works of Bryant and Longfellow.

The American Magazine of Useful and Entertaining Knowledge, while not specifically a literary magazine, was written by Nathaniel Hawthorne for six months in 1836.

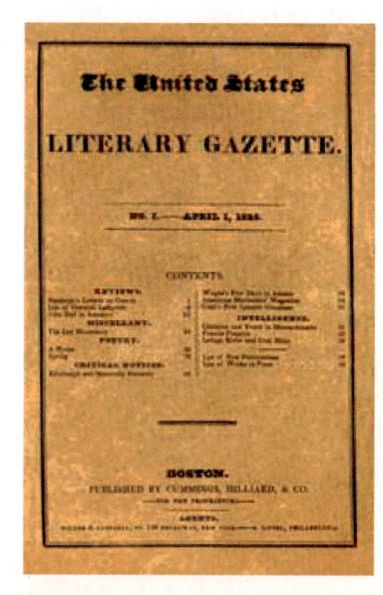

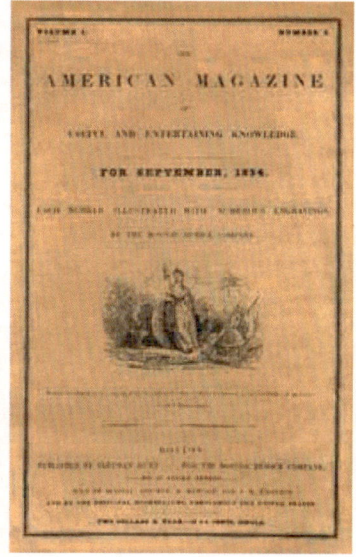

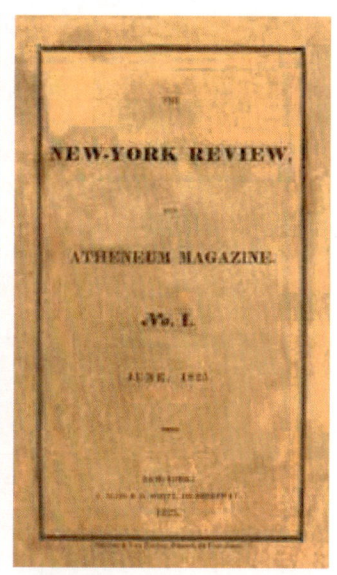

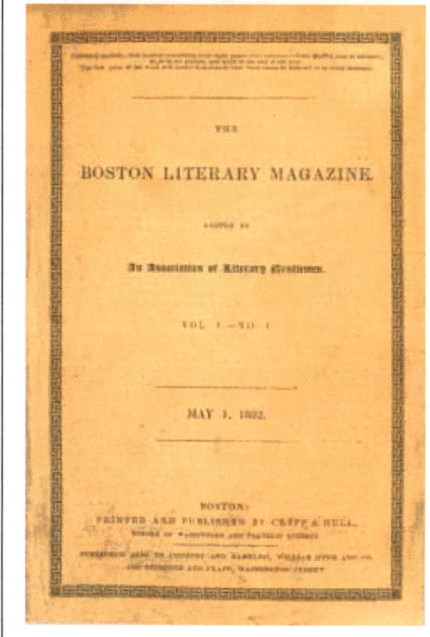

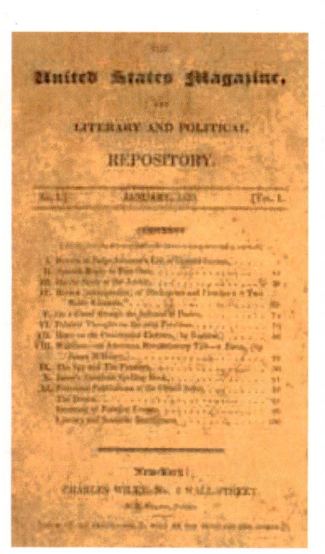

The Great American Magazine: Literature

The origins and development of **Transcendentalism**, a uniquely American blend of literature, religion and philosophy, can be found throughout its periodicals. The earliest roots are found in *The Western Messenger*, followed closely by one of America's most important magazines, *The Dial*, replete with the writings of Ralph Waldo Emerson, Henry David Thoreau and Margaret Fuller. Orestes Brownson's *Boston Quarterly Review*, William Henry Channing's *The Present* and *The Massachusetts Quarterly Review* helped disseminate the message of the movement.

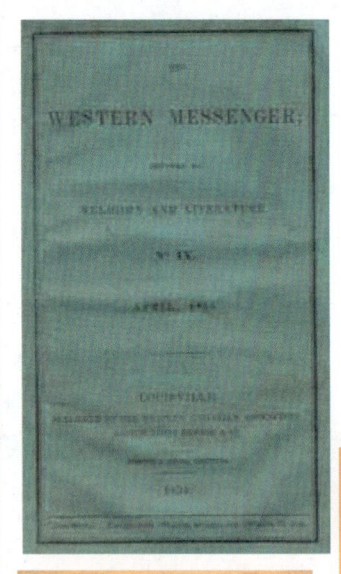

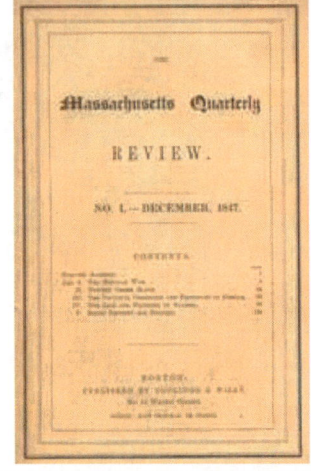

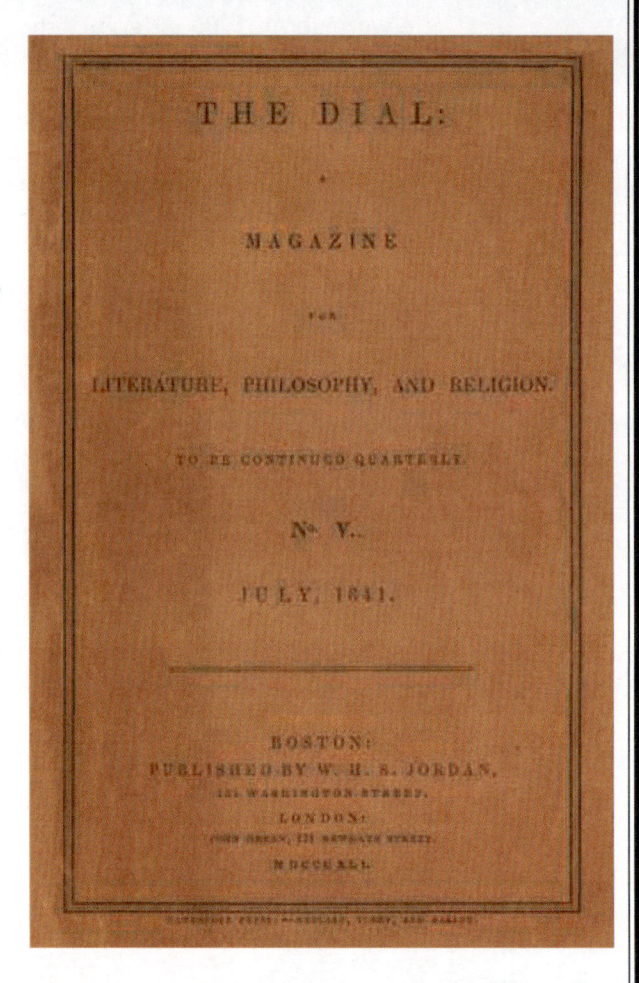

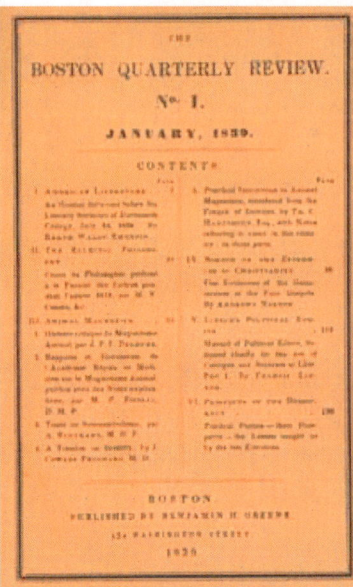

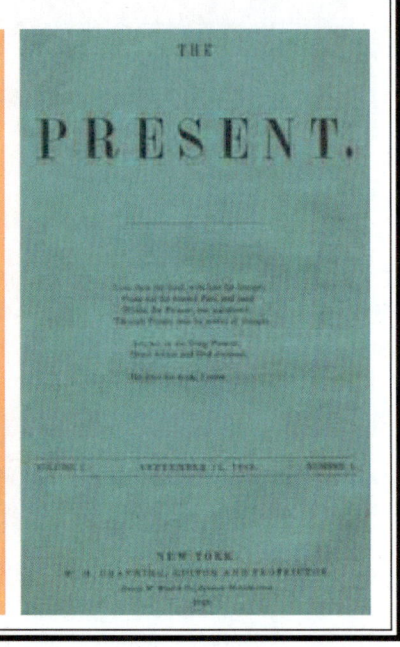

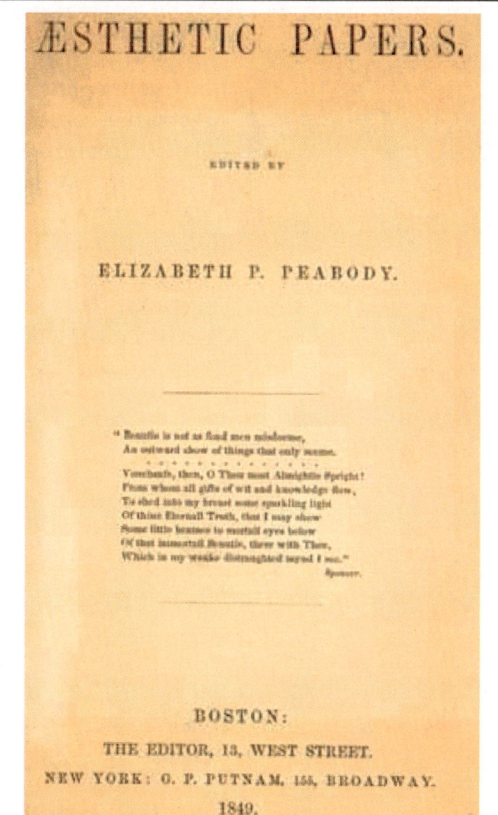

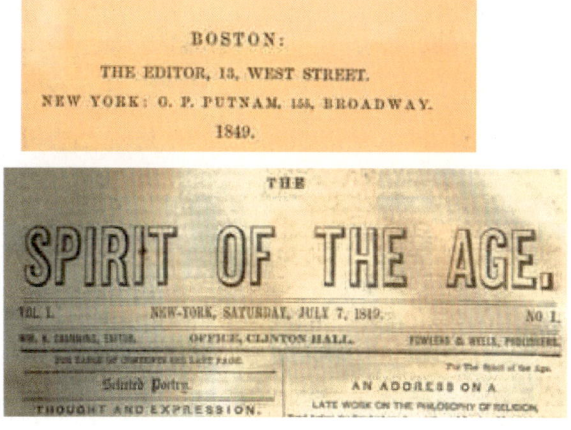

Aesthetic Papers edited by Elizabeth Palmer Peabody, another member of the inner circle also known for her pioneering efforts in childhood education, first published one of the most well-known and influential cornerstones of all transcendentalist treatises, Thoreau's essay "Resistance to Civil Government", now more commonly known as "Civil Disobedience".

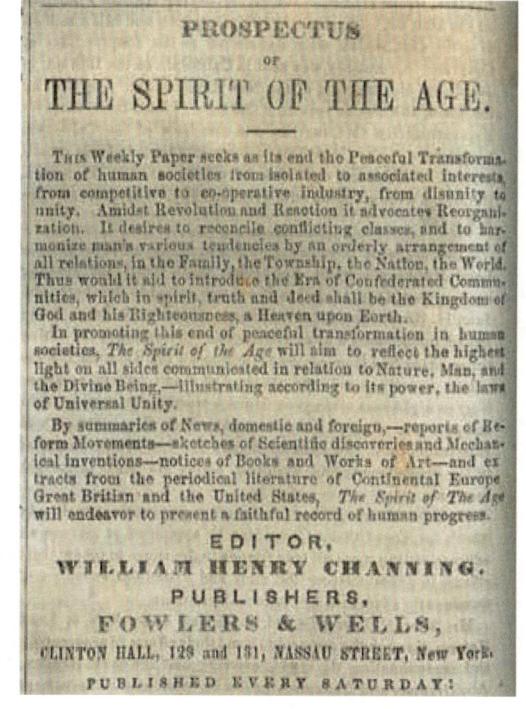

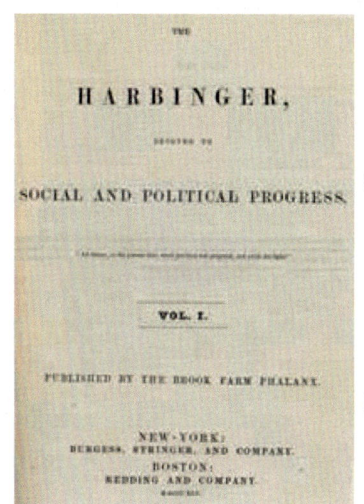

The free-thinking spirit of the 1840's fostered the appearance of a number of Utopian movements, including the Brook Farm Community, which expounded its philosophy in its own periodical, *The Harbinger*.

The Dial had a brief resurrection in Cincinnati in 1860.

Many transcendentalists went on to become leaders in the Abolitionist movement.

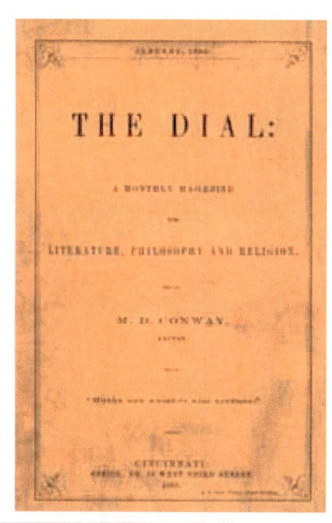

The Great American Magazine: Literature

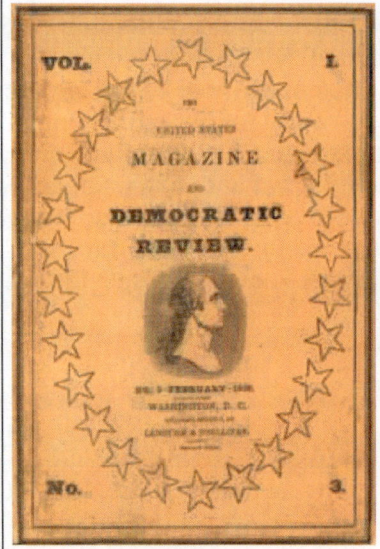

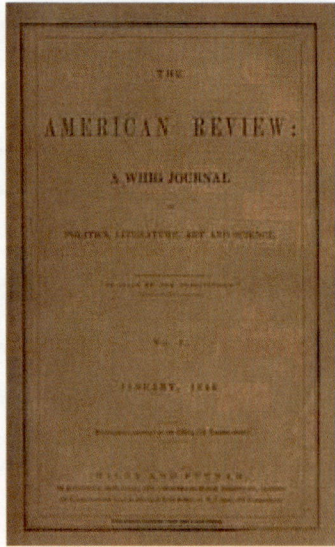

Even political parties issued their own literary magazines! *Boston Miscellany*, John Inman's *Columbian Lady's and Gentleman's Magazine*, and Sartain's *Union Magazine* were among the top tier of dozen's of new literary ventures in the 1840's. *Dollar Magazine's* first issue featured a detailed cover engraving and an early appearance of Santa Claus!

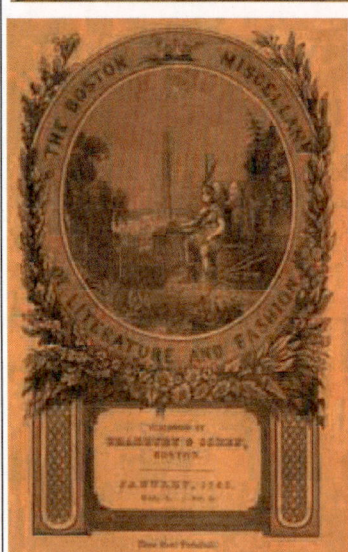

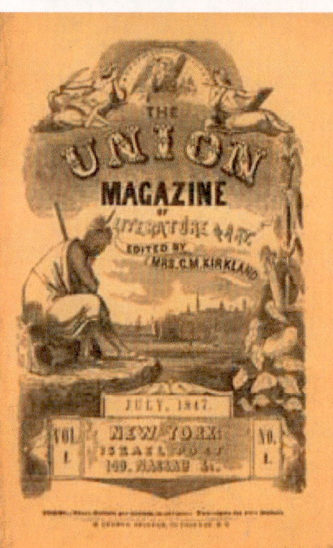

The Great American Magazine: Literature

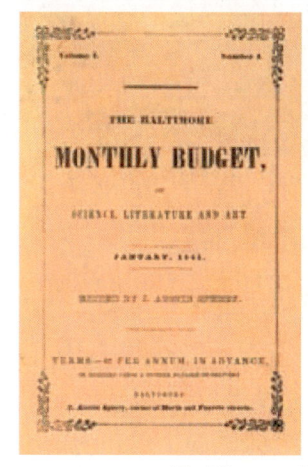

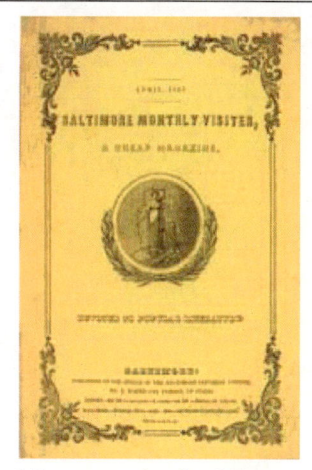

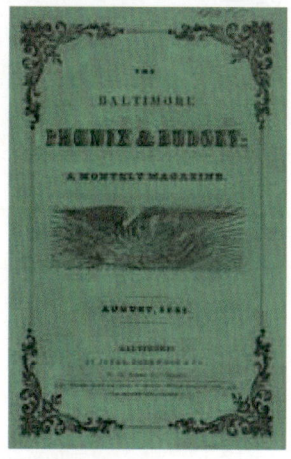

Baltimore had its own stock of literary magazines.
In the 1840's, "western" meant Cincinnati or the newly settled Chicago.
Western Literary Journal was the inaugural literary effort of E. Z. C. Judson,
more familiarly known as Ned Buntline, a colorful self-promoting author, adventurer,
racist (co-founder of the "Know Nothings") and "discoverer" of Buffalo Bill.

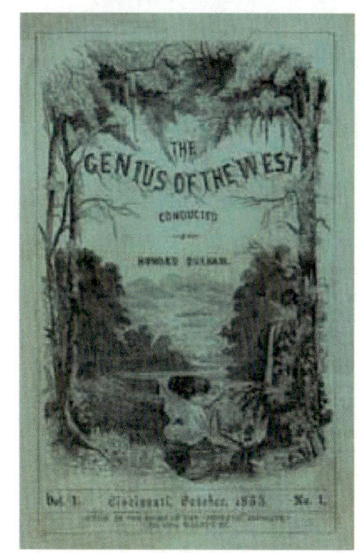

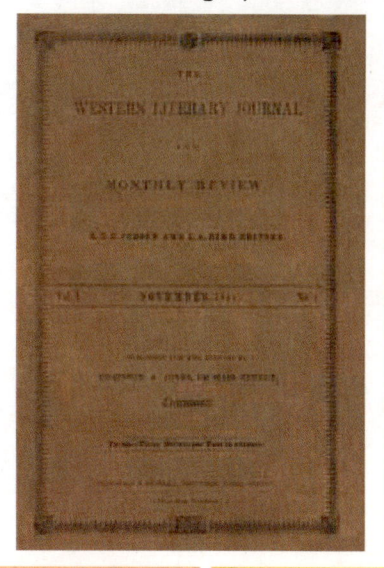

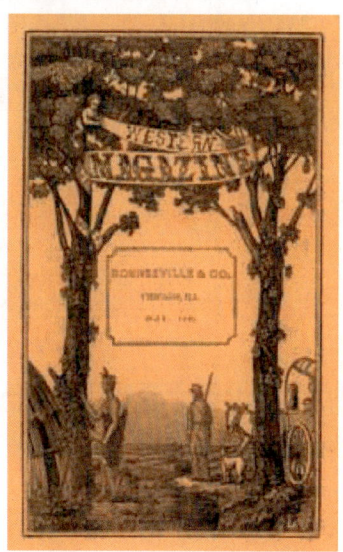

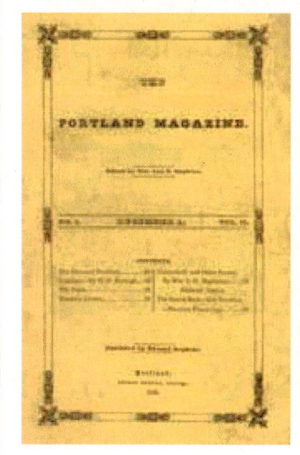

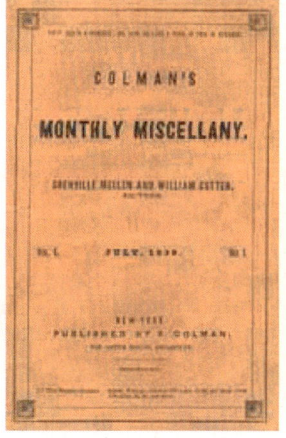

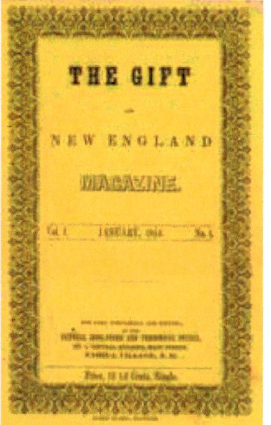

In the first half of the nineteenth century, magazines provided a remarkable cornucopia of original poetry and prose from every corner of the growing nation.

47 The Great American Magazine: Literature

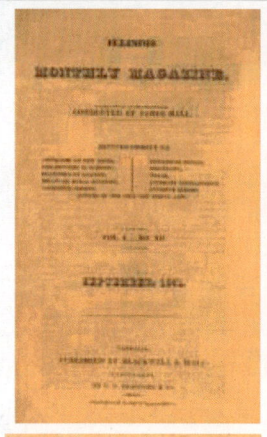

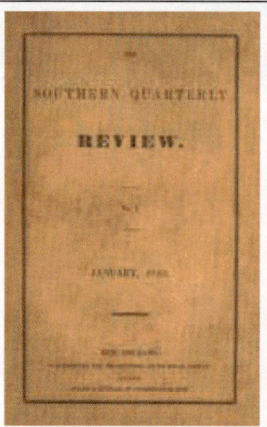

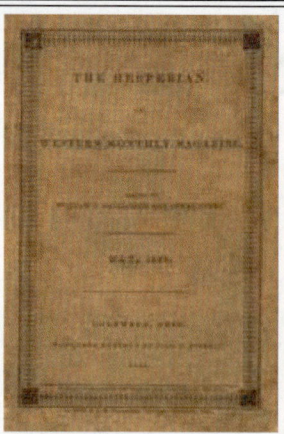

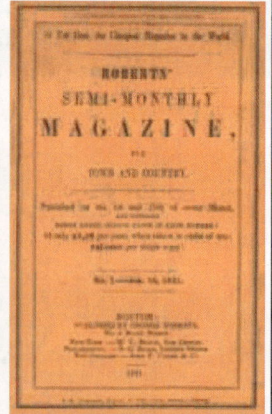

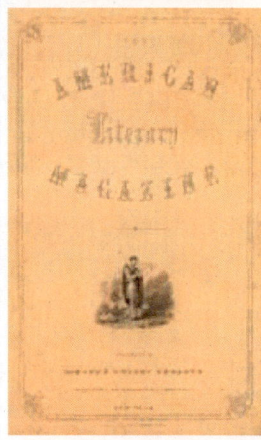

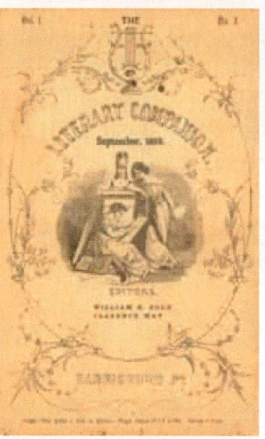

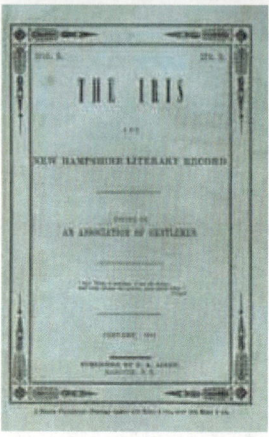

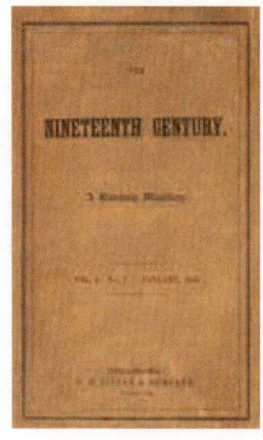

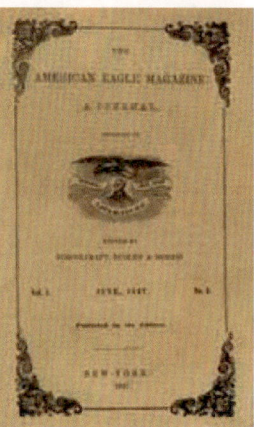

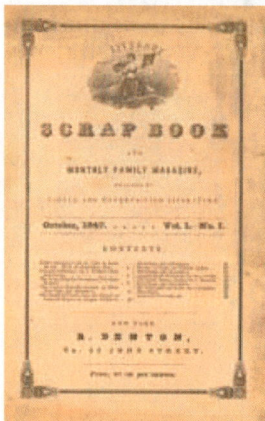

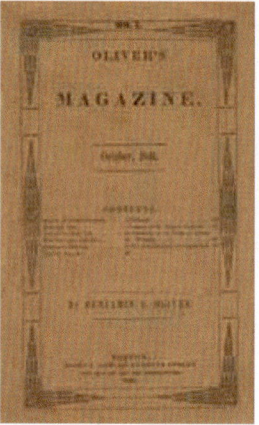

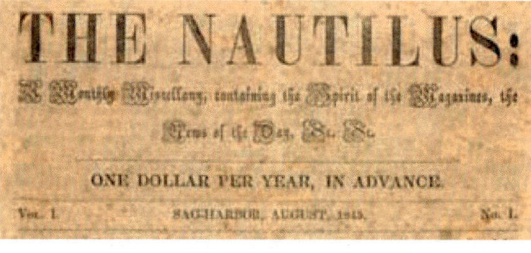

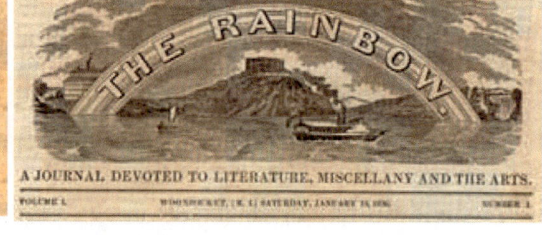

The Great American Magazine: Literature

As demonstrated on the cover of the first issue of *Littell's Living Age*, some magazines concentrated on reprinting European literature. *The Daguerrotype* had nothing to do with photography other than its title, implying the contents presented an accurate textual representation. In contrast, *The American Magazine,* by Brother Jonathan was published in London in 1850. Brother Jonathan preceded Uncle Sam as a symbol of America.

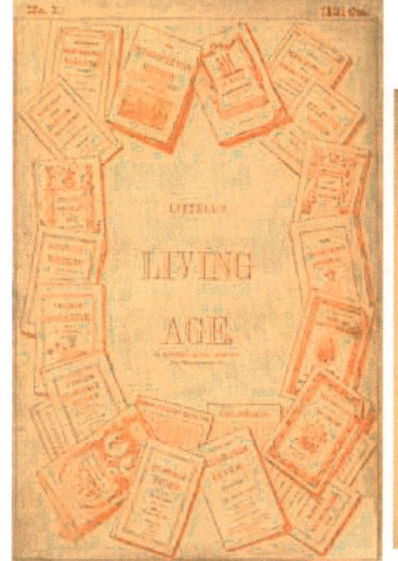

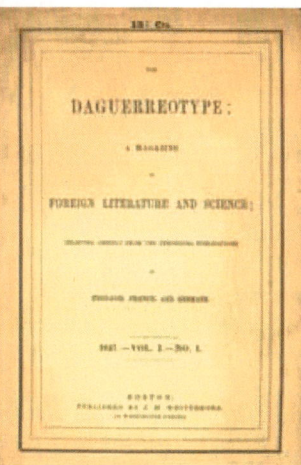

The 1850's saw the emergence of three giants of American periodical literature. *Putnam's Magazine* focused on American writers. During its brief run it brought readers the original works of Thoreau, Cooper, Longfellow, Bryant, Emerson and, most notably, Herman Melville, including his most important short story "Bartleby, the Scrivener" in 1853. *Harper's New Monthly Magazine* also featured Melville but made its name reprinting the works of popular British and French writers including Dickens and, in later decades, original works of Whitman, Twain and Henry James. *Atlantic Monthly* featured works of virtually every major author of the day. *Harper's* and *Atlantic* are still being published.

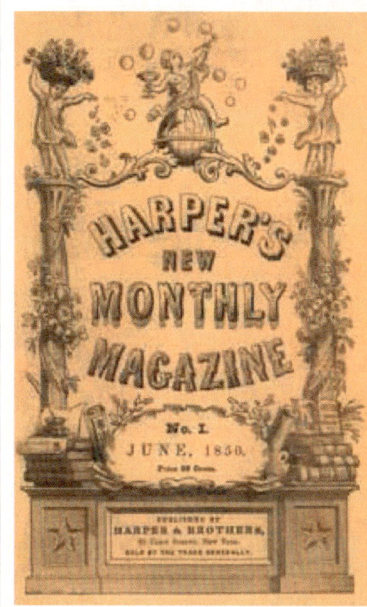

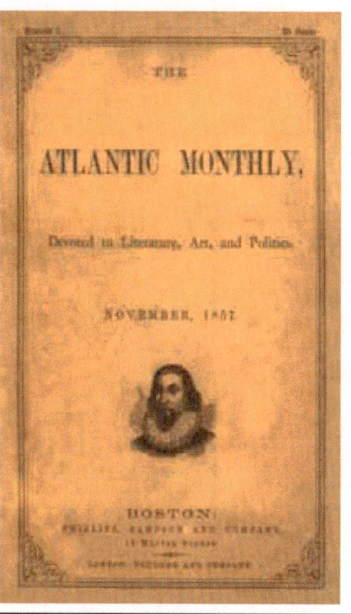

Harriet Farley's *Lowell Offering* and *New England Offering* featured literature written by women working in the mills of Massachusetts.

Despite their relatively large initial circulation, the fragility and emphemeral nature of magazines often renders them very scarce, especially in their original state. Despite extensive research, no other copies of any of these five well-produced titles has been found.

The Companion, aside from literature, contains a long unrecorded overland narrative. *The Empire Ladies and Gentlemen's Magazine* is especially interesting, containing unique references to Edgar Allan Poe.

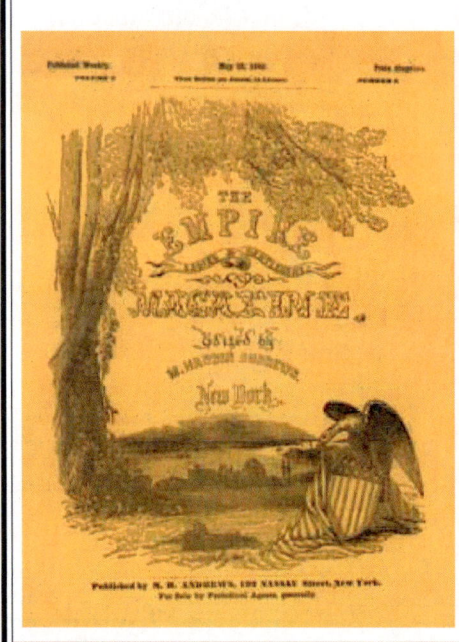

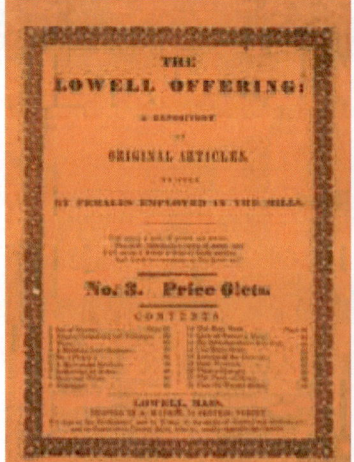

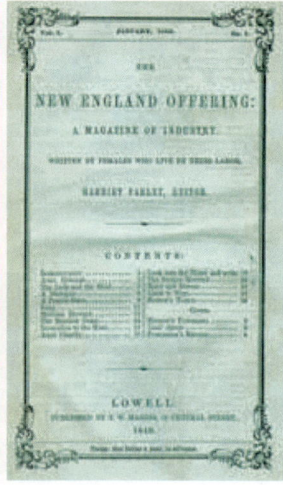

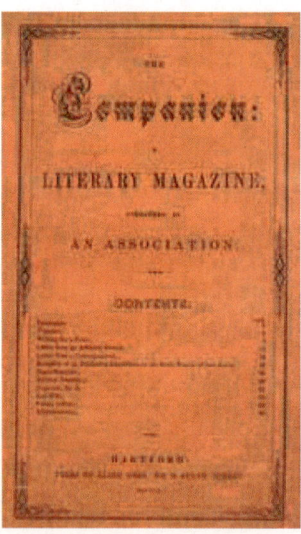

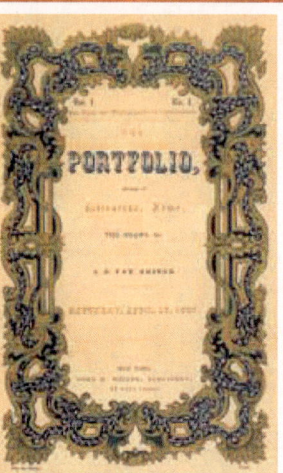

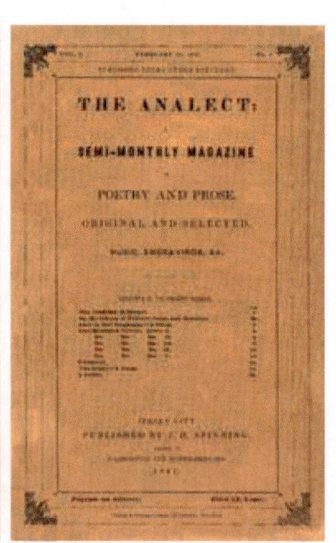

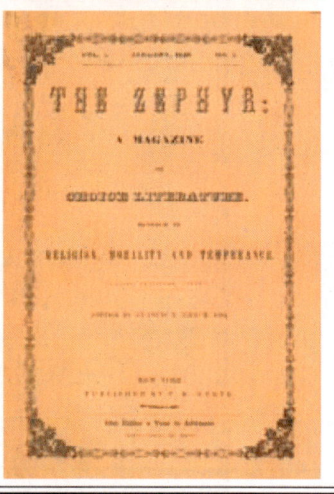

The Great American Magazine: Literature

African American literature in America began with the slave Phillis Wheatley's poetic tribute to George Washington in *Pennsylvania Magazine* in 1776. Appearances of black authors in the following one hundred fifty years were notably sparse.

One glaring exception was the rare *Anglo-African Magazine*, published monthly in 1859 and 1860 and edited by Thomas Hamilton, which featured an incomplete serialized first printing of "Blake: or, the Huts of America", by Martin Robinson Delaney, the third novel written in America by an African American.

It wasn't until the nineteen thirties that the works of African-American writers such as Langston Hughes regularly appeared in the "mainstream" periodical press.

Harriet Beecher Stowe's "Uncle Tom's Cabin" first appeared serially in John Greenleaf Whittier's abolitionist journal *The National Era* and was, in large part, responsible for inciting The Civil War.

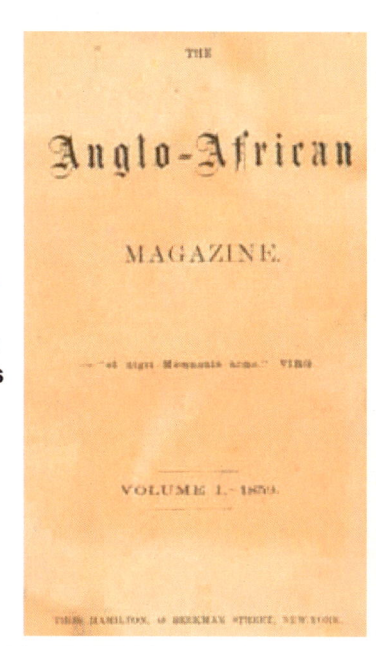

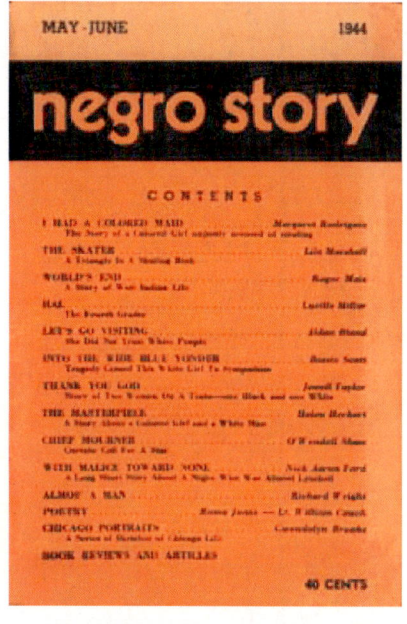

51   The Great American Magazine: Literature

Edgar Allan Poe's association with magazines is legendary. The vast majority of his most important works appeared in magazines and he was, at one time, editor of *Southern Literary Messenger, Broadway Journal, Burton's Gentleman's Magazine* and *Graham's Magazine.*

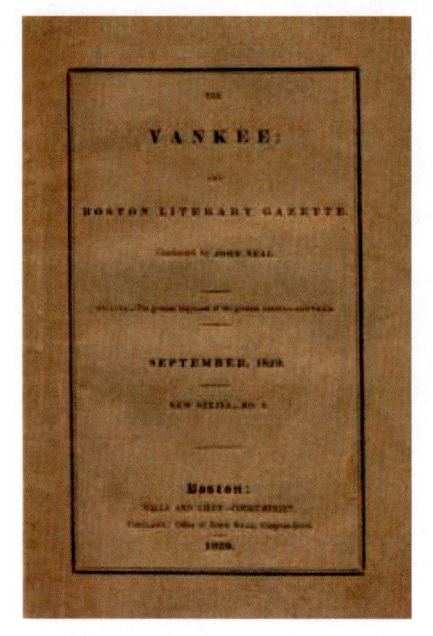

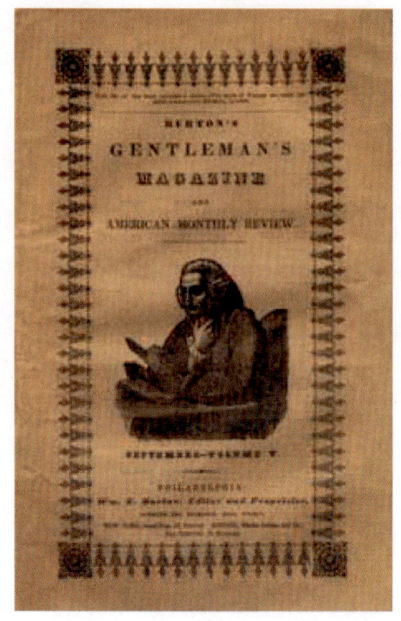

Poe's work first appeared in print in a favorable review of his work in this issue of John Neal's *Yankee* in 1829. The December issue contains long excerpts and critique of "Al Aaraaf" and "Tamerlane". The first horror story, "The Fall of the House of Usher" appeared in this issue of *Burton's Gentleman's Magazine* in 1838 while Poe was editor.

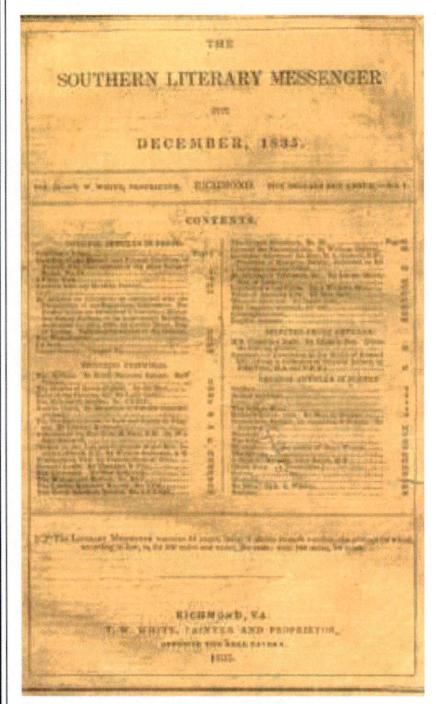

Poe's editorship of the important *Southern Literary Messenger* began with this issue.

Poe edited and was often published in *The Broadway Journal* and frequently appeared in N.P. Willis' *Weekly Mirror.*

The Great American Magazine: Literature

XIX. Our Book-shelves, - - - - - - - " 234 — Edgar A. Poe

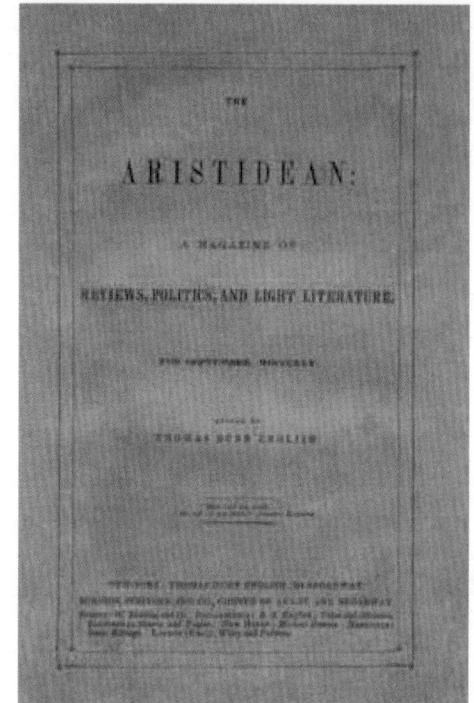

Poe probably reviewed his own works in this issue of the rarely seen *Aristidean*, edited by Thomas Dunn English. This may have been Poe's own copy!

"Murders in the Rue Morgue", America's first detective story, appeared in the newly formed *Graham's Magazine*. Under Poe's editorship it rapidly grew in circulation. This scarce, early issue contains another Poe classic "The Descent into the Maelstrom".

"The Mystery of Marie Roget" was originally serialized in William Snowden's *Ladies' Companion* in three parts, beginning with this November 1842 issue.

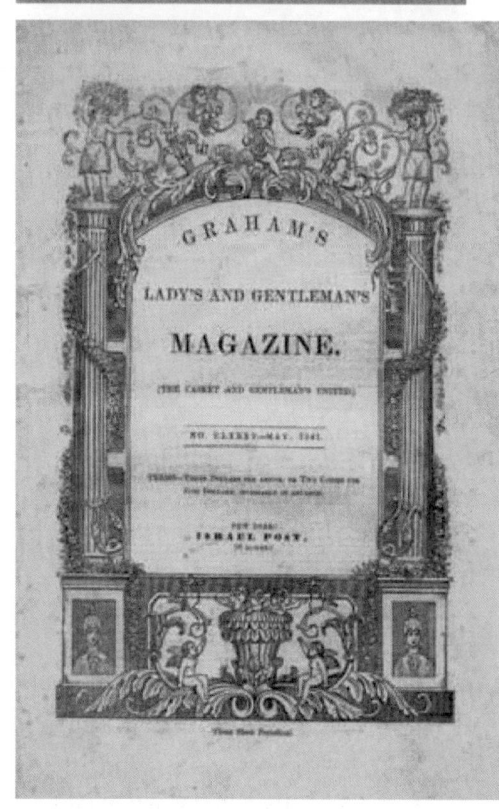

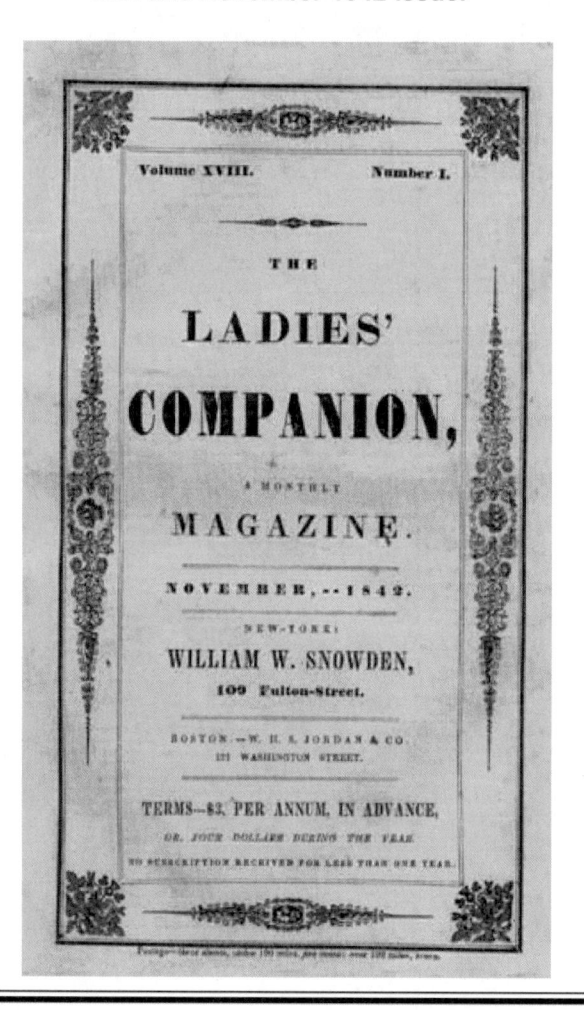

The Great American Magazine: Literature

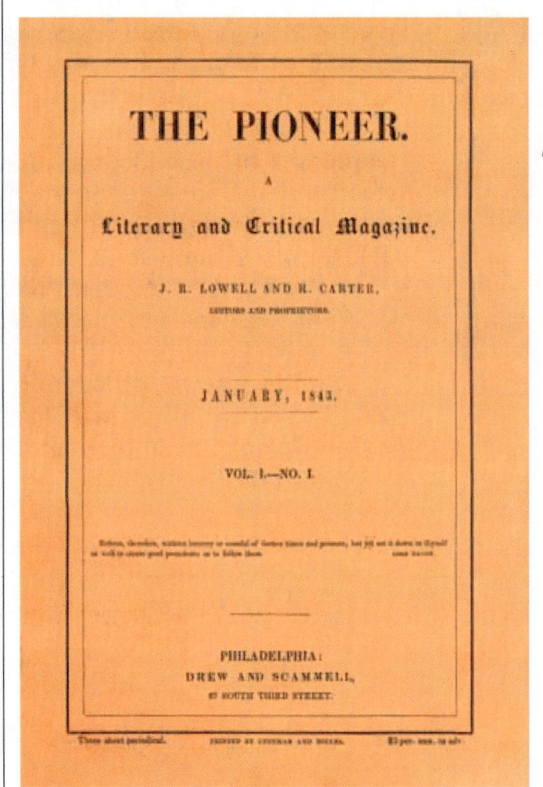

"The Tell Tale Heart" first appeared in the inaugural issue of James Russell Lowell's rarely seen *Pioneer* after being rejected by *Boston Miscellany* due to its provocative content. This is the rare Philadelphia edition.

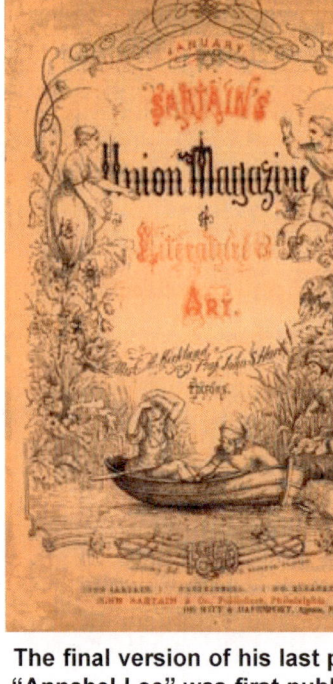

Poe's best known poem, "The Raven", first appeared in the second issue of *American Whig Review* in 1845.

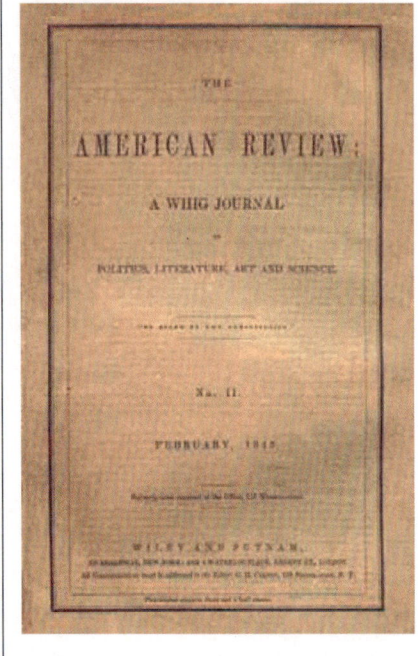

The final version of his last poem, "Annabel Lee" was first published posthumously in this 1850 issue of *Sartain's Union Magazine*.

Mark Twain's original work appeared in magazines over 200 times.

His first literary effort, a short humorous story "The Dandy Frightening the Squatter" appeared in this issue of Benjamin Shillaber's satirical literary weekly, *The Carpet Bag*. Shillaber's creation, Mrs. Partington, was later adapted by Twain as Aunt Polly in "Tom Sawyer". The very scarce *Kelley's Weekly* first printed any portion of "Innocents Abroad". *Packard's Monthly* contained three Twain appearances in 1869. *The Galaxy* featured eleven contributions between 1868 and 1871 and *The Century* published three chapters of "Huckleberry Finn" prior to their appearance in book form, as well as "A Connecticut Yankee in King Arthur's Court", "Pud'nhead Wilson" and nine other works as late as 1901.

The first publication of any part of "Tom Sawyer" appeared in the August 23, 1876 issue of *Wild Oats*, a rare satirical weekly.

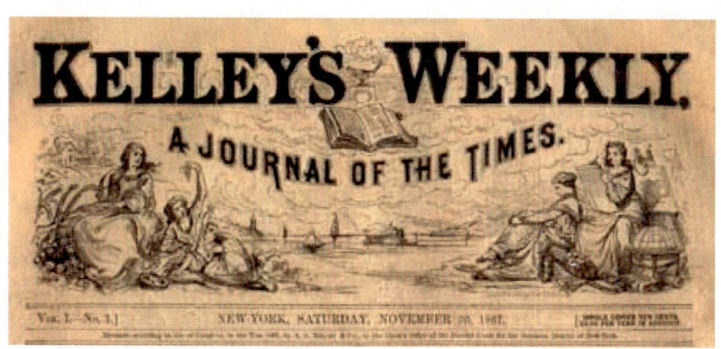

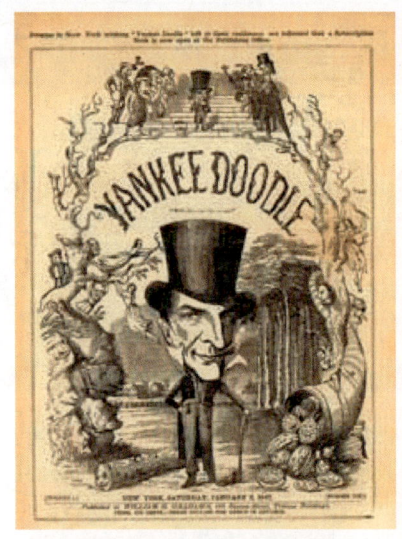

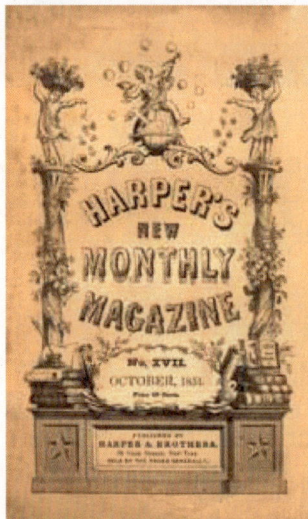

The humor magazine *Yankee Doodle* published many of the earliest squibs from the pen of Herman Melville in 1847, including the serialization of the satirical "Authentic Anecdotes of Old Zack".

The earliest published excerpt of Melville's classic "Moby Dick" was in this issue of *Harper's Monthly*.

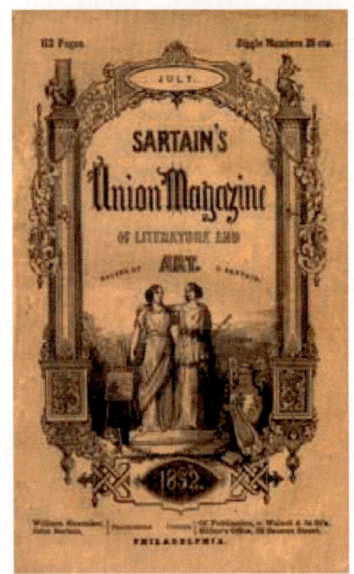

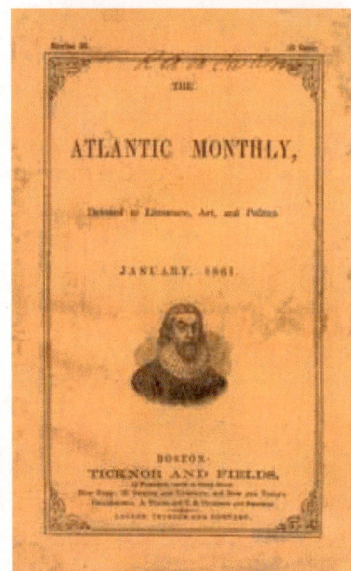

The first printing of any part of "Walden" by Henry David Thoreau appeared in one of the last issues of *Sartain's Magazine*. The first American appearance of Jules Verne is found in the May 1852 issue. This January 1861 issue of *Atlantic Monthly* contains Longfellow's legend-making "Paul Revere's Ride". Julia Ward Howe's "Battle Hymn of the Republic" was first published in *Atlantic* in February 1862.

Emily Dickinson had only a few anonymous works published during her lifetime. An Amherst College magazine, *The Indicator*, contains her first appearance in 1850 and, a few years later, this issue of *The Round Table* featured her first publication in a national magazine, an essay entitled "My Sabbath".

The Great American Magazine: Literature

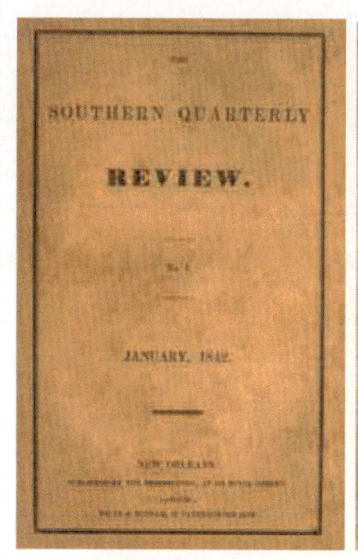

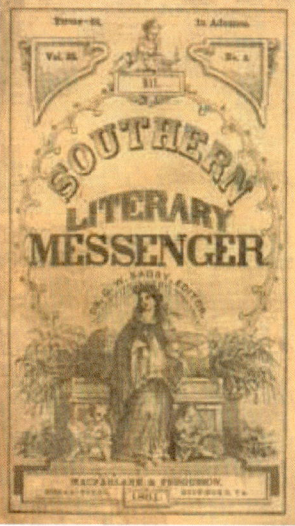

As the schism between the north and south deepened, a number of distinctly Southern magazines appeared, such as *Southern and Western Monthly Magazine*, edited by the noted regional author, W. Gilmore Simms. *Southern Literary Messenger,* the foremost, continued publication after secession.

This issue of the short-lived, rare *Wheler's Magazine* contains an original contribution by John Neal.

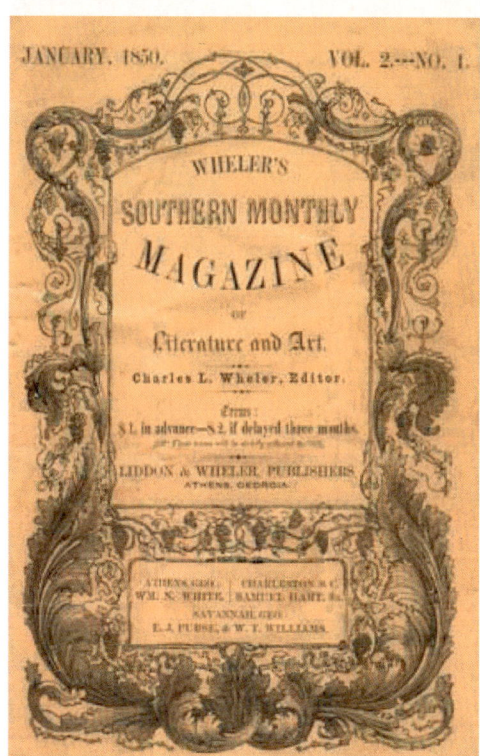

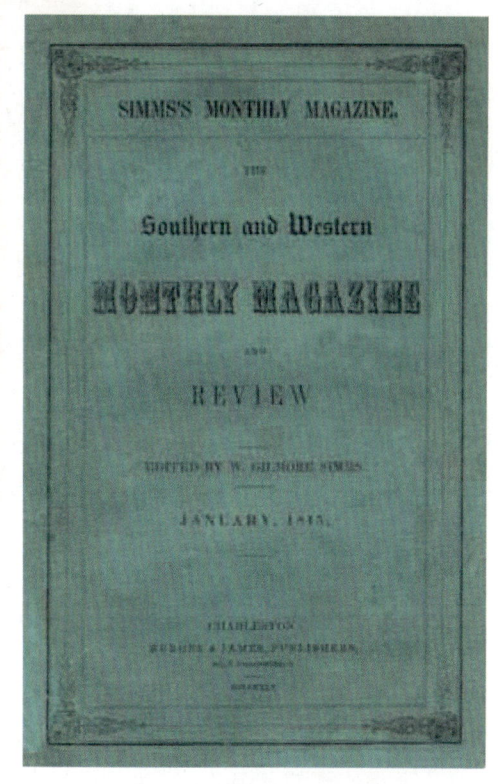

The Countryman was published on an obscure plantation in Georgia. This issue contains the first literary appearance of one of the typesetters, Joel Chandler Harris.

The Great American Magazine: Literature

Only a very few literary magazines, such as *The Age,* were published in the Confederacy. A shortage of paper often dampened circulation.

The Confederate analog of *Harper's Weekly, Southern Illustrated News,* and the miscellany *The Magnolia* combined news and literature.

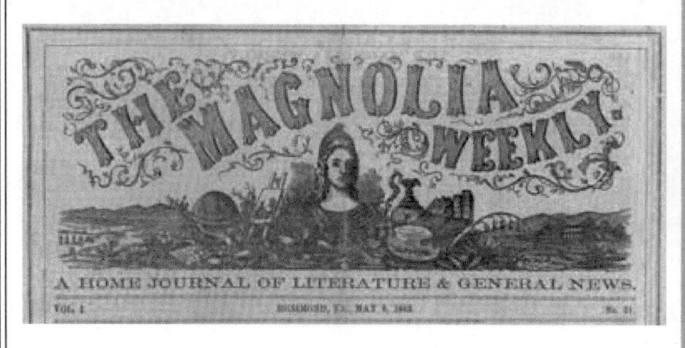

Immediately after the Civil War, former General D. H. Hill began *The Land We Love* in North Carolina.

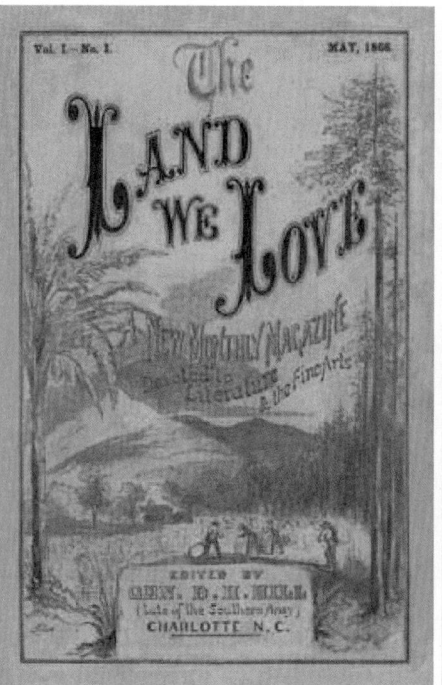

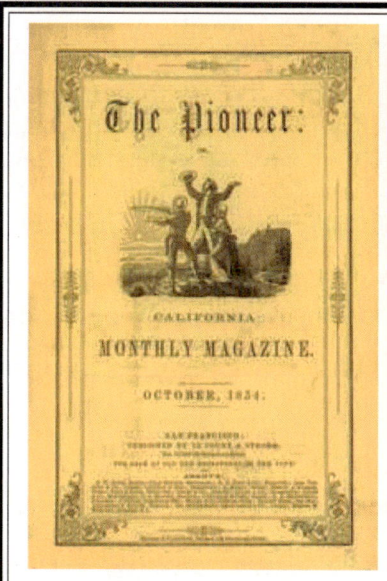

In 1854, Ferdinand Ewer started California's first literary magazine, *The Pioneer*, modeling it after *The Knickerbocker*. *Hutching's California Magazine* followed a few years later and featured stories with western themes "to picture California life". *Gazlay's Pacific Monthly* was published in New York but was devoted to stories about the west. Begun in 1868, *Overland Monthly* did more than any other magazine to establish the market for serious literature in the far west. It was edited by Bret Harte and had contributions from Harte, Mark Twain and Ambrose Bierce.

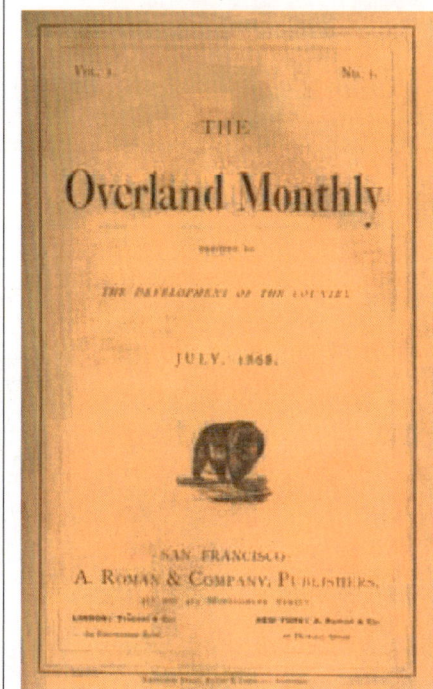

The rare *North Pacific Review*, edited by Robert F. Greeley, lasted only eight issues.

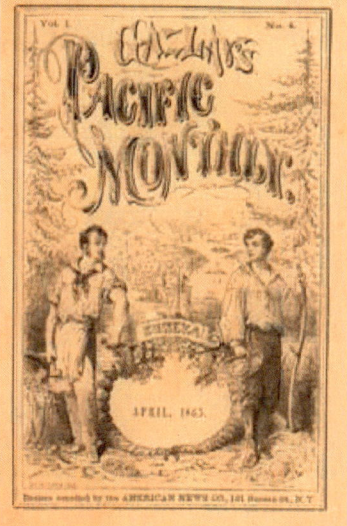

The Great American Magazine: Literature

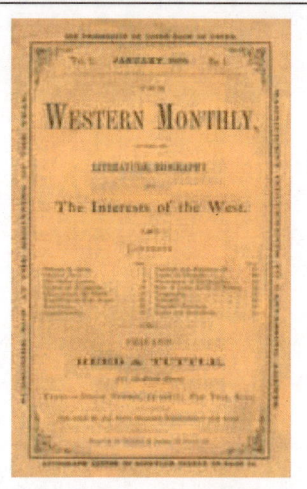

Western Monthly was Chicago's most important pre-fire periodical and literary magazine. In 1871, it changed its title to *Lakeside Monthly*.

The very rare Chicago-based *Outlook* is not related to the later literary review of the same name.

Charles Scribner's first magazine publication was a religious miscellany, *Hours at Home* in 1865. His earliest literary venture was *Scribner's Monthly* in 1870, which became the successful *The Century* in 1881. In 1887, *Scribner's Magazine* was reincarnated and remained a mainstream literary force through the middle of the twentieth century, publishing the works of the most important authors, including Ernest Hemingway and F. Scott Fitzgerald.

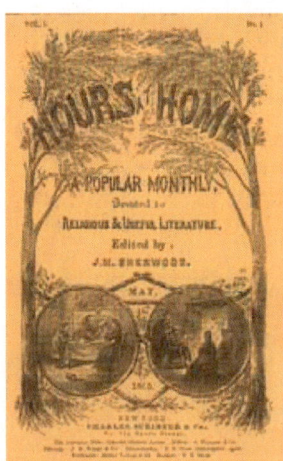

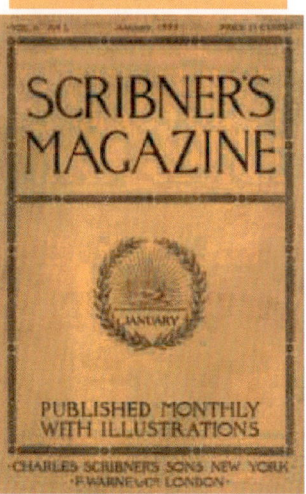

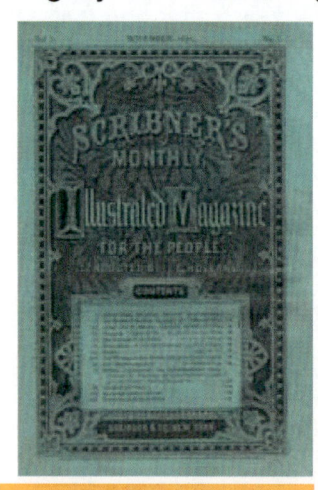

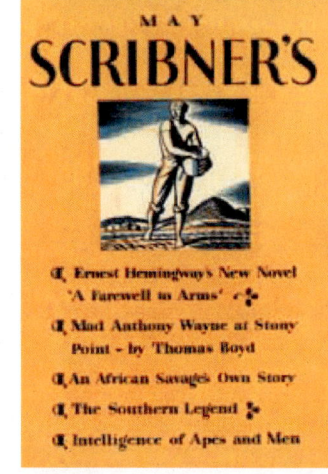

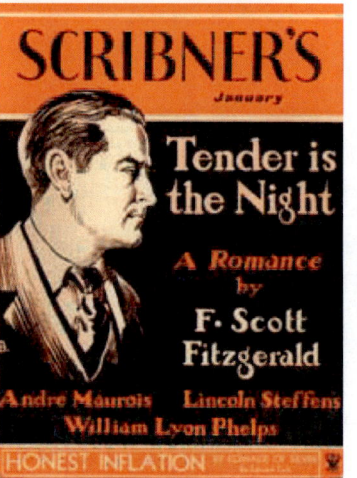

The Great American Magazine: Literature

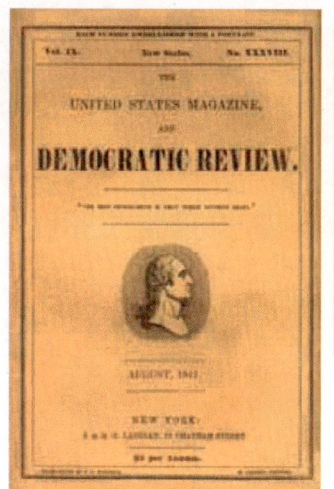

After his earlier life as a newspaper editor, **Walt Whitman's** first literary appearance in a national publication, a short story, "Death in a Schoolroom, A Fact" appeared in this issue of *United States Magazine and Democratic Review*. His only novella "Franklin Evans" is in a rare and valuable supplement issue of Park Benjamin's *The New World*.

The Critic, an important literary review that lasted until 1906, featured twenty-nine Whitman contributions, from its first issue in 1881, through 1891. The prolific Whitman was a frequent contributor to periodicals throughout his lengthy career.

As a result of one of the most productive literary lunches in history, the editors of *Lippincott's Magazine* in 1890 first published Oscar Wilde's "The Picture of Dorian Gray" and Sir Arthur Conan-Doyle's "The Sign of (the) Four", the first American appearance of Sherlock Holmes.

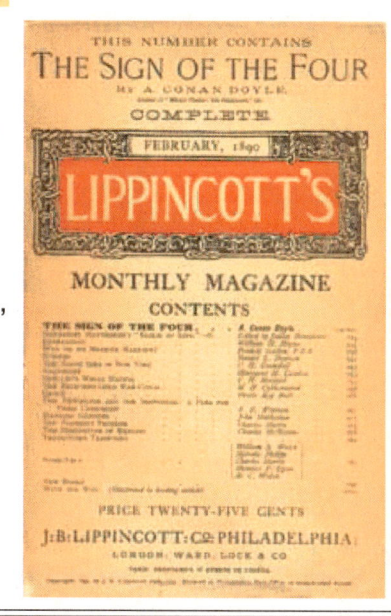

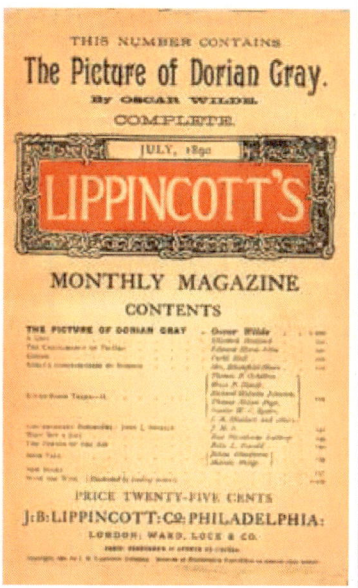

The Great American Magazine: Literature

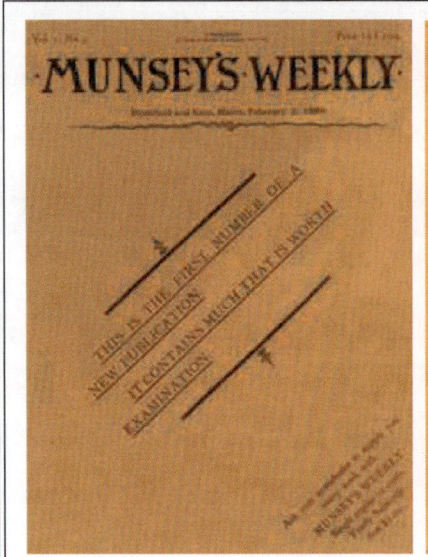

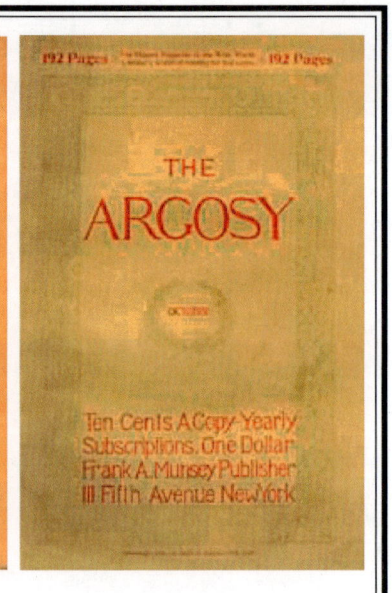

In the early eighteen-nineties, in order to complete with the reigning stalwarts of the industry, *Scribner's*, *Harpers*, *Century* and *Atlantic*, Frank Munsey and S.S. McClure reduced the price of their magazines and created an explosion of popular interest and increased circulation. Munsey's *The Argosy* was originally a children's magazine, publishing author's like Horatio Alger and Oliver Optic. He converted it from a miscellany to a smaller-sized purely fiction publication with the issue above, October 1896, considered to be the first "pulp" magazine. *Argosy* went on to enjoy a long and successful run. *The Cosmopolitan* began in Rochester and was soon moved to New York. It published many notable authors, including the original serialization of "War of the Worlds" by H.G. Wells beginning in April 1897.

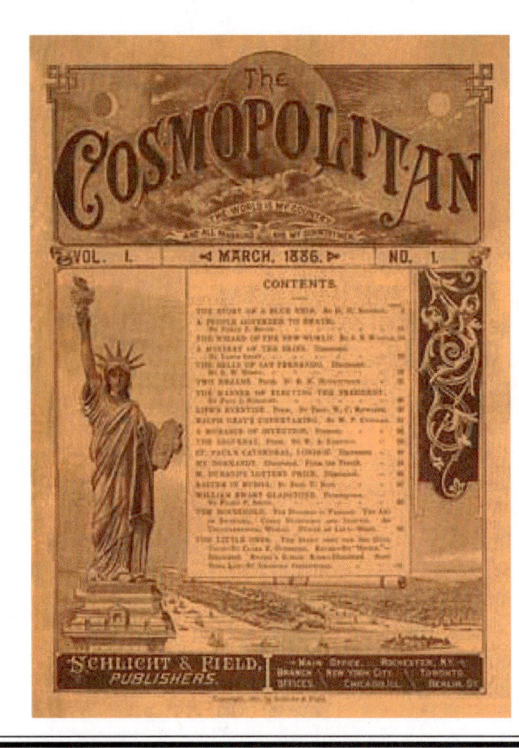

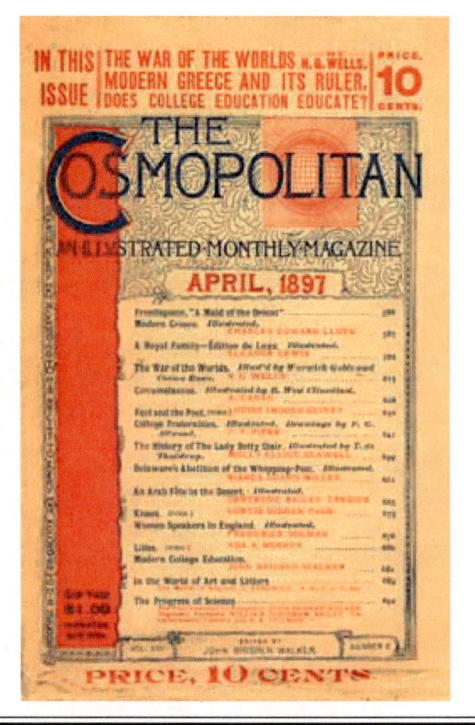

The Great American Magazine: Literature

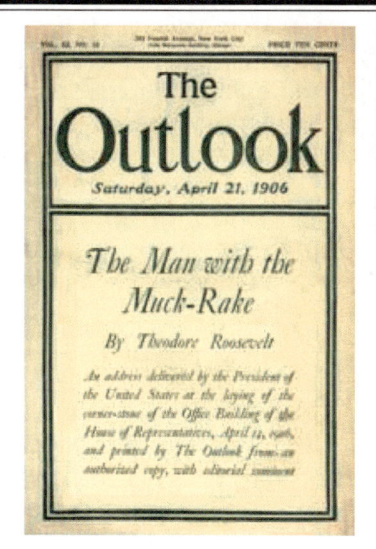

In the first decade of the Twentieth Century, *McClure's Magazine* pioneered a form of investigative journalism designed to expose unscrupulous business practices and political corruption known as muckraking, taken from a term adapted by President Theodore Roosevelt in a speech criticizing the journalists that was first circulated in the important literary review *The Outlook*. After his presidency, Roosevelt briefly became an editor of *Outlook*. One of muckraking's most notable examples was a series of articles by Ida Tarbell exposing the practices of the Standard Oil Company. Upton Sinclair's novel "The Jungle" was a major factor in the legislation of the Pure Food and Drugs Act and the Meat Inspection Act. After making a considerable impact, the movement lost momentum by 1912.

Women of this era made significant and multifaceted contributions to magazines, from anarchist Emma Goldman's important journal *Mother Earth* to the feminist writings of Charlotte Perkins Gilman in *The Forerunner* to the quaint and beautifully illustrated chapbook devoted to stories of life in the Lower East Side of Manhattan, *The East Side*, by the nearly forgotton Zoe Anderson Norris.

The Great American Magazine: Literature

Story papers were weekly eight-page tabloids, often combining material and themes to appeal to the whole family. The largest had enormous national circulations, some reaching 400,000 copies. They were fragile, printed on cheap paper and exceedingly ephemeral. Few copies of even the most popular titles have survived to the present day. Unlike the dime novels, which generally confined illustration to the cover, the story papers integrated text and illustration throughout. Story papers originated in the early 1840's with such titles as *Brother Jonathan* and *Flag of Our Union*. They reached their peak between the end of the Civil War and the turn of the century, replaced by dime novels, short story magazines and widely-circulated "slick" magazines.

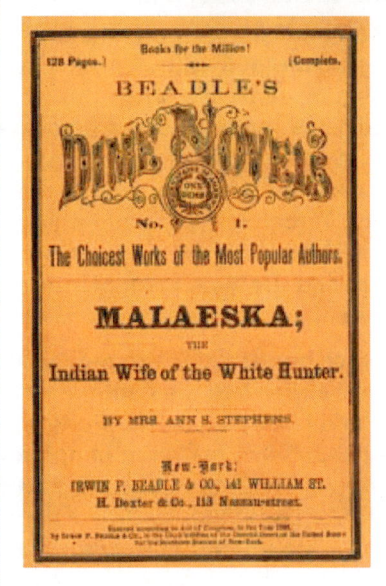

Dime novels were aimed at a youthful, working-class readership and widely distributed in massive editions. As with the story papers, only a few examples remain. Illustration was usually confined to the cover. Erastus and Irwin Beadle, later Beadle and Adams pioneered the genre in 1860, reprinting "Malaeska" by Ann S. Stephens in a small cheap format, followed very shortly afterwards by "Seth Jones" a western hero that created a huge following, selling over half a million copies! At this point, many other publishers, including De Witt and Munro jumped on the bandwagon. A wide variety of themes were depicted; tales of urban outlaws, detective stories, working-girl narratives of virtue defended, and costume romances, though the western was the most popular, likely fueled by the scurrilous Ned Buntline and the first American superhero, Davy Crockett.

While most baby boomers identify with Crockett by conjuring up fond memories of Walt Disney's television adventure starring Fess Parker and Buddy Ebsen, Crockett was spinning his own legend even before his death at the Alamo in 1836.

The Crockett Almanac began in 1835 and continued into the 1850's, elevating him to a larger than life figure, laying the groundwork forthe enormous popularity of later western heros like Seth Jones, Buffalo Bill and Wild Bill Hickok.

The Great American Magazine: Literature

The publishing empire of Francis Scott Street and Francis Shubael Smith began in 1855 when they bought *The New York Weekly Dispatch* and began *New York Weekly,* which soon became one of the highest circulation story papers.

Their second publication, *Street and Smith's Literary Album*, followed ten years later.

In an era of rampant anti-semitism, the notion of a Jewish hero was, to say the least, unusual!

Frank Leslie was one of the most colorful and prolific publishers of the nineteenth century. Born Henry Carter in England, an engraver by trade, he used the pseudonym "Frank Leslie" on his early drawings after coming to New York in 1848. After briefly working for P. T. Barnum, in 1854 he started *Frank Leslie's New York Journal*, the first of twenty two magazines that would bear his name in the next quarter century.

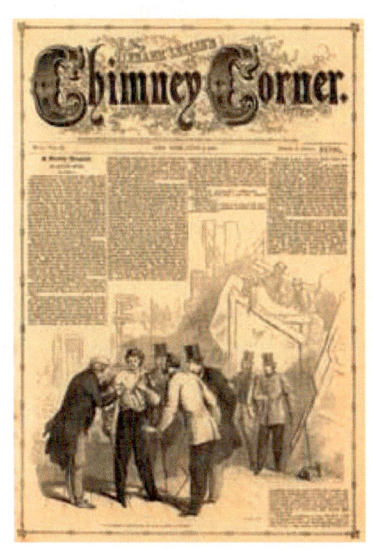

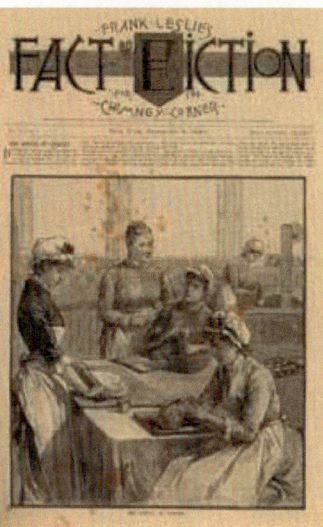

The story paper *Frank Leslie's Chimney Corner* was a popular title. *Stars and Stripes* and *Fact and Fiction* were not as successful.

65   The Great American Magazine: Literature

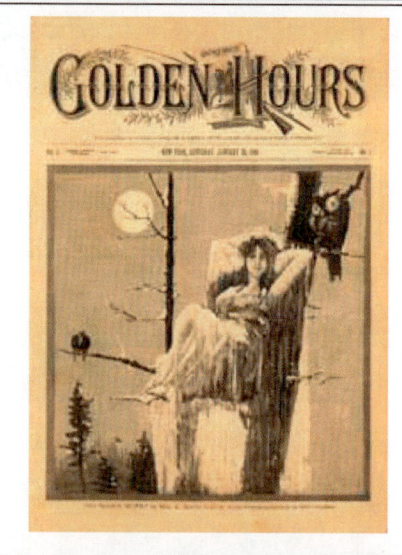

The New Sensation was the first story paper to employ color printing. Robert Bonner's more conservative *New York Ledger* was one of the longest-running and influential titles, even publishing an original story by Charles Dickens.

The Wild Fire is a good example of the many well-produced tabloid scandal sheets of this era which are now virtually lost.

Frank Tousey's *Boys of New York* was one of the longer running and popular titles. This issue features one of the many futuristic Frank Reade stories.

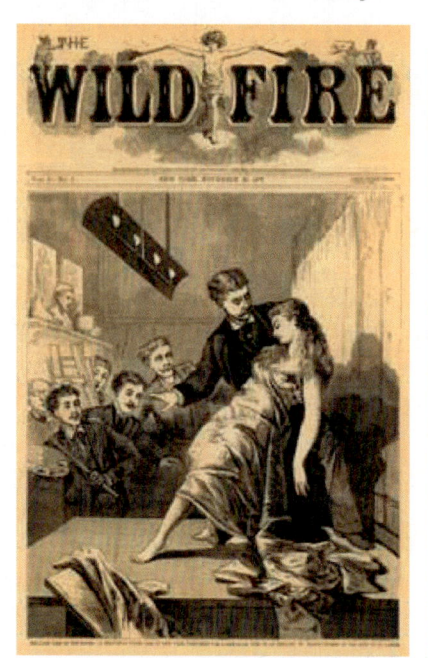

The Great American Magazine: Literature

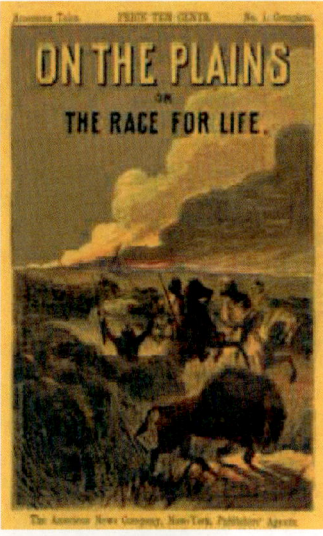

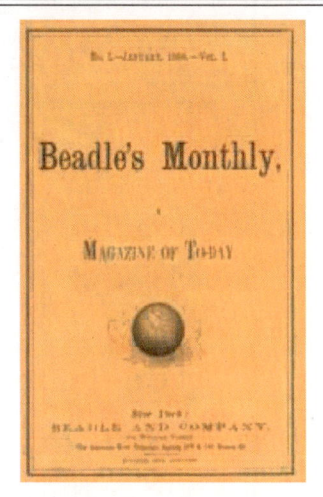

The Beadles also had an short-lived literary magazine

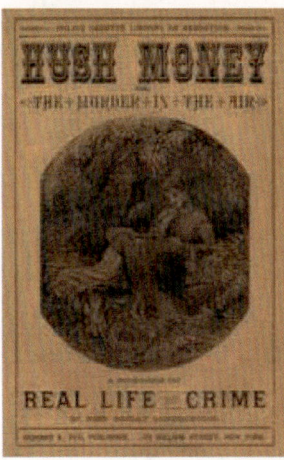

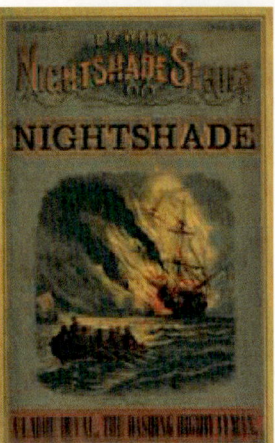

The earliest dime novels were small in format with a potpourri of themes like war and adventure. Many were sensationalistic. Even the notorious Richard K. Fox, publisher of the tabloid *National Police Gazette* tried his hand. Dime novels and story papers were the earliest fuel of the American public's insatiable appetite for crime and sensationalism. Tabloid journalism likely got much of its inspiration from them.

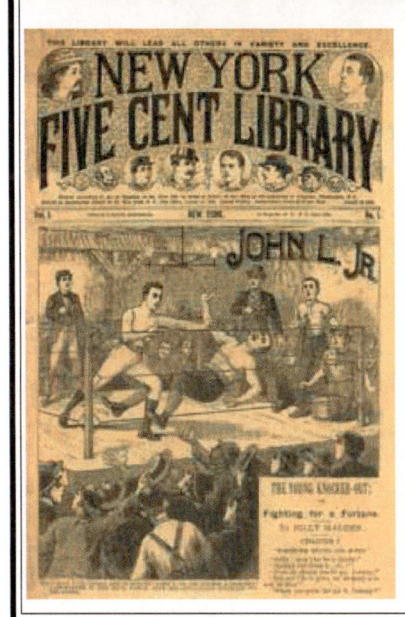

Frank Reade Library was the earliest serial dealing with the yet unnamed genre of science-fiction. The steam man was actually built and patented!

Boxing has always had a special low-brow appeal. This made it an ideal topic for dime novels.

67 The Great American Magazine: Literature

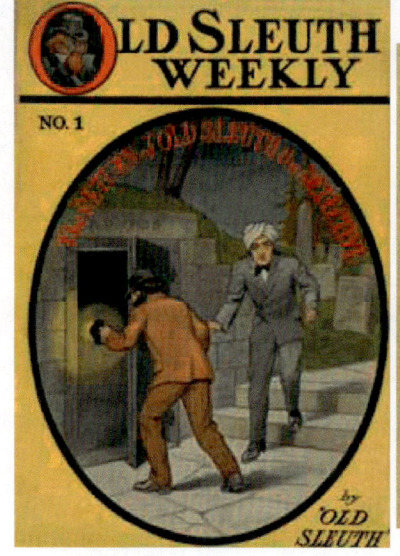

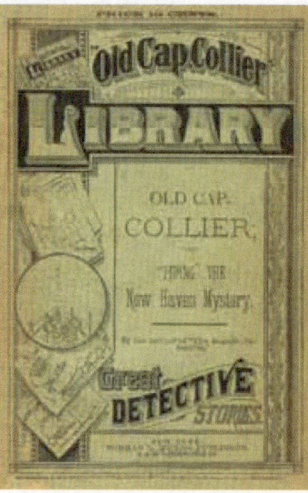

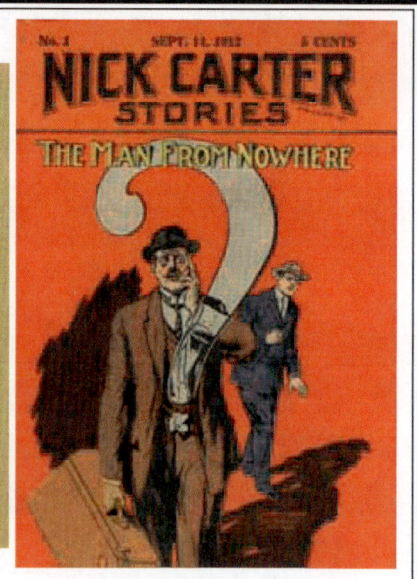

Harlan Halsey's *Old Sleuth* was the first serial detective character; so popular, in fact, that a lawsuit was needed to determine which publisher could use the name. *Old Cap Collier* and *Nick Carter*, who persisted into the pulp era, followed shortly and enjoyed large readerships as well.

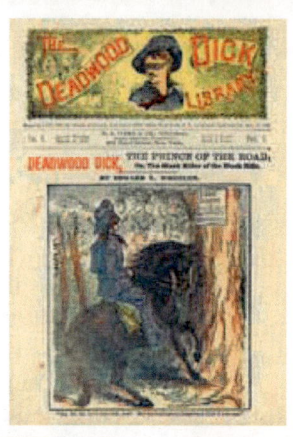

Western themes continued to be popular and profitable. *The James Boys* and *Deadwood Dick* were the most popular bad guys and the self-promoting showman and former scout, William F. Cody, Buffalo Bill, was the most widely read hero. *Buffalo Bill Stories* evolved into *Western Story Magazine*, the first western pulp.

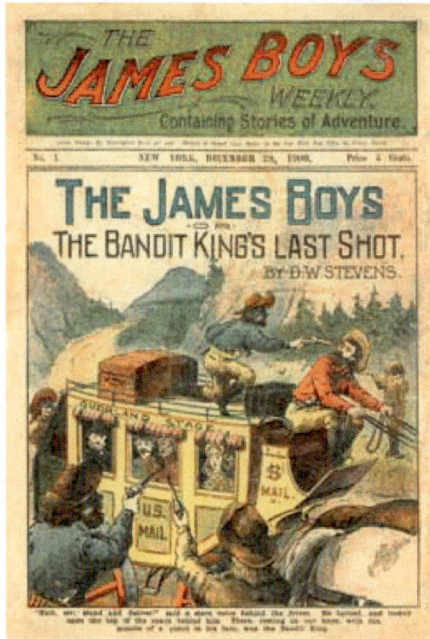

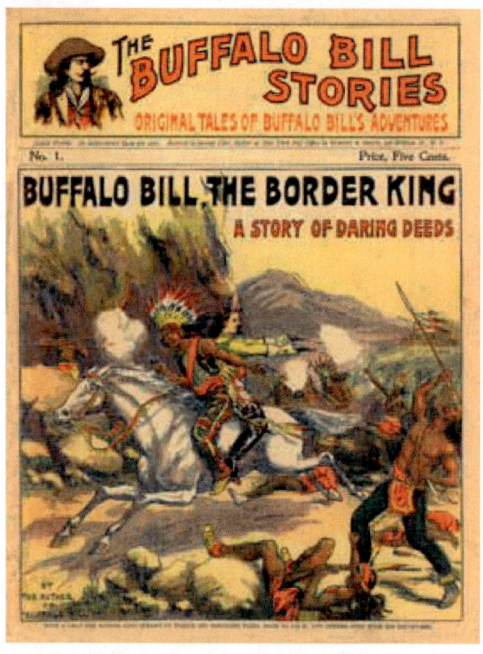

The Great American Magazine: Literature

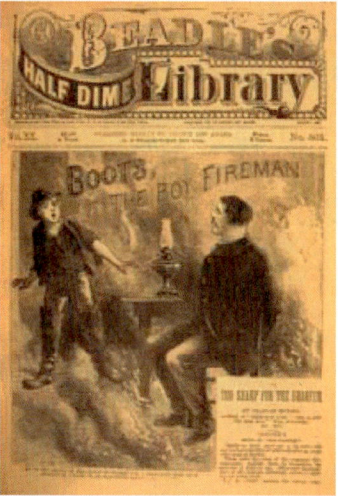

Dime novel format evolved first to a larger size, then a reduced price and as technology improved, color covers.

The patriotism brought about by the Spanish-American War did not escape dime novel publishers Frank Tousey, Howard Ainslee and Street and Smith. American wars became a frequent theme, from The Revolution to the war of the present day.

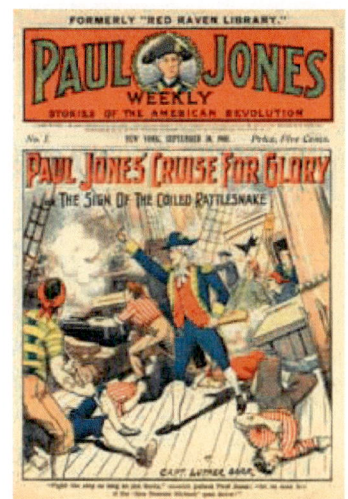

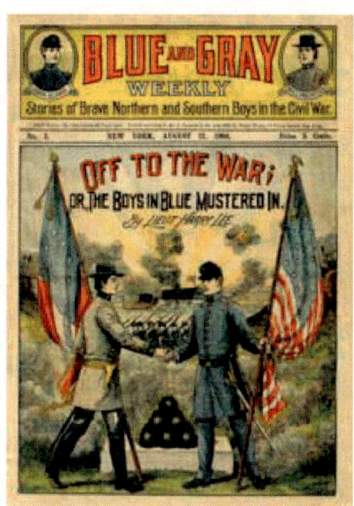

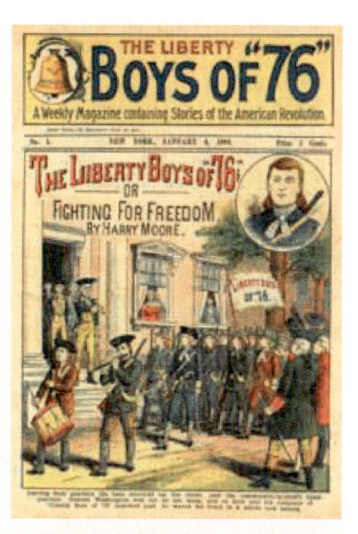

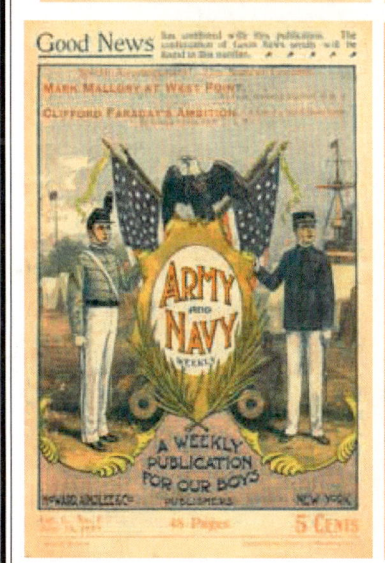

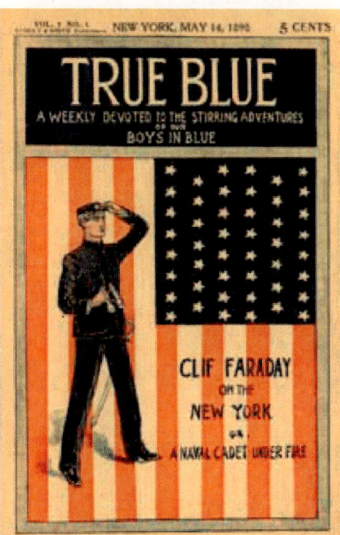

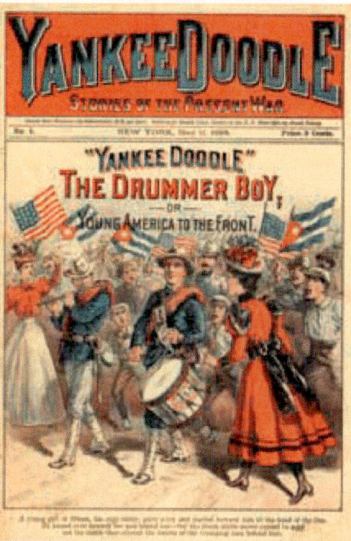

The Great American Magazine: Literature

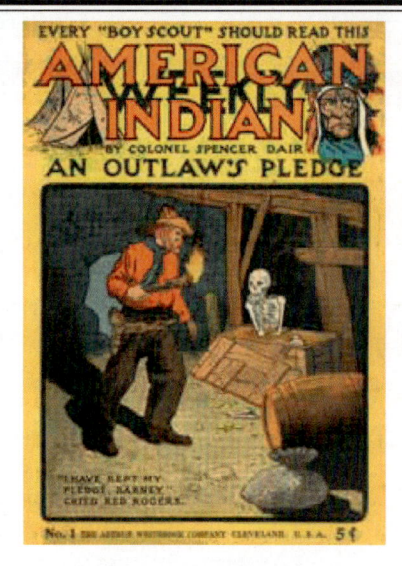

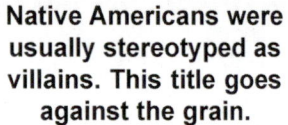

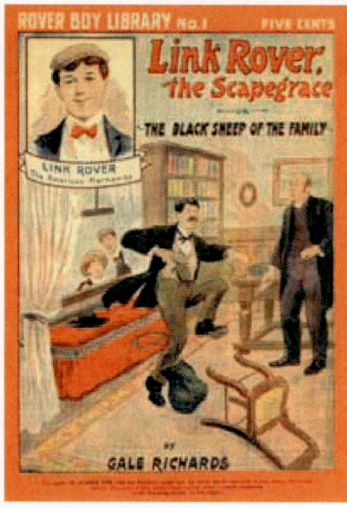

Native Americans were usually stereotyped as villains. This title goes against the grain.

Horatio Alger-like boy heros were a frequent theme. Girl characters were often included in an effort to appeal to a female readership as well.

Dime novel publishers constantly searched for new and popular themes. The Alaska goldrush and the automobile were fresh topics at the turn of the twentieth century, but by the time the pulps took over as the predominant source of cheap serial fiction, their appeal was gone.

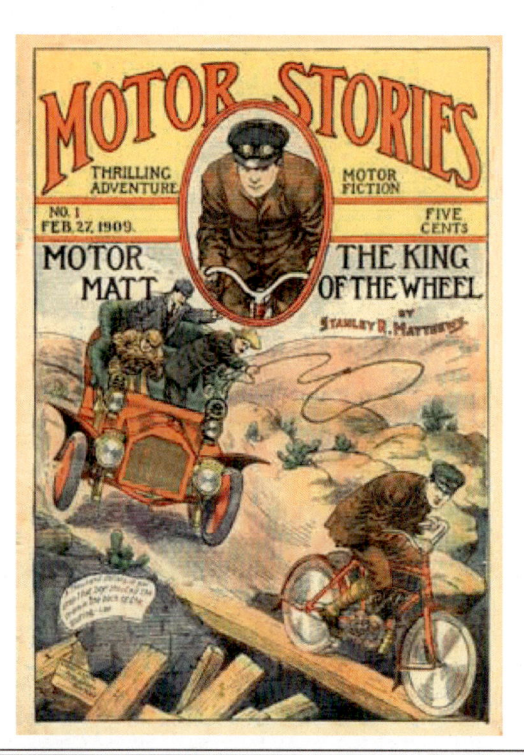

The Great American Magazine: Literature

The list of contributors to *Smart Set* during its distinguished run included Jack London, Sinclair Lewis, F. Scott Fitzgerald, Eugene O'Neill and O. Henry. Between 1914 and 1923 it was edited by H. L. Mencken and George Jean Nathan.

Ayer's Magazine is virtually unremembered. The first issue had illustrations by Penrhyn Stanlaws and Rose O'Neill Latham.

Booklover's Magazine failed in its attempt to compete with *Harper's* and *Scribner's* though it published important authors like Booth Tarkington and Theodore Dreiser.

National Post lasted for only five issues. The first features a story by Zane Grey and a cover illustration by Will Bradley Studios.

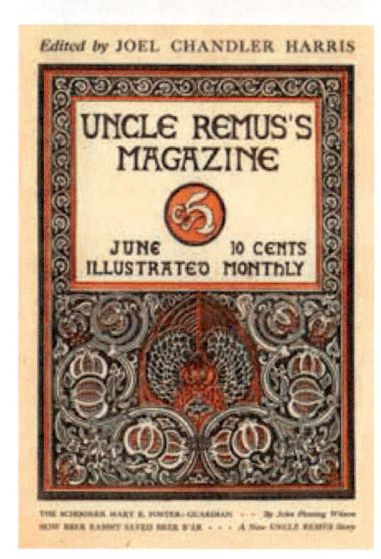

Joel Chandler Harris founded and published *Uncle Remus's Magazine* in Atlanta from June 1907 until his death in May 1908.

The first issue of the little known *Neale's Monthly* has contributions by Katherine Lee Bates and Ambrose Bierce.

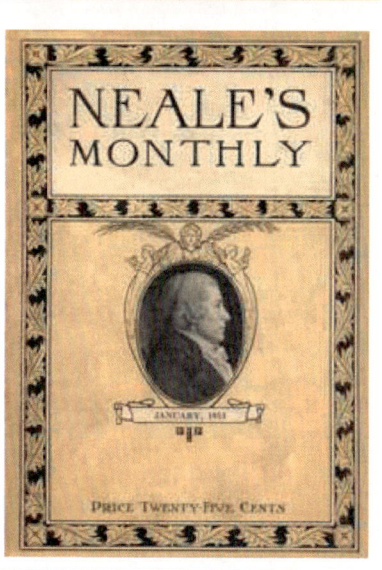

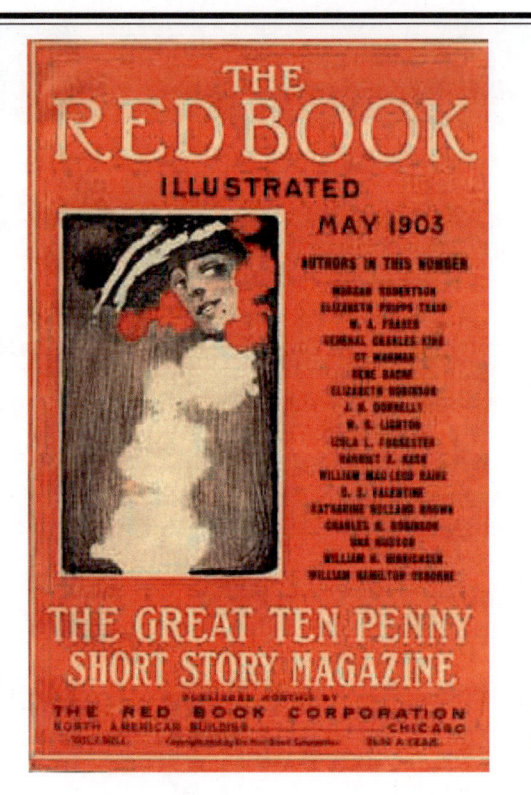

The first issue of *The Pocket Magazine* featured one of numerous original American magazine appearances of Sir Arthur Conan Doyle.

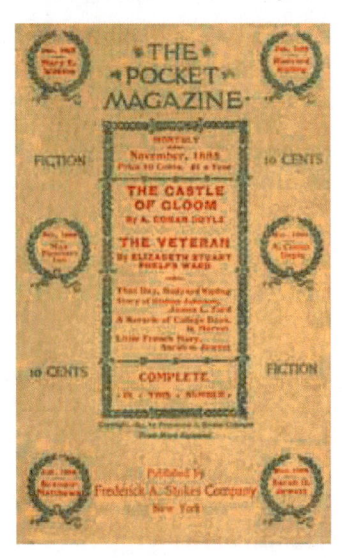

Short story magazines were very popular around the turn of the 20th century. *The Red Book* was ultimately the most successful of all and is still published today. In 1930, it introduced Nick and Nora Charles to the world with the first publication of Dashiell Hammett's "The Thin Man".

Despite its magnificent cover design, there just weren't enough card game stories to keep *Poker Chips* going more than a few issues.

The Great American Magazine: Literature

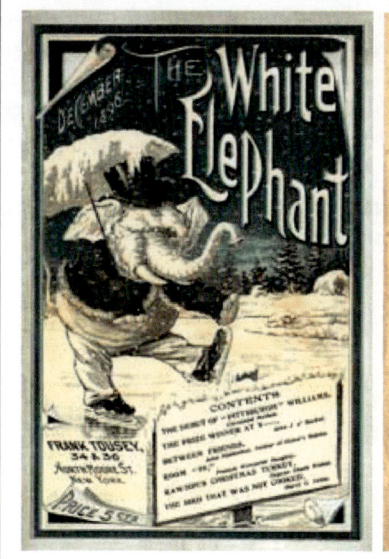

These three short story magazines all had animal themes. *The White Elephant* was published by the dime novel giant, Frank Tousey. *The Black Cat* had nothing to do with magic or superstition. It did, though, publish an early literary effort of Jack London, a short story entitled "A Thousand Deaths" in May 1899. *The Owl* contains London's first publication in 1897.

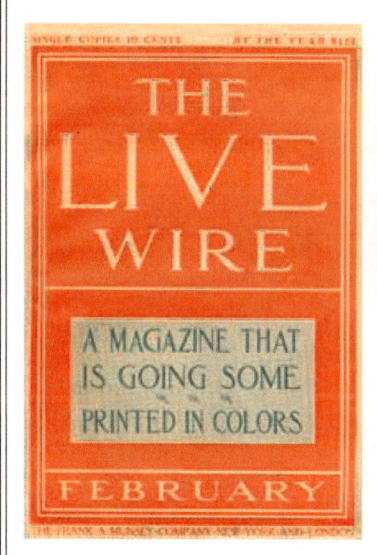

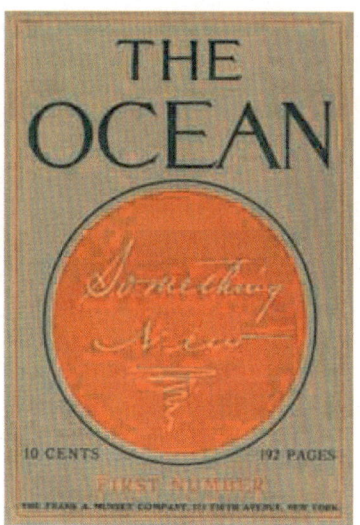

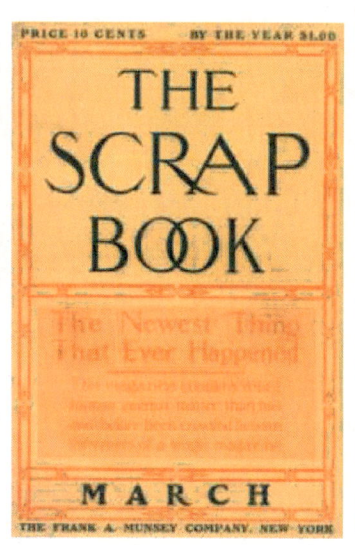

The prolific Frank Munsey supplied magazine readers with a wide variety of titles.

The first decade of the twentieth century was a crossroads in magazine publishing; story papers and dime novels were on the wane, short story magazines and chapbooks were at their zenith and illustrated weekly "slicks" and pulps were just starting to blossom.

The eighteen-nineties saw the birth of a distinctive genre of literary magazines called Chapbooks, born out of the success of Stone and Kimball's Chicago based semi-monthly. They were characterized by small or odd-shaped pages, fine typography and printing, and cleverness and radicalism in criticism. The inexpensive format and relatively small circulation presented a literary opportunity for editors and writers who could not find their way into the major literary magazines of the day. Aside from the archetype, *The Chap-Book*, the most important were Elbert Hubbard's *Philistine*, Gelett Burgess' *Lark* and Thomas Mosher's *Bibelot*.

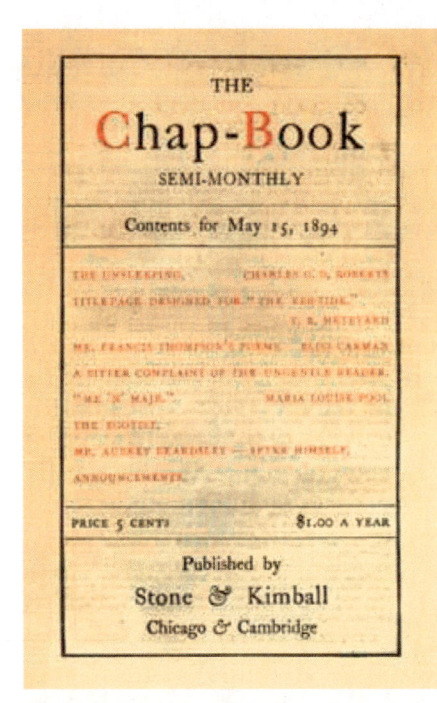

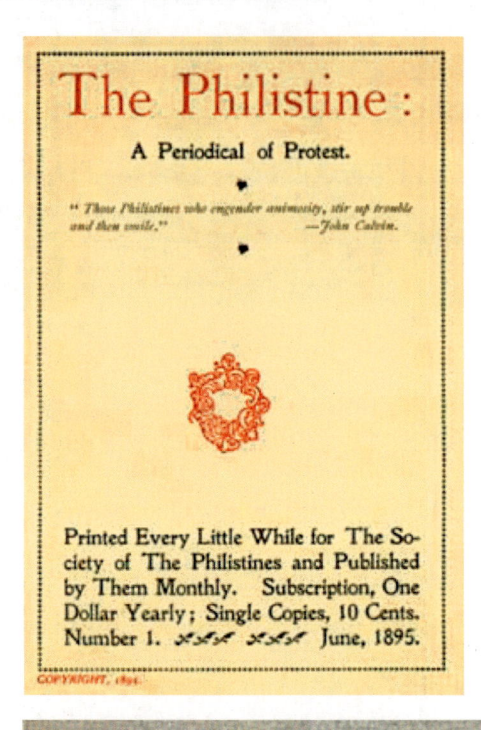

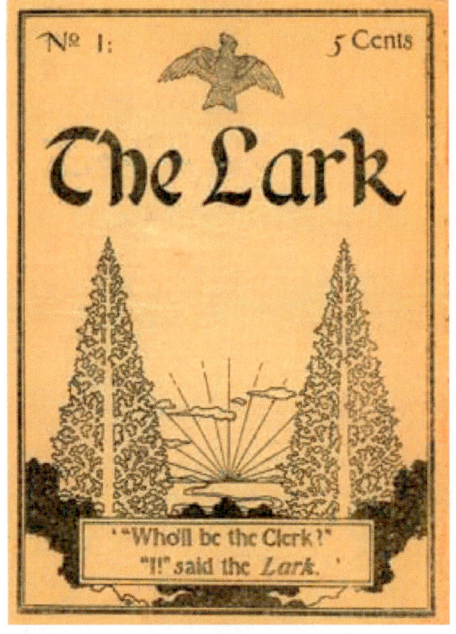

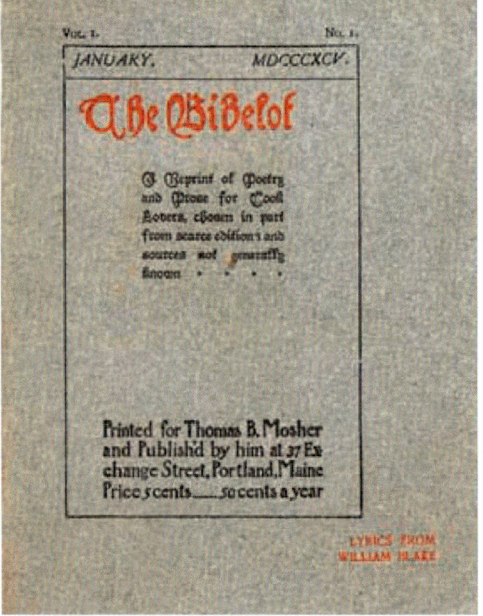

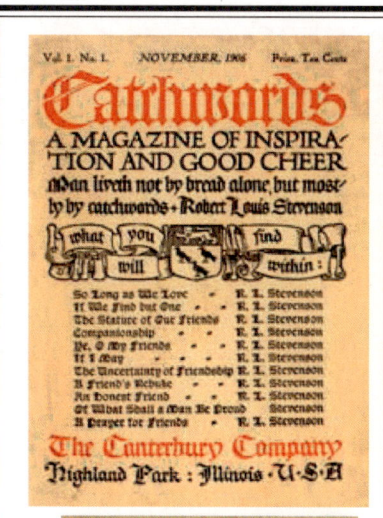

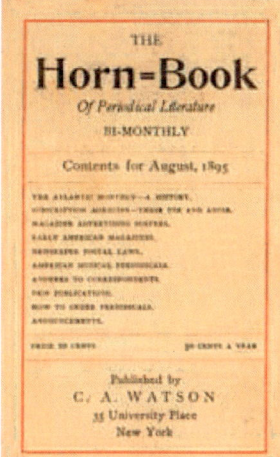

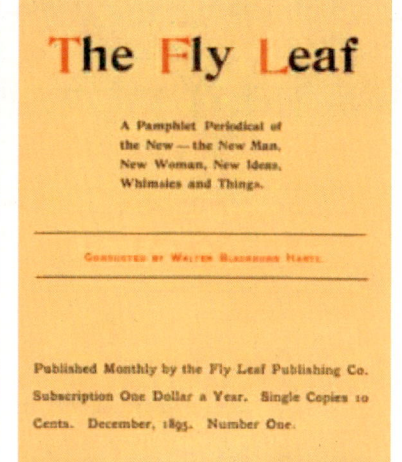

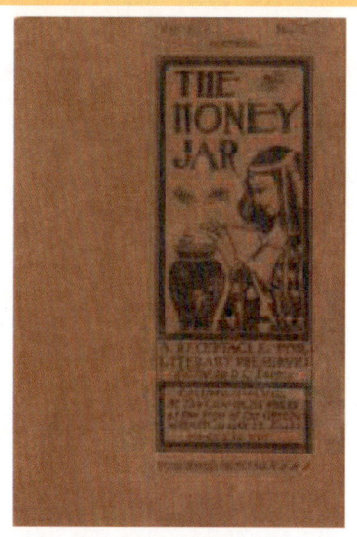

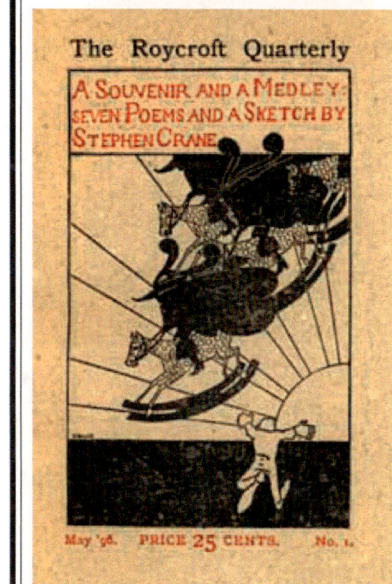

A number of chapbooks like *The Lotus* and *The Honey Jar* were produced by college literary societies. The first issue of *The Roycroft Quarterly*, produced by Elbert Hubbard, was devoted exclusively to Stephen Crane.

75   The Great American Magazine: Literature

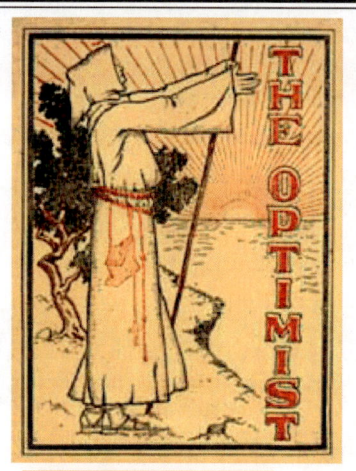

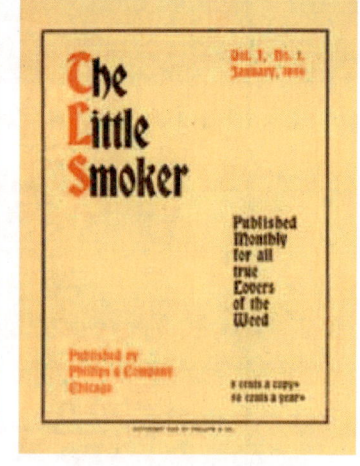

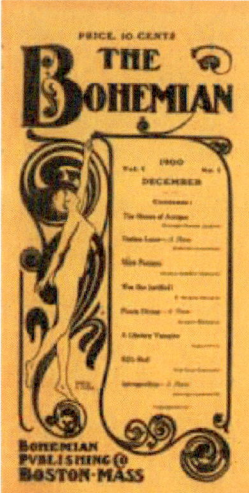

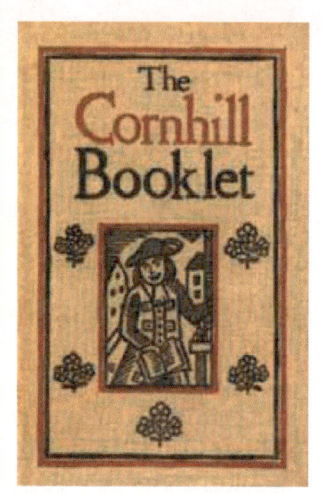

Some chapbooks had a more singular purpose like *Lucifer's Lantern*, published in Utah with a distinctly anti-Mormon flavor and *The Little Smoker*, published for "lovers of the weed".
The Story Teller was for children.

Storyland is probably unique. A handwritten note inside identifies the ediitor as fifteen year old Beatrice Beck, who had to suspend publication after one month when she couldn't keep up with her homework!

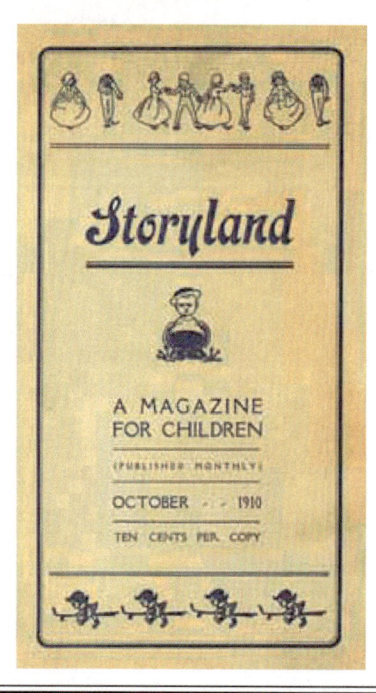

The Great American Magazine: Literature

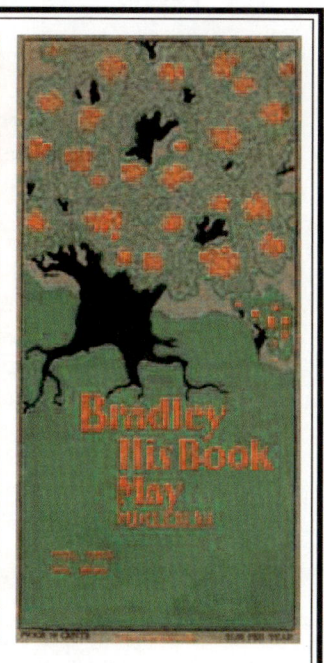

At the time of the chapbooks, the Art Nouveau and the Arts and Crafts Movements were at their peak in the world of art and illustration. Magazines provided a fine venue for the works of Will Bradley, Edward Penfield and Maxfield Parrish.
The Blue Pencil was issued by an exclusive New York literary club whose members included Richard F. Outcault, most famous as the creator of
The Yellow Kid and Buster Brown.

The rare and highly collected *Yellow Kid Magazine* is considered to be the first periodical based on a comic character. The content of the magazine, though, was purely literary with "the kid" appearing only on the covers.

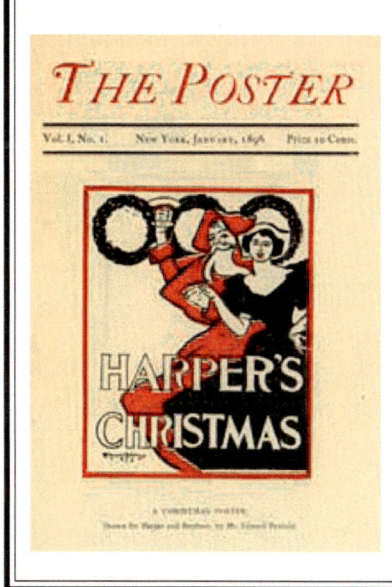

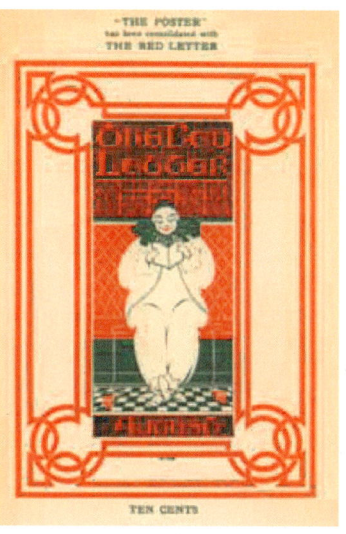

The Great American Magazine: Literature

"Little Magazines" published creative, often innovative work, with little or no regard for commercial gain. In their time, they introduced the vast majority of important new writers and poets to the American public and provided an outlet for new creative work that, in many cases, had a latitude well outside the criteria governing most mainstream journals. They sometimes had very small print runs and most were quite short-lived.

While Hoffman et. al. (the classic reference on the topic) traces the earliest precursors of this diverse genre back to the *The Dial* of the 1840's, the universally recognized premiere was Harriet Monroe's *Poetry*, the most important American poetry journal ever published. Margaret Anderson's *Little Review* followed in 1914. Both of these cornerstone publications were significantly influenced by Ezra Pound. Alfred Kreymborg was another early, influential force, editing a number of the most highly regarded journals such as *Others* and *The Glebe*.

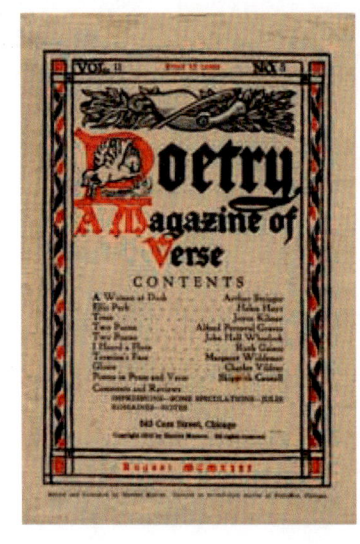

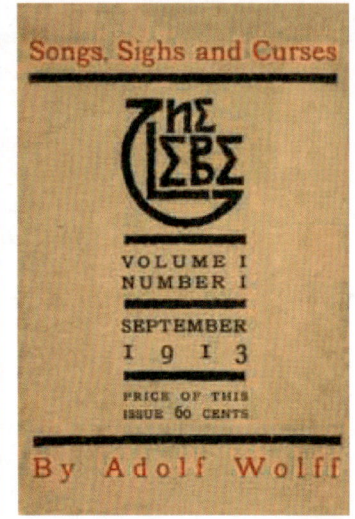

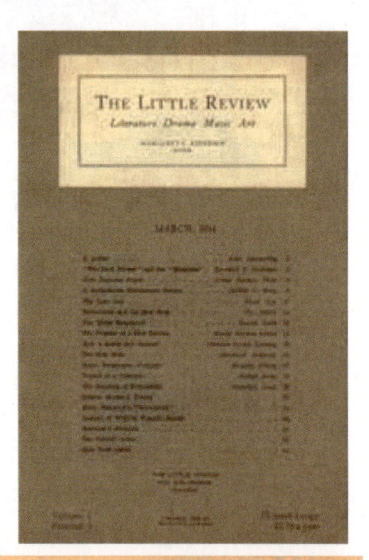

One of America's most beloved poems, Joyce Kilmer's "Trees" was first published in this 1913 issue of Harriet Monroe's monumentual magazine, *Poetry*.

No, Hugh Hefner was not the first to use *Playboy* as a magazine title! The distinction goes to this eclectic, elegantly illustrated little magazine edited by Egmont Arens, published at the Washington Square Bookshop in New York City between 1919 and 1924.

The Great American Magazine: Literature

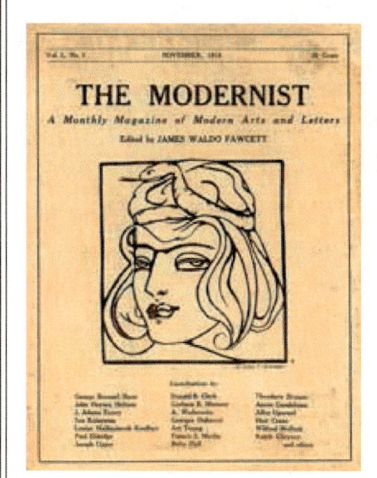

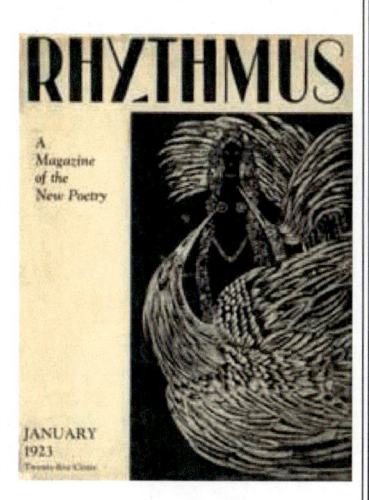

The avant garde creativity seen in little magazines also extended to the accompanying illustration. *Aesthete 1925* was issued by the "younger generation of writers" in response to an article critical of them in the mainstream *American Mercury*.

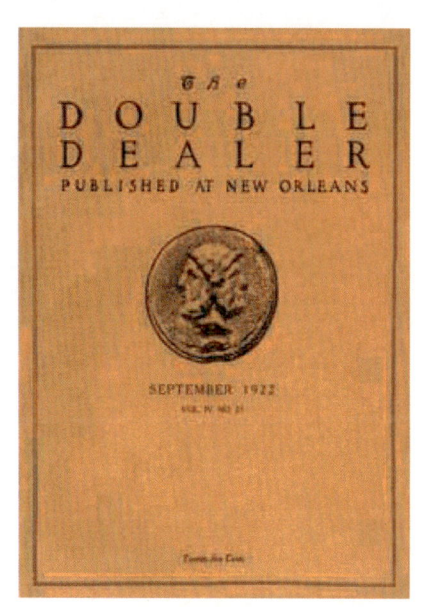

The Quill came to represent the spirit of New York's Greenwich Village. The first issue was edited by Harold Hersey, who is best remembered for his later editorship of dozens of pulp magazines. *The Double Dealer*, published in New Orleans, had an almost uncanny ability to discover new literary talent. This 1922 issue included the first appearances of Thornton Wilder and Jean Toomer.

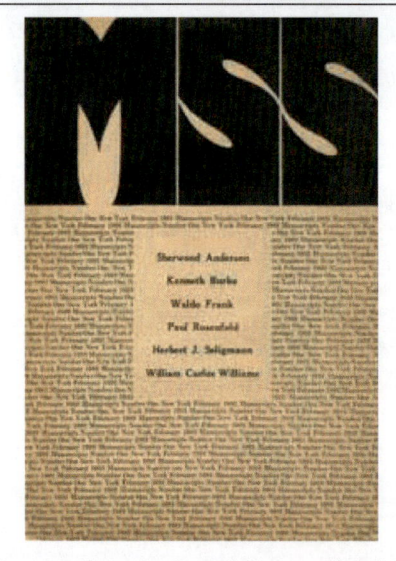

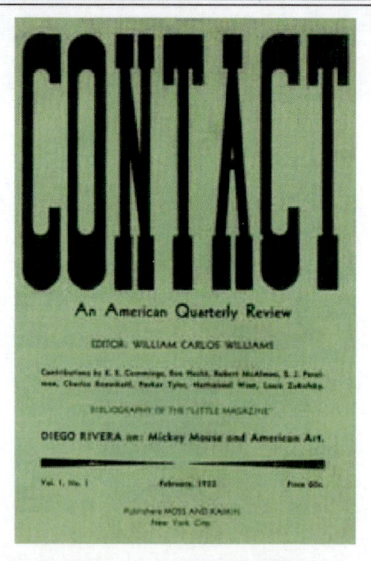

Manuscripts featured the work of Sherwood Anderson and New Jersey pediatrician/poet William Carlos Williams, who also edited two journals entitled *Contact*. This is the first issue of the second series.

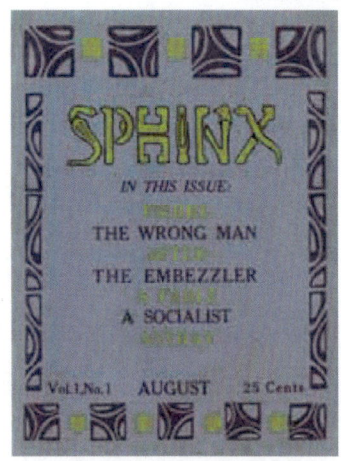

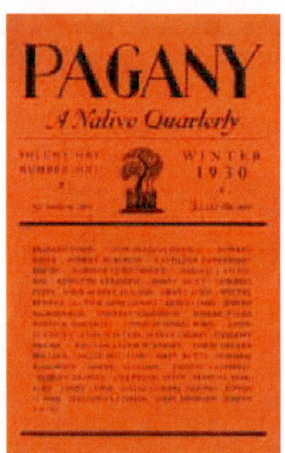

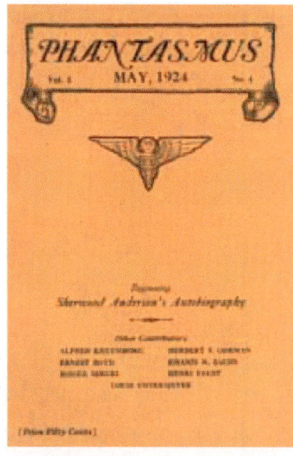

Over six-hundred little magazines appeared between 1912 and the mid-1940's, comprising a wide variety of focuses, including poetry, short stories and radical literature.

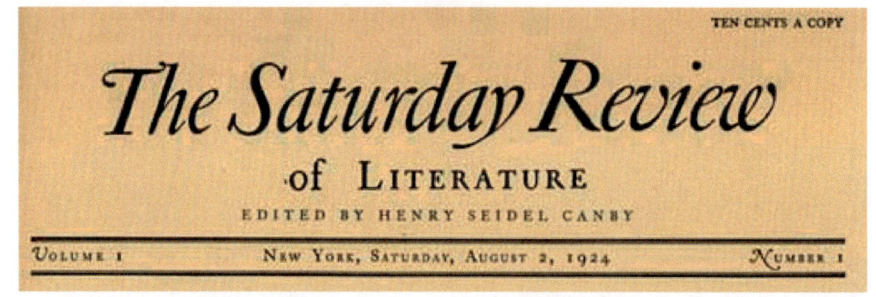

Born out of the demise of the literary section of *The New York Evening Post*, the venerable *Saturday Review of Literature* edited by Henry Seidel Canby, William Rose Benet and Amy Loveman became one of the most influential forces of literary criticism of the twentieth century.

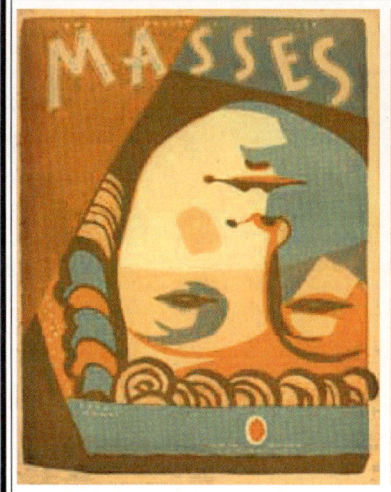

Three of the "unmailable" 1917 issues of *The Masses*

Under the editorship of Max Eastman, assisted by Floyd Dell, *The Masses* was the most important radical magazine of its time, publishing articles by John Reed, who was briefly an editor, and virtually all of the most important radical or liberal literary figures. In late 1917, it was banned from the mails because of its anti-war content and ceased publication with the November/December issue. The editors were brought to trial, resulting in two hung juries. Eastman started *The Liberator* using the same staff in March 1918 with a more concrete political stance, publishing until October 1924. *New Masses* was started in 1926 by some of *The Liberator's* literary editors but soon became increasingly Stalinist and alienated much of the left.

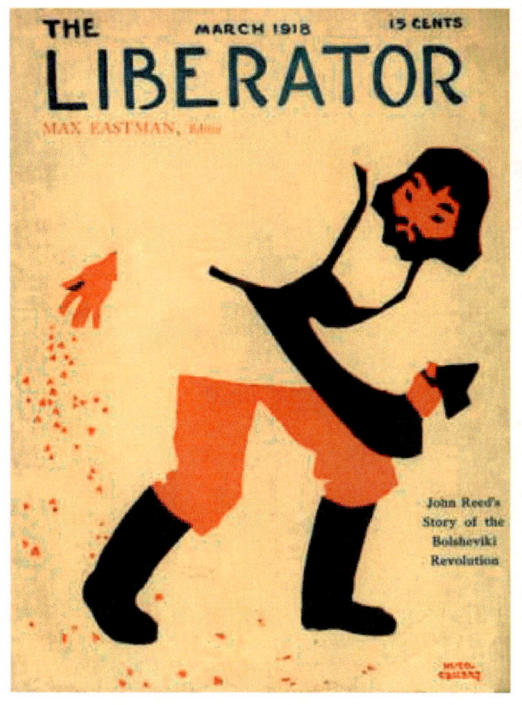

The Great American Magazine: Literature

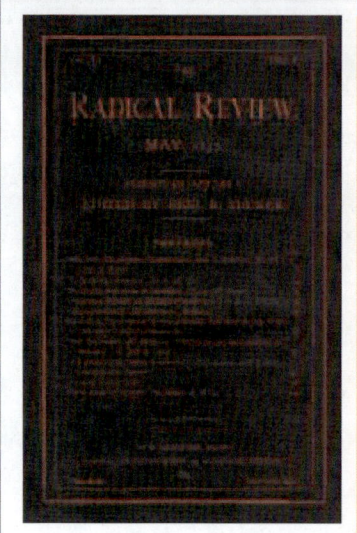

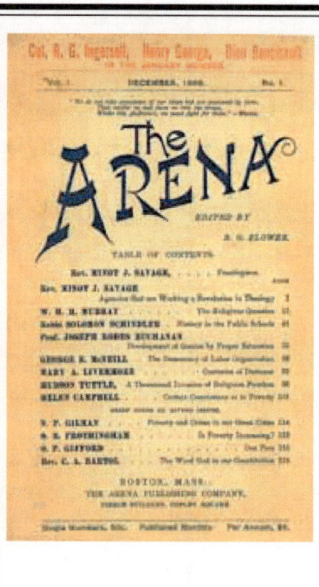

Radical Review, started in 1877, was one of America's earliest anarchist publications.
The Comrade was an early Socialist magazine.
The first issue included an article by Jack London.
B. O. Flower's *Arena* was the most widely circulated and important radical magazine of its era, mixing literature and criticism with a fervent advocacy for women's rights and political, socioeconomic and religious reform.
Left wing magazines such as *The Left* were commonly published until World War II. The very rare *Proletariat* was published by the Jack London Memorial Institute and is typical of the many Bolshevik-leaning magazines of its era. *The Anvil* was the second and most successful of Jack Conroy's three magazines, focused on the social and economic woes of the working class. 1000 copies of the first issue were printed and circulation eventually peaked at 5000. In 1935, it merged into *Partisan Review*.

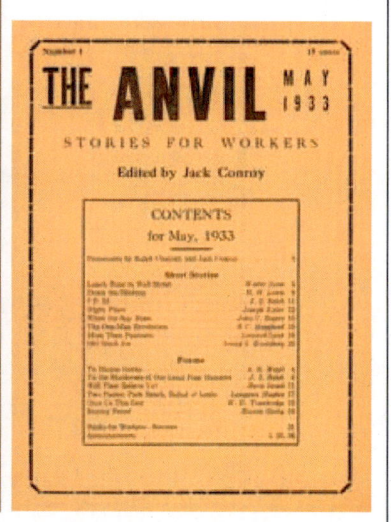

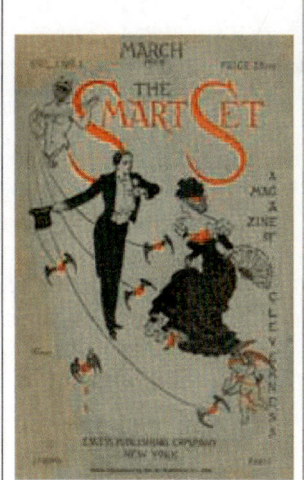

The first issue of *Smart Set* and the first appearance of Dashiell Hammett, October 1922

H. L. Mencken and George Jean Nathan had an interesting and duplicitous publishing career; high-brow magazines they proudly put their name on and less socially acceptable pulps to pay the bills. After acquiring *Smart Set*, Mencken and Nathan surreptitiously published the "louse magazines" *Parisienne*, *Saucy Stories* and, most successfully, *Black Mask*. *Black Mask* pioneered hard-boiled detective fiction with the works of Dashiell Hammett and Raymond Chandler. Hammett's first appearance (as was that of F. Scott Fitzgerald) was in *Smart Set*, after which he developed his "Continental Op" in *Black Mask*. His best known appearance is "The Maltese Falcon", serialized in five issues in 1929 and 1930, introducing Sam Spade, later portrayed by Humphrey Bogart in the film noir classic. With the success of the previous venture, Mencken and Nathan proudly embarked on another less profitable, yet highly reputable, literary venture, *The American Mercury*.

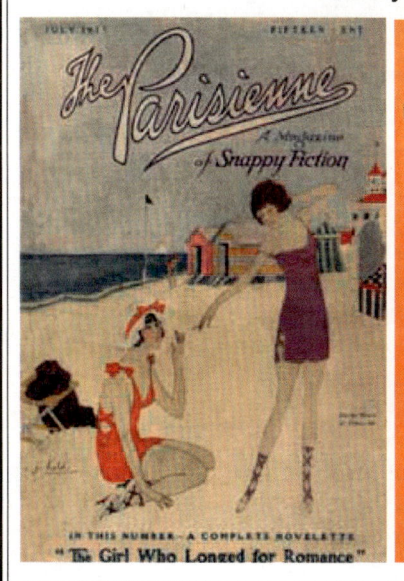

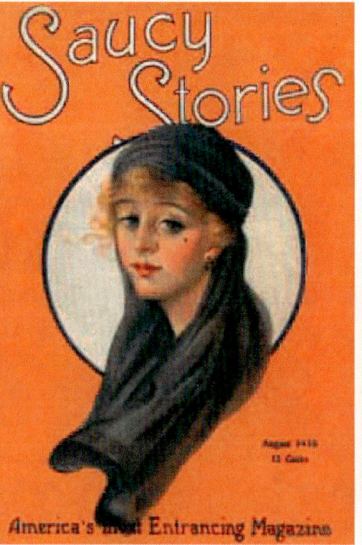

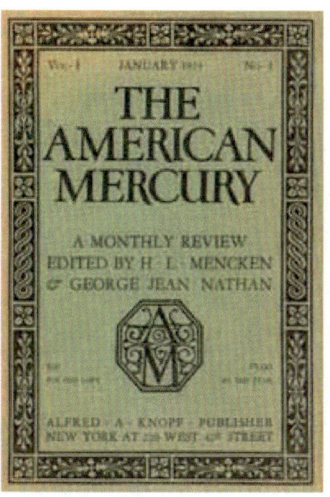

The Great American Magazine: Literature

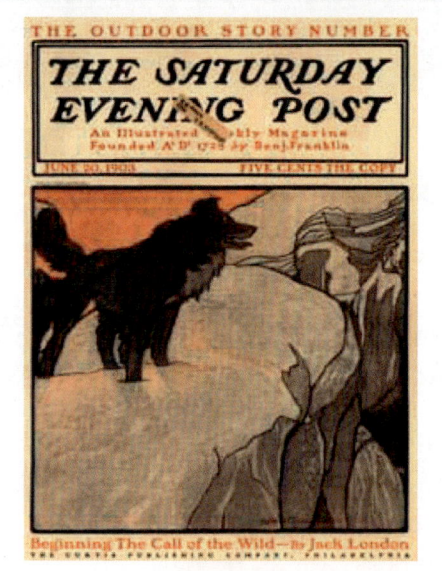

In 1897, Cyrus Curtis bought the floundering and undistinguished *Saturday Evening Post* for one thousand dollars. With editor George Horace Lorimer, they built it into the highest circulation literary periodical of the first half of the twentieth century. Beginning by fabricating a "heritage" to Benjamin Franklin, *The Post* then utilized the most popular writers and illustrators. The many literary highlights include the first printing of Jack London's "The Call of the Wild".

In 1898, the first of 320 *Post* covers illustrated by the well-regarded J. C. Leyendecker appeared. In 1916, the twenty-two year old Norman Rockwell presented his work to editor Lorimer and soon became the most popular magazine artist of all, illustrating 321 covers thru 1963.

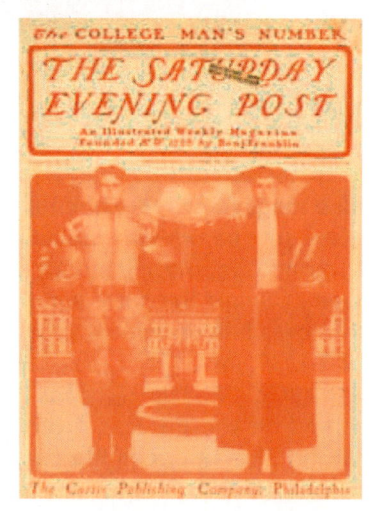

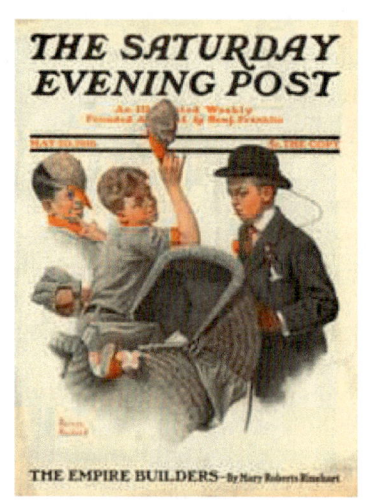

Leyendecker's and Rockwell's first *Post* covers.

The prolific and immensely popular Rockwell illustrated the cover of magazines more than five-hundred times. These are among the rarest, from an obscure magazine supplement to a Boston newspaper and this first issue of *Milestones* a monthly issued by a tire manufacturer, which contained a story by Ring Lardner.

The Great American Magazine: Literature

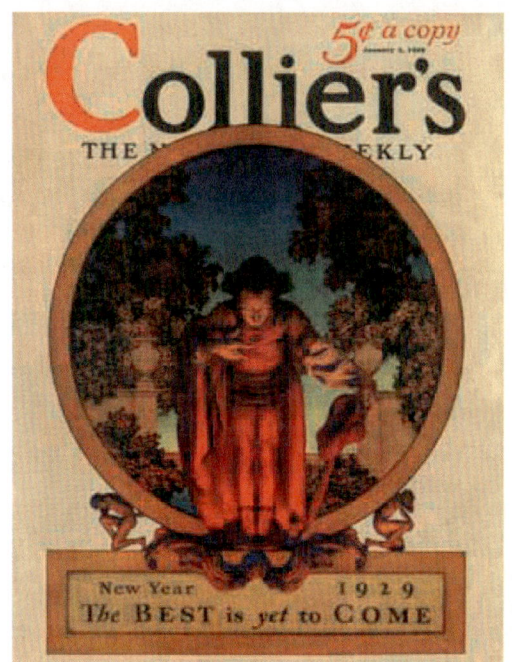

Beginning as a minor illustrated miscellany, *Once A Week*, *Collier's* was only a short step behind *The Post* in popularity. The many covers illustrated by Maxfield Parrish are particularly notable. This one was adapted from Louise Saunders' "Knave of Hearts".

Parrish's magazine covers are among the most beautiful ever created. This cover is one of his finest. *Hearst's Magazine* was a short-lived monthly that merged with *Cosmopolitan*.

Jack London's "White Fang" was initally serialized in 1906 in Caspar Whitney's elegantly illustrated *Outing Magazine*. At this time, *Outing* also published Clarence Mulford's "Bar 20 Range Yarns", the first appearance of the western hero Hopalong Cassidy, illustrated by Frank Schoonover and N.C. Wyeth.

The Great American Magazine: Literature

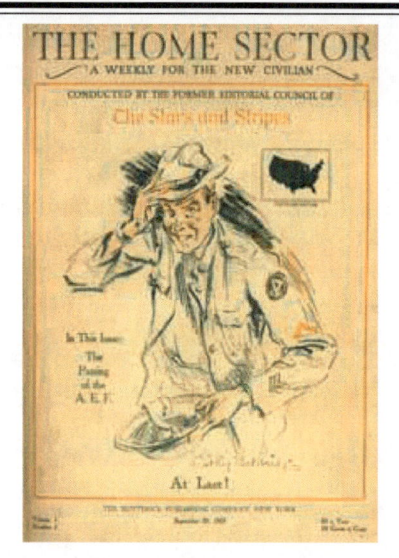

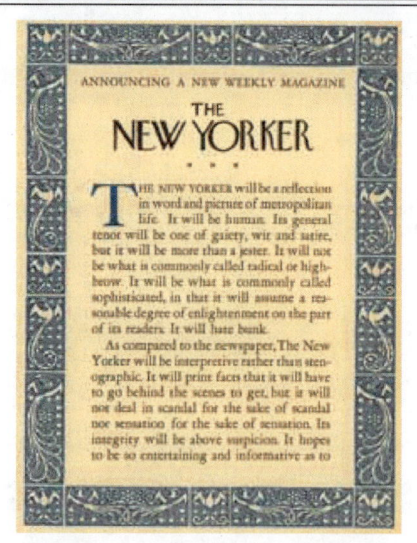

After returning from military service during the First World War and his stint as editor-in-chief of *The Stars and Stripes*, the boorish Harold Ross, with his friend Alexander Woolcott, started his first publication *The Home Sector*. In the early twenties, he became associated with the effete group of writers of the Algonquin Round Table. This led to the formation of his master opus, *The New Yorker*, which he edited until his death in 1951. True to its prospectus, *The New Yorker* has been the prototype of urbane wit and the journal of "the aristocracy of New York sophistication" since its inception. Among its many literary highlights are the 1946 issue entirely devoted to John Hersey's "Hiroshima" and the original appearances of J. D. Salinger's "Franny" and "Zooey".

The issue of November 6, 1926 below was never published. It was created by the magazine contributors on the one year anniversary for the amusement of the staff and friends. The cover is by Rea Irvin (Penaninksky) and features a silhouette of Ross (with the ever-present cigarette hanging from his mouth) as the now familiar Eustace Tilly, gazing upon the arachnoidian Woolcott.

The Great American Magazine: Literature

Ernest Hemingway was intimately associated with magazines throughout his career. His first published literary effort was a short story in this 1916 issue of *Tabula*, his high school literary magazine. *Double Dealer*, a rare and important little magazine published in New Orleans, provided his first national appearance in 1922. In 1923, *Poetry* published a number of his poems which were later included in his first book. Even after his national reputation was made, *Scribner's* serialized "A Farewell to Arms" prior to publishing it in book form. In the late thirties and forties, Hemingway wrote articles as a war correspondant for *Ken*, *PM* and *Collier's*. One of his last works "The Old Man and the Sea" was first published as a feature in *Life* in 1952.

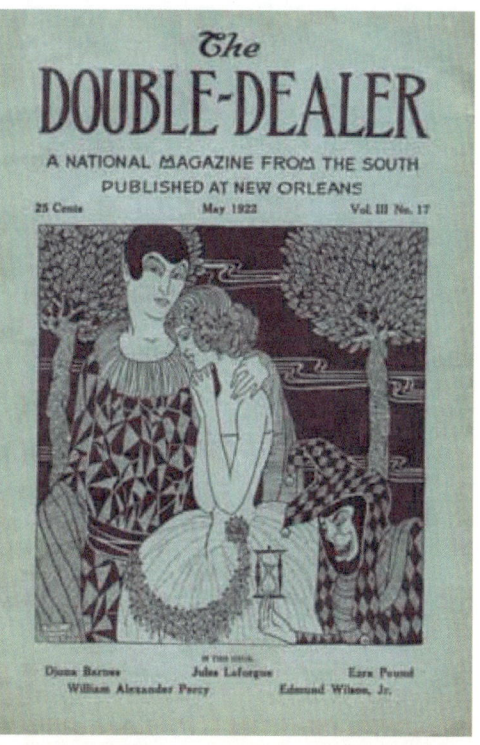

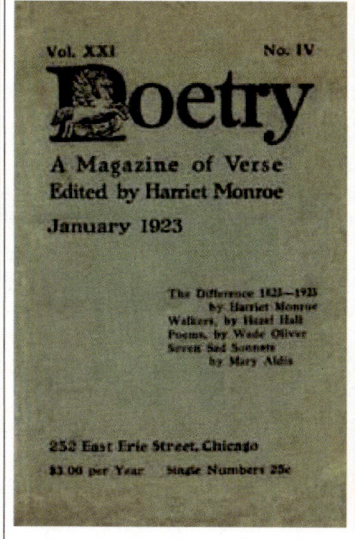

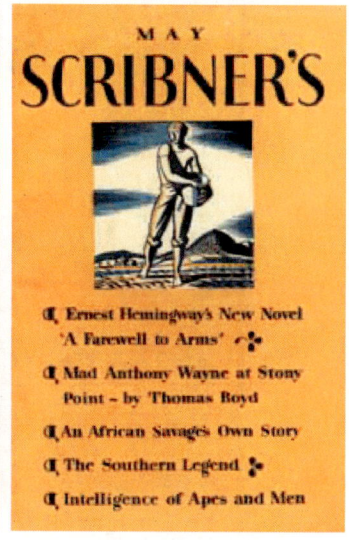

Much of the most important literature of the post-World War One era emanated from the community of writers living in Paris, including the "lost generation" of American expatrites such as Gertude Stein, who coined the term, Hemingway and F. Scott Fitzgerald.

One of the most important and controversial literary works of the twentieth century, James Joyce's "Ulysses" was first seen in *The Little Review* beginning in March 1918, largely due to the efforts of Ezra Pound, who brought Joyce's manuscript to editor Margaret Anderson. The work made a profound impression on Anderson, as seen by the announcement on the rear wrapper of the issue prior to its initial publication. In 1919, after 14 of the 17 parts had been serialized, it was banned by the Society for the Suppression of Vice. Four issues were impounded by the Post Office and editors Anderson and Jane Heap were arrested and tried as purveyors of obsenity. The first book edition was published in Paris in 1922 and it wasn't until 1934, after two pirated editions, before an authorized American edition finally appeared.

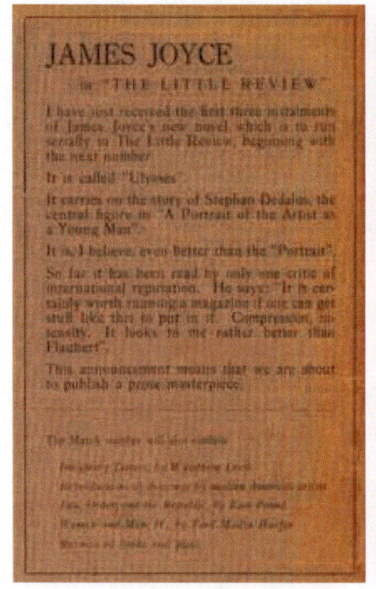

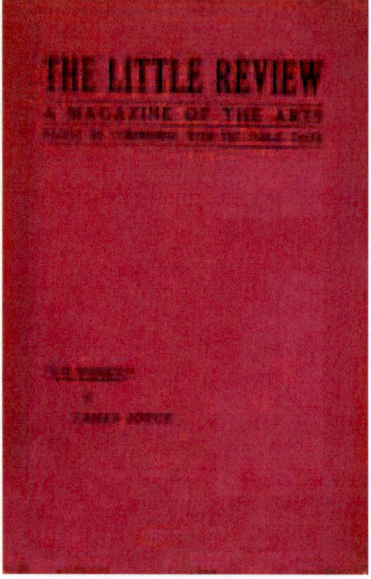

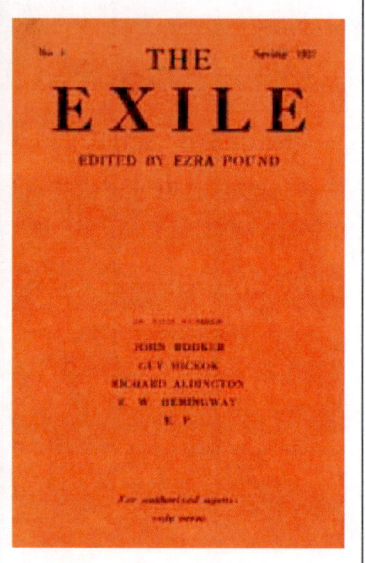

The intermingling of the aesthetic community was remarkable. At the behest of the great photographer Edward Steichen, Gertrude Stein wrote in support of the then controversial post-impressionists Picasso and Matisse in a 1912 supplementary issue of Steichen's rare and valuable *Camera Work*.

Ezra Pound published the work of Hemingway and other expatriates, from Paris in *The Exile*.

In 1924, Hemingway helped Ford Maddox Heuffer edit *Transatlantic Review*, another important vehicle for Stein's lost generation.

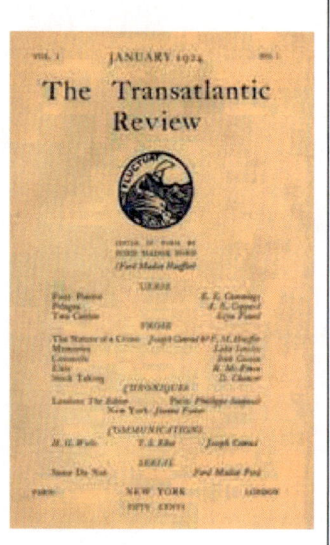

The Great American Magazine: Literature

The legendary avant-garde literary magazine, *Broom* was first published in 1921 in Rome, from 1922 in Berlin and lastly in New York from 1923-24, "selecting from the continental literature of the present time the writings of exceptional quality most adaptable for translation into English". Literary contributors include Ezra Pound, William Carlos Williams, John Dos Passos, E. E. Cummings, Jean Cocteau, Gertrude Stein, Jean Toomer and Hart Crane. It also reproduced the works of prominent artists including Picasso, Matisse, Rockwell Kent, Derain, Gris, Lipchitz, and Wanda Gag and photographers such as Man Ray. The original editor Harold Loeb was one of the owners of a New York bookshop "The Sunwise Turn" and sold his interest in that to start, along with Alfred Kreymborg, this periodical in Rome. It ended its existence in New York under Malcolm Cowley, being censored by the postal authorities.

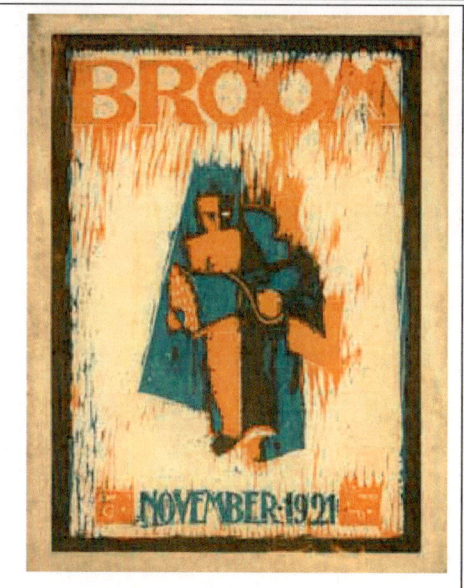

Edited by Eugene Jolas and associates, *Transition* was the most important expatriate journal of its time. The first issue was published from the legendary Shakespeare and Company, Paris, though also with an American price of fifty cents. Highlights include the first installment of James Joyce's "A Work in Progress" (Finnegan's Wake). Quoting Wm. Reese Company, catalog 237, "with *The Little Review* and *The Dial*, (*Transition* was)...one of the cornerstone periodicals nurturing the advent and progress of literary Modernism".

In January 1920, Scofield Thayer assumed editorship of *The Dial* and transformed it into a journal of art and culture; incorporating liberal politics with a radical and clearly focused aesthetic agenda. The list of artists published in *The Dial* is astonishing. Among those who appeared in the first year alone were Sherwood Anderson, Hart Crane, E. E. Cummings, Kahlil Gibran, Marianne Moore, Ezra Pound, Bertrand Russell, Carl Sandburg and W. B. Yeats. In 1922, it first published T.S. Eliot's "The Wasteland".Thayer became ill and, after a brief editorship by Marianne Moore, the magazine ceased publication in 1929.

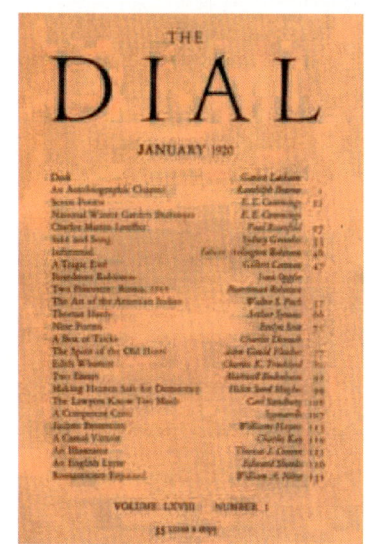

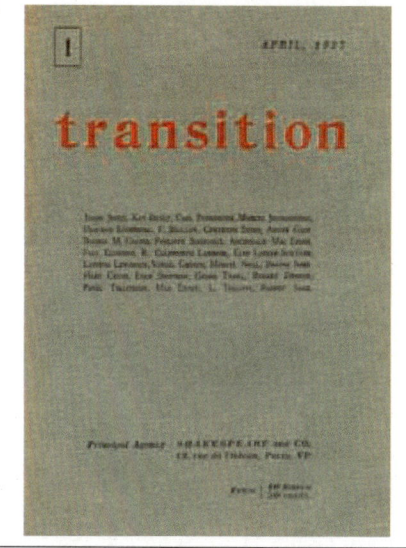

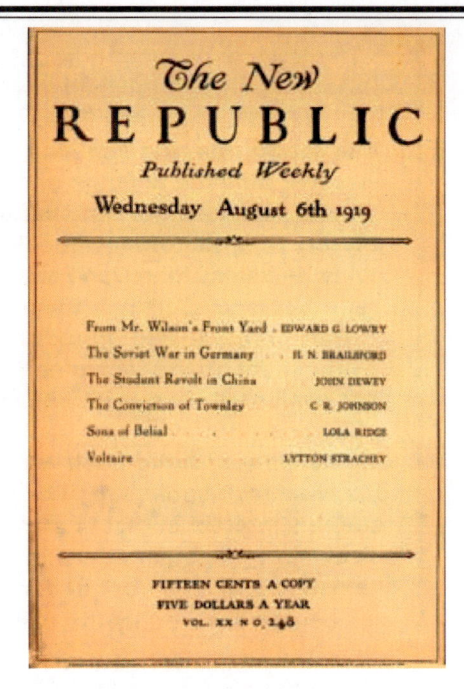

Wiilliam Faulkner's literary debut was a short poem entitled "L'Apres-Midi D'un Faune" in this 1919 issue of *The New Republic*.

The first literary appearance of Thomas Lanier "Tennessee" Williams was in, of all places, this 1928 issue of the pulp magazine *Weird Tales*. The cover is an illustration of a story by the short-lived but highly regarded Robert E. Howard.

Whit Burnett first published *Story Magazine* on a mimeograph machine in Vienna, Austria in April 1931. After eleven issues he brought it to America, where it flourished, discovering such prominent authors as J.D. Salinger, Joseph Heller and Tennessee Williams and also publishing the early works of such notable writers as William Saroyan, Norman Mailer and Truman Capote.

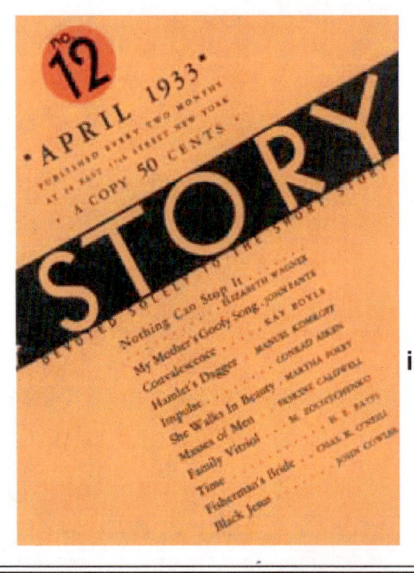

The reclusive Salinger's first publication was in this 1940 issue of *Story*.

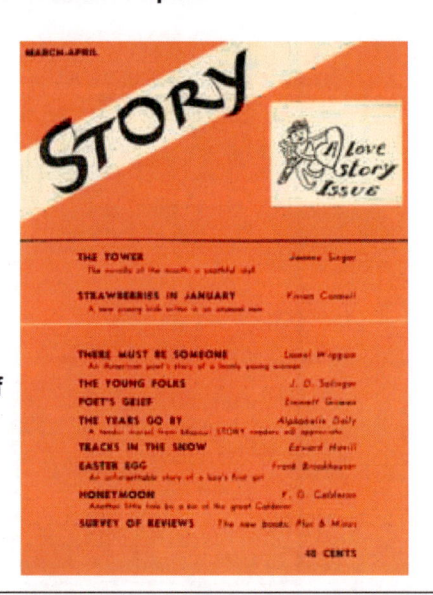

The Great American Magazine: Literature

In the first decade of the twentieth century, "pulp" fiction magazines began to flourish. Some were converted from pre-existing "slicks". *Everybody's* retained its title after changing format, while *Gunter's Magazine* became *New Story* and *Monthly Story Magazine* became the very successful *Blue Book*. *Tip Top Semi-Monthly* was converted from a dime novel. *Railroad Man's Magazine,* a Munsey publication, was the first pulp magazine designed to appeal to a specialized readership. *Adventure* began and flourished as a true pulp. The most important pure adventure pulp magazine, it ran for over 800 issues, starting in 1910. It was financed by Butterick & Co., the publishers of the fashion magazine *Delineator*. It attracted the best writers of the genre and, for a time, was edited by Sinclair Lewis. One of its features led to the founding of The American Legion. Rockwell Kent provided illustrations in the 1920's.
Racial prejudice was not very subtle at this time. The cover of the first issue is an excellent example of a "Yellow Menace" theme, later perpetuated by Sax Rohmer, with his villain, Fu Manchu.

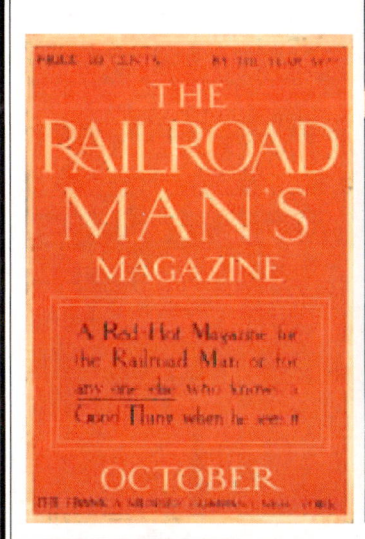

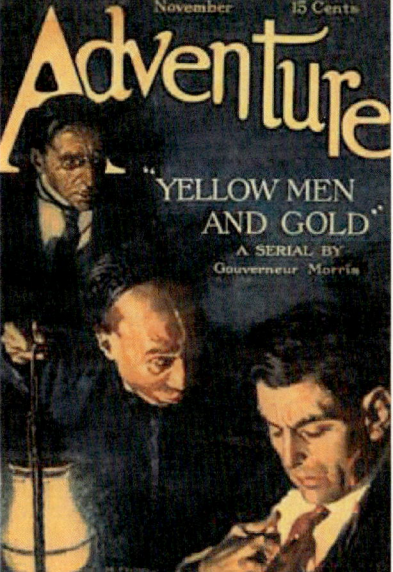

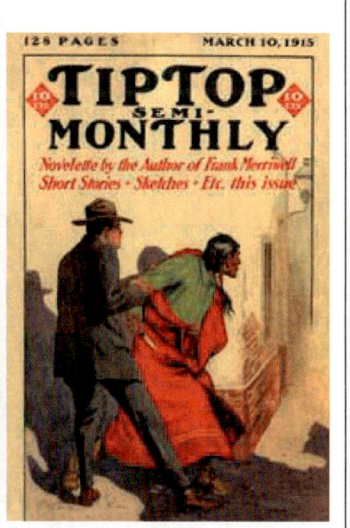

The Great American Magazine: Literature

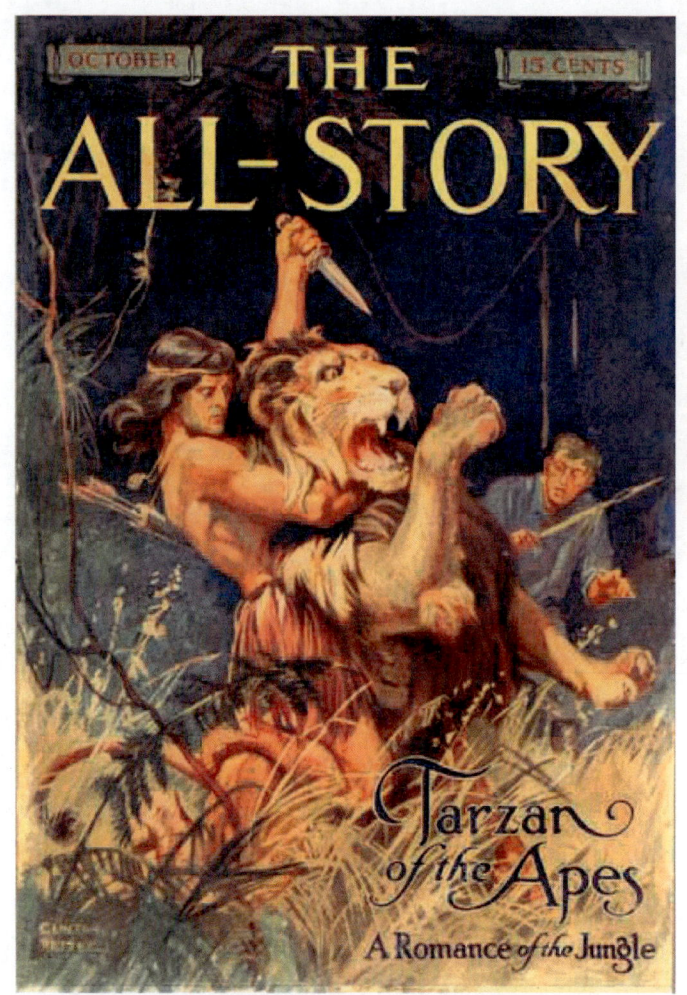

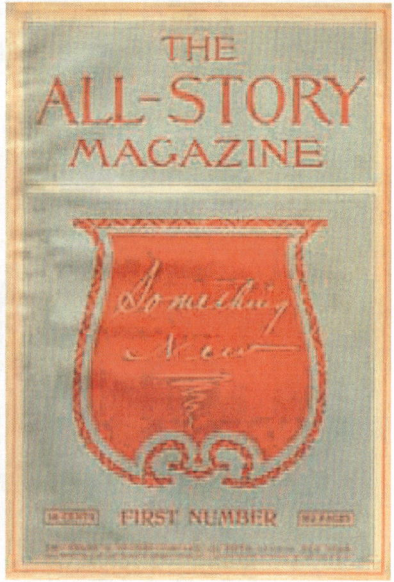

All-Story Magazine began as a Munsey pulp in 1905. The October 1912 issue introduced Edgar Rice Burroughs' "Tarzan of the Apes". This is arguably the single most valuable issue of any magazine ever published. Many Tarzan stories originally appeared in *All-Story*. The first appearance of Johnston McCulley's "Zorro" is in the August 9, 1919 issue.

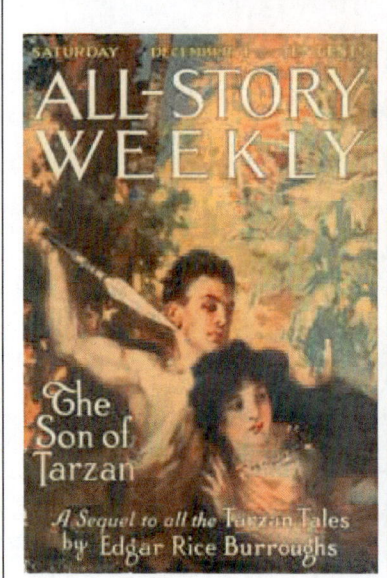

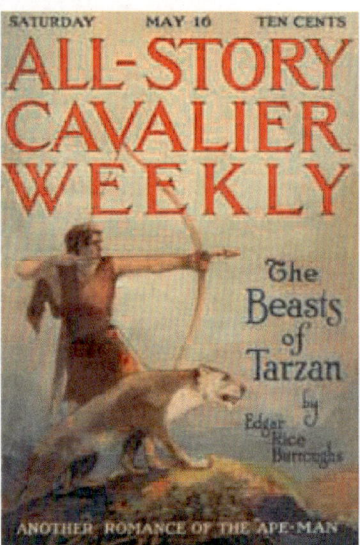

The Great American Magazine: Literature

The universe of Pulp magazines is about 900 titles with 40,000 issues between 1896 and the mid nineteen-fifties. Satisfying the American public's ongoing demand for cheap and readily available fiction, pulps replaced dime novels and story papers and eventually succumbed to a combination of "slick" magazines, paperbacks, comics and the new visual medium, Television.

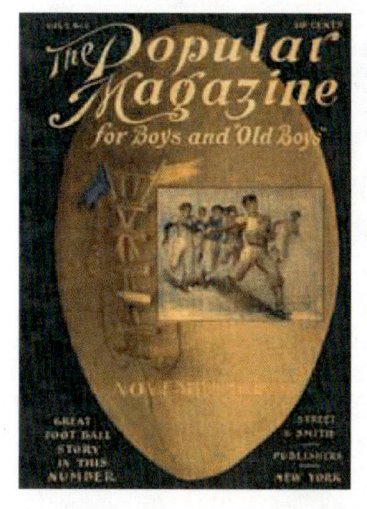

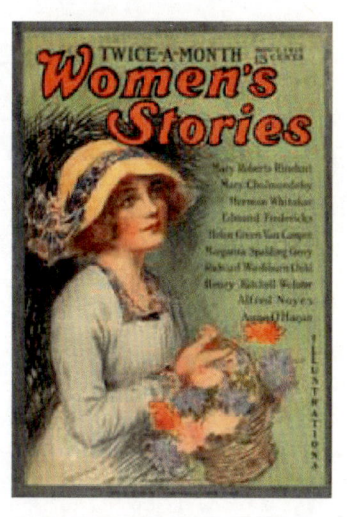

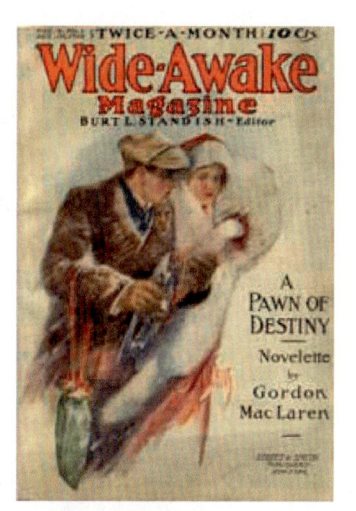

Pulps are fiction magazines that get their name from the cheap paper they were printed on. Most were printed in a small format though some were in a larger "bedsheet" size.

Most of the earliest pulps featured a variety of story types. As their popularity grew, more specialized titles and new genres appeared.

Publishing giant Street and Smith issued *Detective Story Magazine*, the first of dozens of detective pulps in 1917. They pioneered the love pulp in 1921 and introduced the first of many sports-themed pulps, *Sport Story Magazine*, in 1923.

Another popular genre was mystery, beginning with *Mystery Magazine,* published by Frank Tousey in 1919.

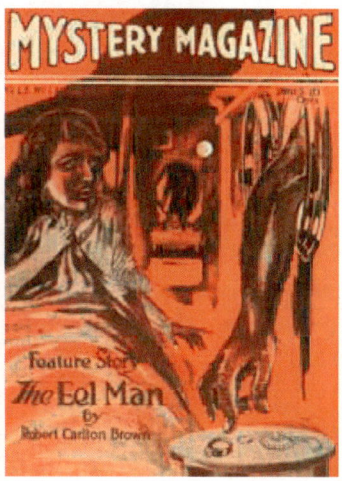

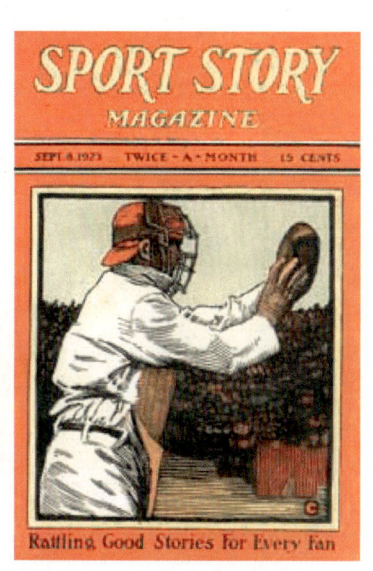

The Great American Magazine: Literature

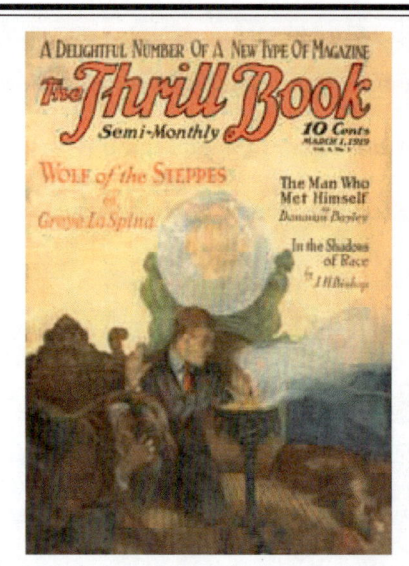

In 1919, the short-lived and rare *Thrill Book* was the first magazine to devote itself completely to occult fiction. In 1923 *Weird Tales* successfully continued the genre, running until the late 1940's. Its highlights include appearances by Robert E. Howard, including his famous "Conan" stories and art by Margaret Brundage.

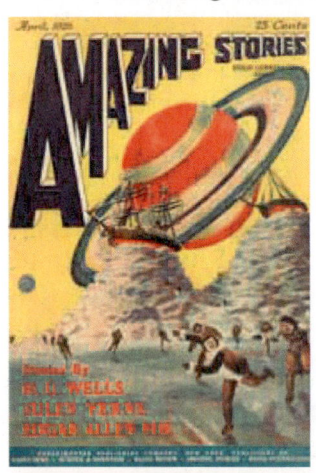

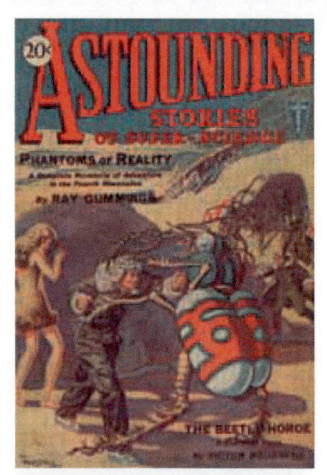

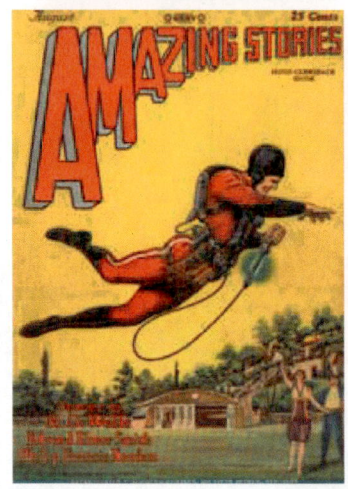

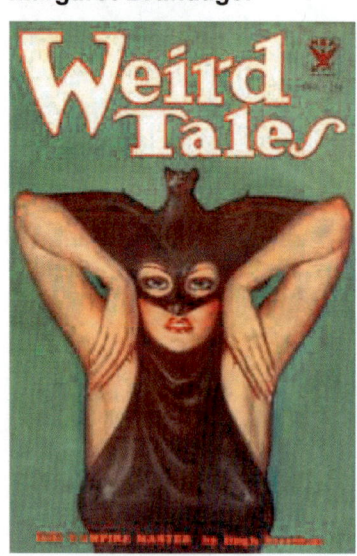

Hugo Gernsback's *Amazing Stories* is considered the first magazine devoted to science-fiction, and with Clayton Publishing's *Astounding* are the two most successful and long-running. The August 1928 *Amazing* introduced Buck Rogers. Flash Gordon made his only pulp magazine appearance in December 1936.

The Great American Magazine: Literature

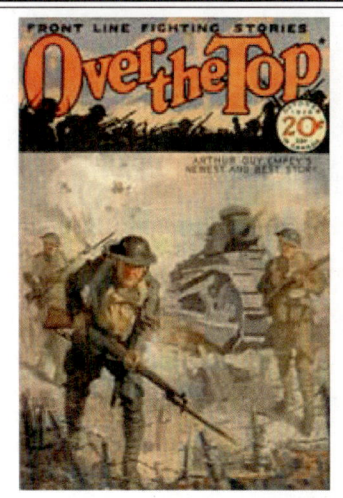

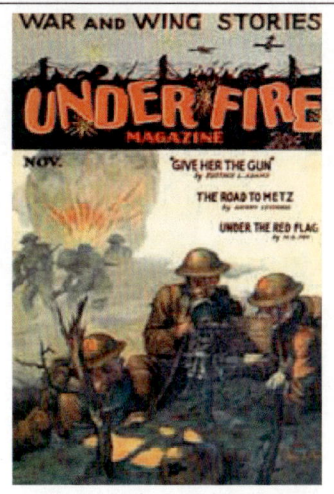

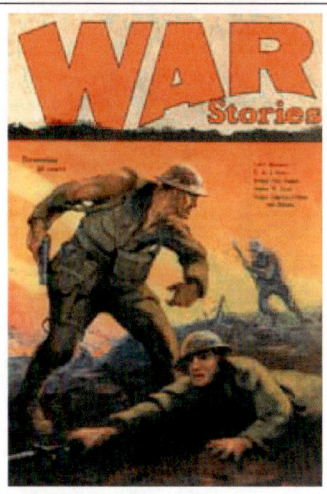

Quite a few Pulps extolled the glories of "The Great War".
The fascination with aviation made it a popular theme as well, beginning with
Air Stories, started just a few months after
Charles Lindbergh's trans-atlantic flight in 1927.

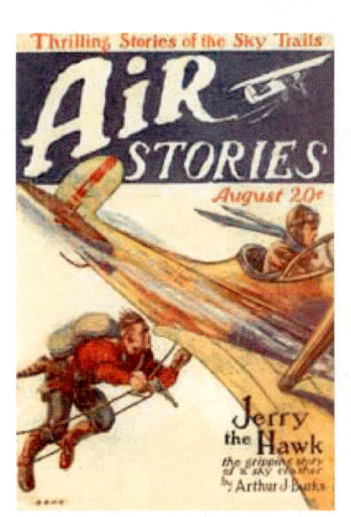

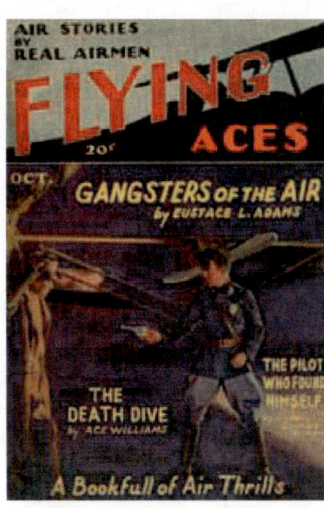

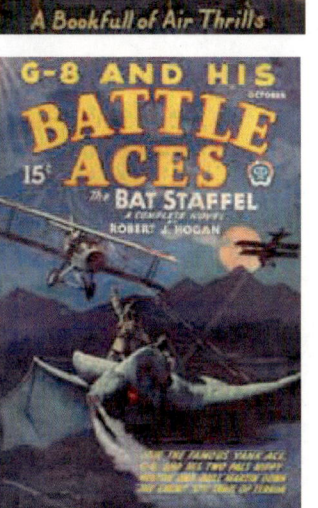

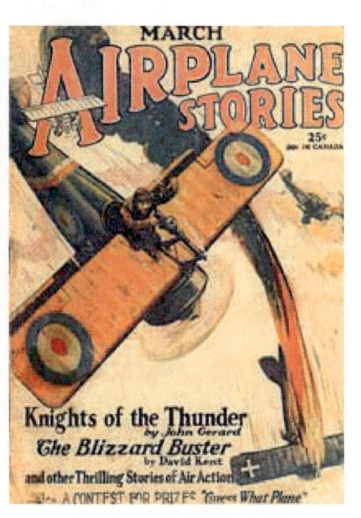

95   The Great American Magazine: Literature

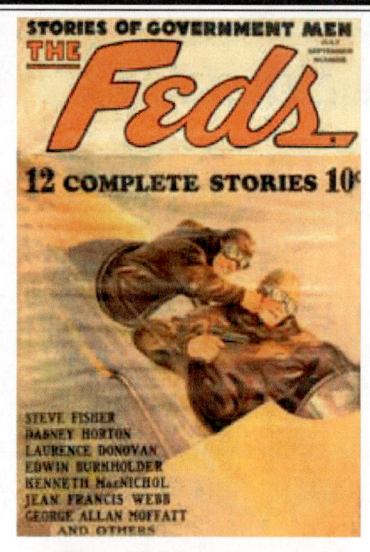

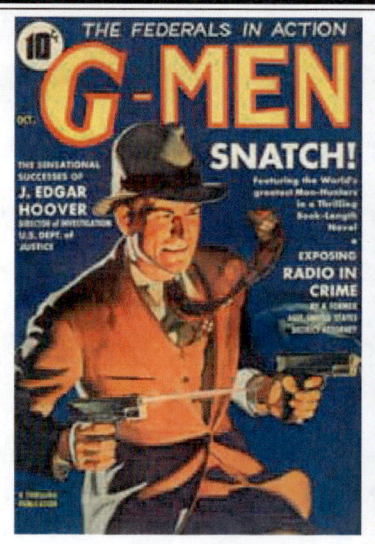

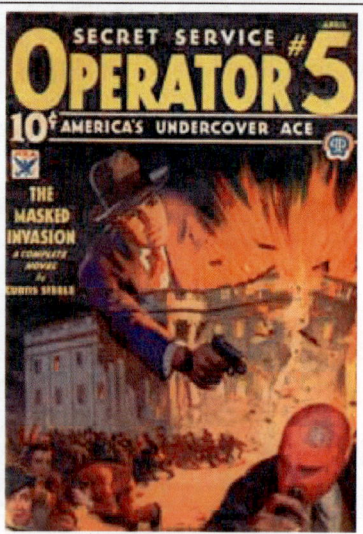

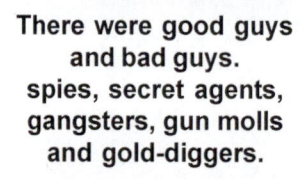

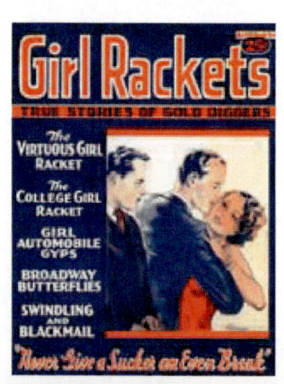

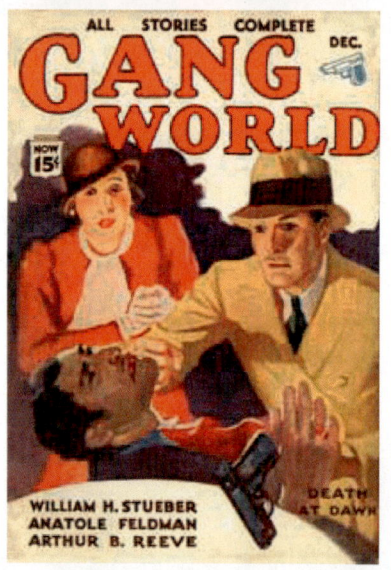

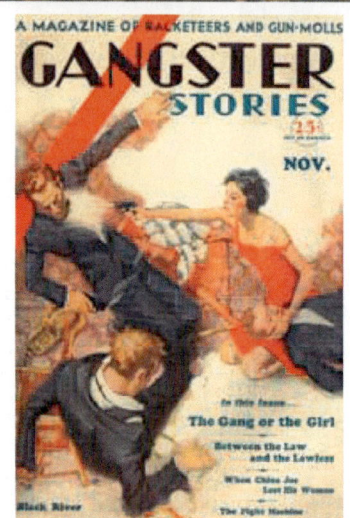

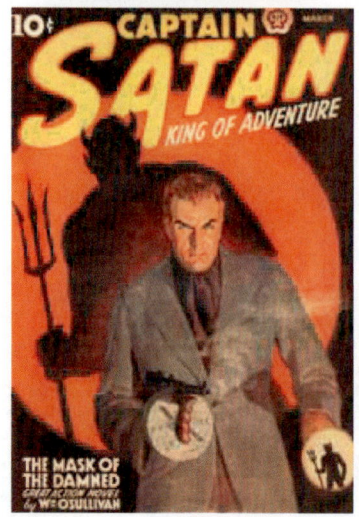

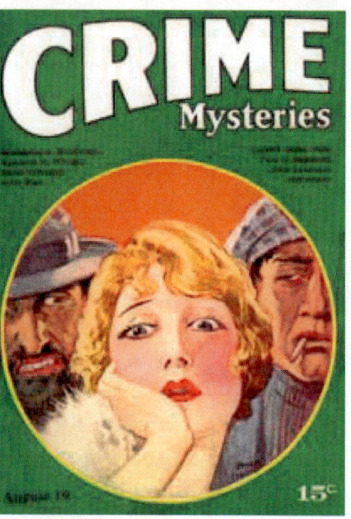

There were good guys and bad guys. spies, secret agents, gangsters, gun molls and gold-diggers.

The Great American Magazine: Literature

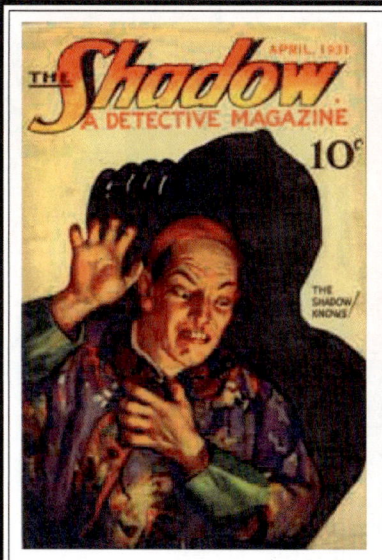

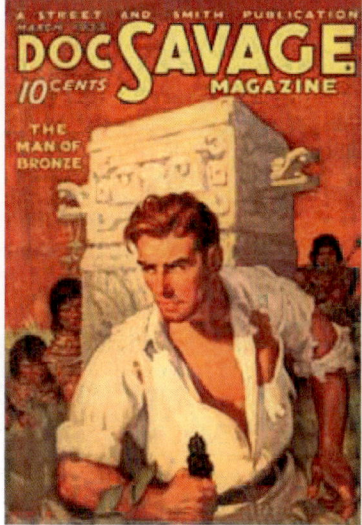

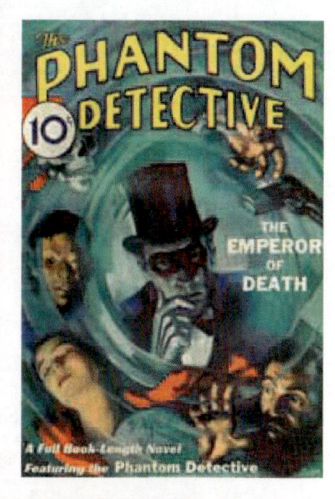

Of all the heros,
The Shadow and Doc Savage
by far had the largest following.
The Spider and *The Phantom Detective*
were also very popular.

In October 1933, The cover of *Dime Mystery* introduced a particularly sadistic and occult form of villainy known as "weird menace". It was immediately in great demand, triggering a variety of "shudder pulps", including *Terror Tales*, *Horror Stories* and *Startling Mystery*. Probably for the better, this genre disappeared in the early forties, but it likely set the groundwork for the likes of Freddie Kreuger and other movie ghouls.

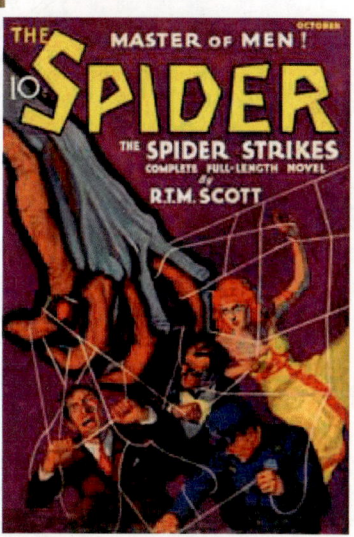

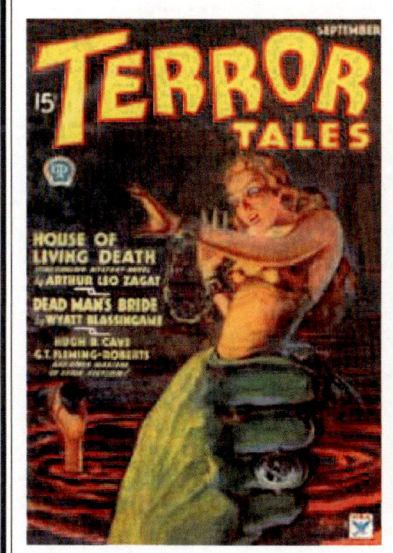

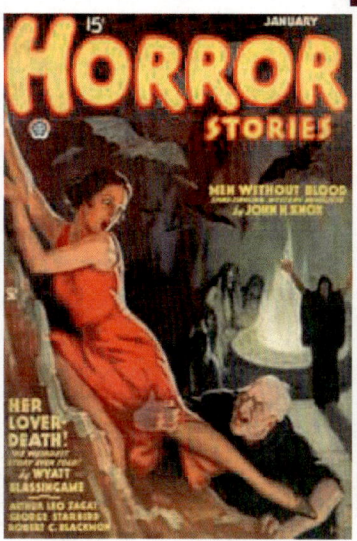

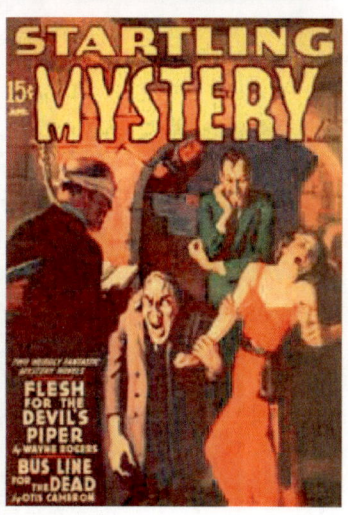

The Great American Magazine: Literature

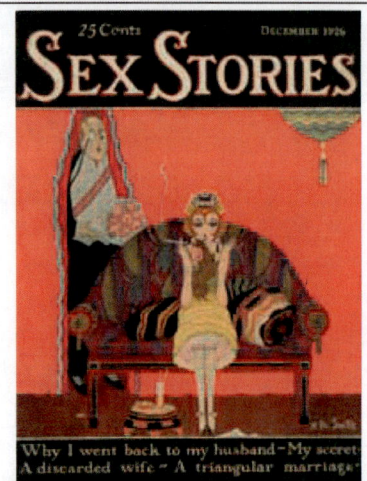

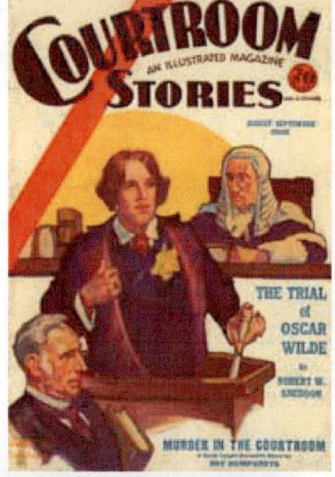

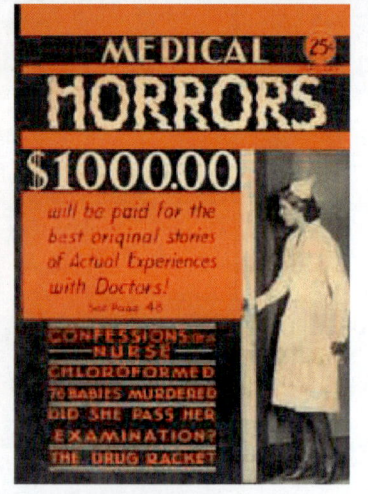

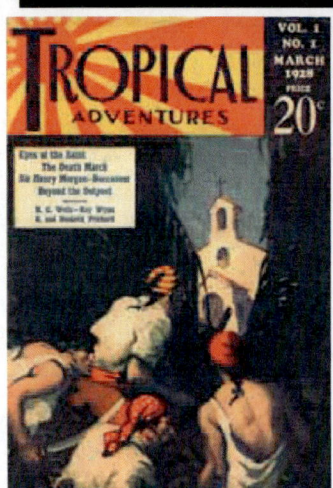

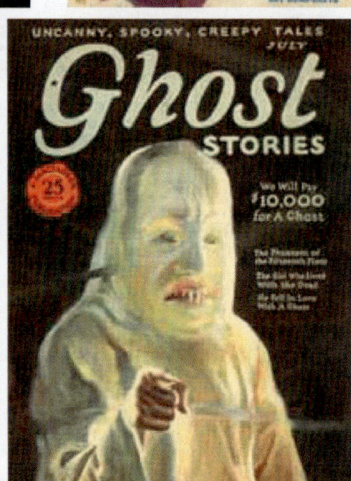

Publishers continually looked for new themes. Even doctors and lawyers didn't escape notice!
Zeppelin Stories and *Fire Fighters* are among the rarest and most highly sought of all of the off-beat titles.

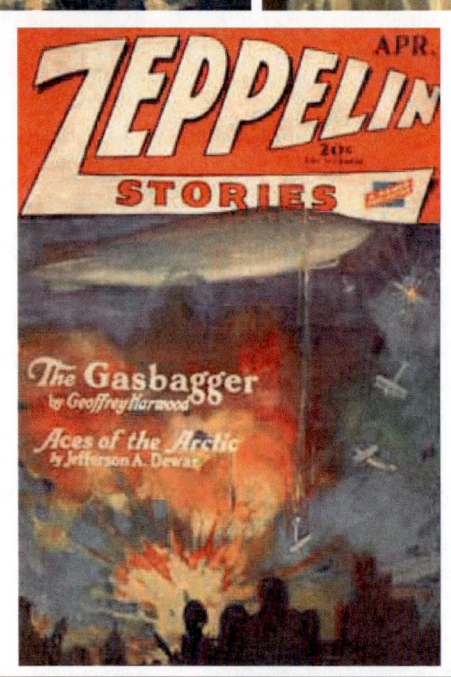

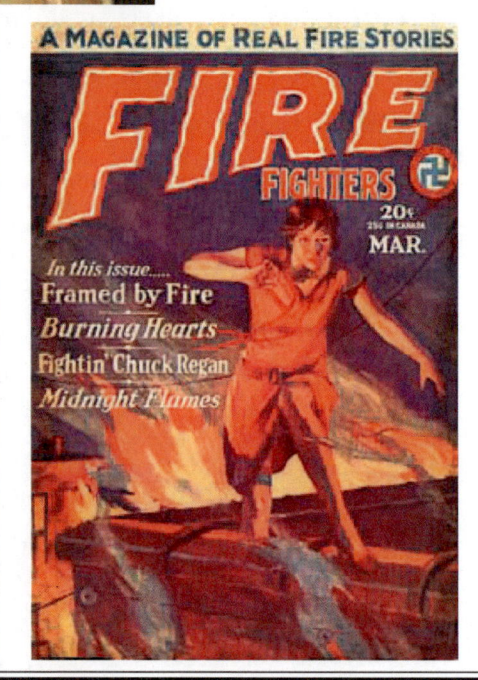

The Great American Magazine: Literature

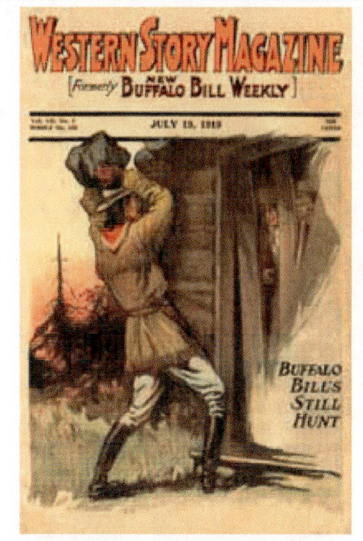

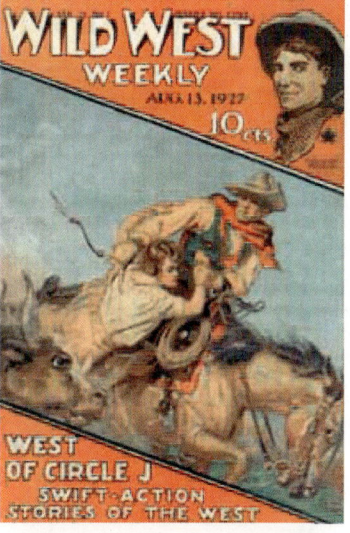

The earliest western pulps evolved directly from Dime Novels. *Western Story Magazine* changed its name. *Wild West Weekly* didn't.

Pulps were no exception to the enduring popularity of western-themed fiction. Dozens of titles were issued.

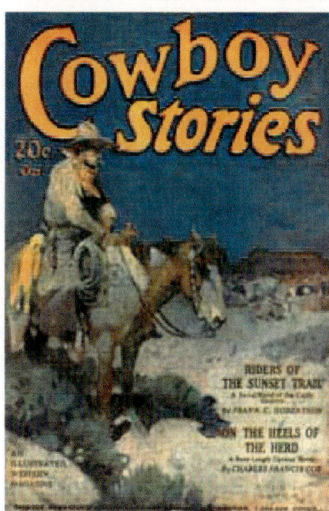

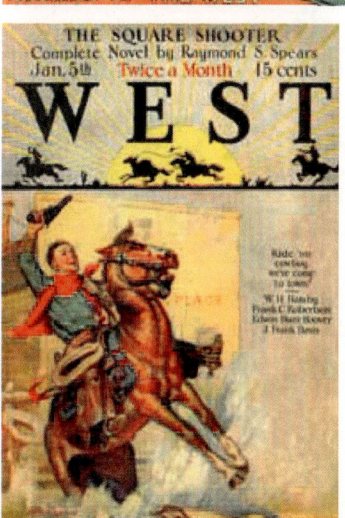

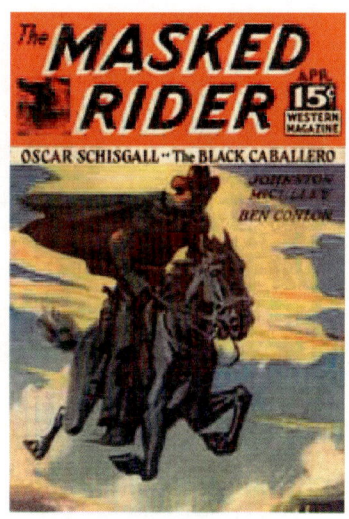

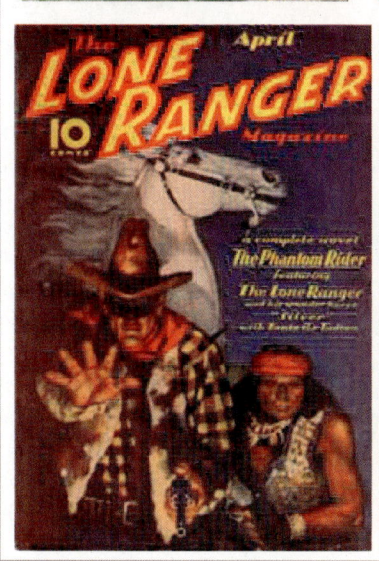

With the great success of *Doc Savage*, Street and Smith followed up with a western hero, *Pete Rice*, though he never achieved "Doc's" popularity. *The Lone Ranger* was later continued in the famous television series starring Clayton Moore and Jay Silverheels. Notice how Silver got second billing over Tonto!

The Great American Magazine: Literature

A few pulps featured female heroines.

The first issue of *Saucy Romantic Adventures* introduced "The Domino Lady".

Scarlet Adventuress ran for three years in the late thirties.

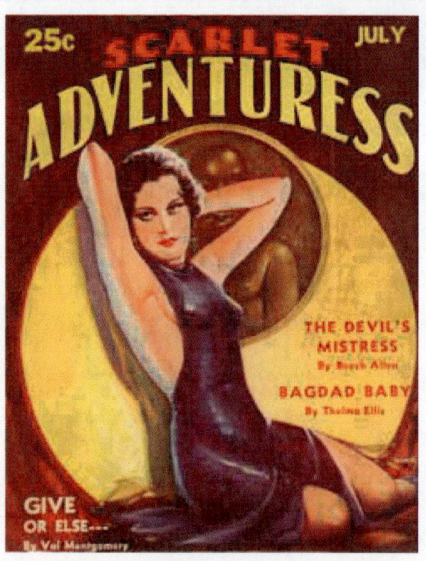

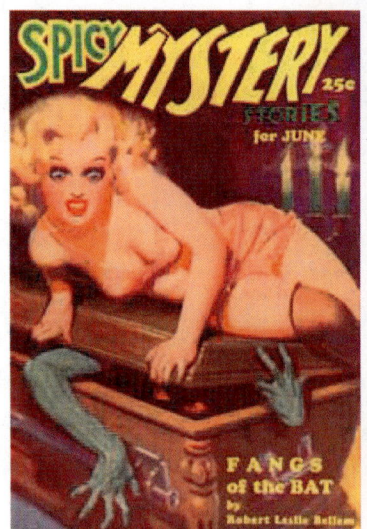

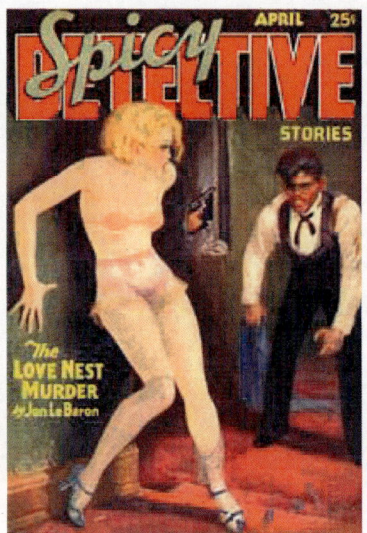

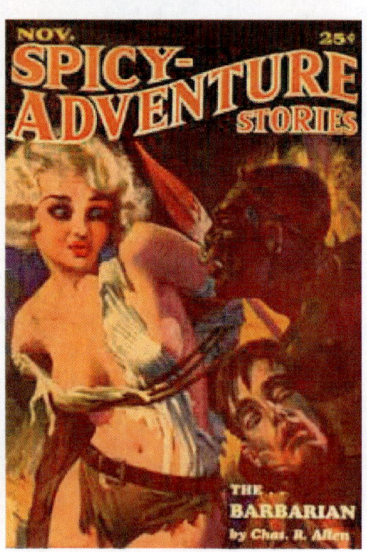

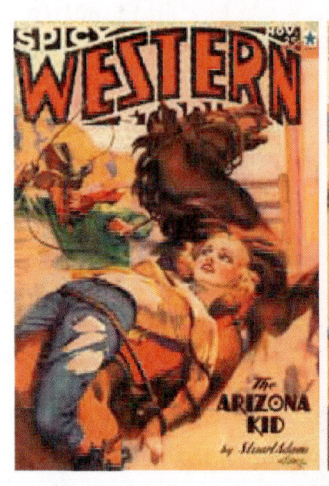

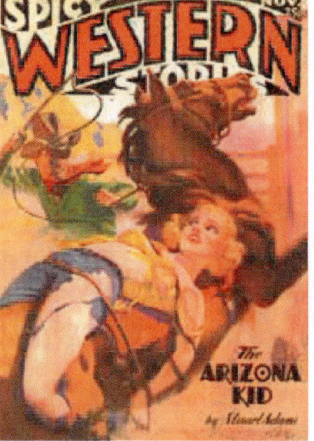

The highly sought Spicy pulps pushed the limits of censorship. *Spicy Mystery* was the most popular. The first issue of *Spicy Western* had two versions, one more provocative and the other, with a star on the cover, more socially acceptable. In the early forties, the censors finally had enough. The artwork was toned down and the first name of the title was changed from "spicy" to "speed".

The Great American Magazine: Literature

103

Despite the enormous popularity and size of the movie industry, there has been very sparse bibliographic study of the magazines issued in conjunction with it. A recent perusal of internet search engines rather amazingly confirms that there is virtually no other comprehensive source, despite the fact that many of the actual early films have been lost and the only remaining documentation exists in printed form. Other than the chapter in my 1996 volume, the following is the only comprehensive visual and textual treatment of the subject, new and improved, emphasizing the pre-1940 era, with a few selected major titles afterwards. All illustrations are from the author's personal collection. The focus has been to obtain the first issue of a title, though when rarity (not infrequently) supervenes, type issues are employed.

Source material is very sparse. The initial list began with the only two existing resources in 1996:

The Union List of Film Periodicals by Brady, Wall and Weiner, Greenwood Press, 1984

International Film, Radio and Television Journals. Edited by Anthony Slide, Greenwood Press, 1985

and was expanded with exhaustive research as well as prospecting for new titles and information at antiquarian bookfairs, ephemera shows and on the internet (primarily Ebay). The latter has been most fruitful. This list has been twenty years in the making. It is now quite unusual to find something new, suggesting that it is getting fairly close to complete (being an avid collector, the author wholly realizes that there is *always* potentially something new in the next booth or listing, hence the fun of it all!). In nine years of intensive searching, only about ten new titles have been added. Many of these have only been seen once. Early Movie Magazines are very rare birds indeed; ephemeral in the true sense of the word, despite their relatively recent vintage.

Movie Periodicals can be roughly divided into five categories:

1) Fan Magazines- intended for the general public as a vehicle to increase viewing interest

2) In-house Magazines- issued by individual studios to promote their films to distributors

3) Exhibitor's or Trade Journals- employed by movie distributors and exhibitors, containing much about the films themselves, especially new releases, often with graphic advertising.

4) Technical Journals- designed for members of the industry for technical and creative information

5) Movie Pulp Magazines- fiction magazines based on either movie screenplays or movie themes

The list is chronological, from the origin of the earliest title. Technical journals are excluded.

A Bibliography of American Movie Periodicals

Fan Magazines

Motion Picture Story Magazine (February 1911) title changed to
Motion Picture Magazine (March 1914)
Photoplay Magazine (August 1911)
Motion Picture Album (June 1912)
Movie Pictorial (1913)
Moving Picture Stories (January 3, 1913)
Motion Picture Times (1915)
Who's Who in Moving Pictures (1915)
Motion Picture Mail (1915) A weekly Supplement to The Daily Mail newspaper
Photoplay Vogue (1915)
Weekly Movie Record (1915)
Movie Magazine (March 1915)
Film Players Herald and Movie Pictorial (March 1915)
Picture Play Weekly (April 10, 1915) title changed to
Picture Play Magazine (October 3, 1915) title changed to
Picture Play (March 1927) title changed to
Charm (March 1941)
Feature Movie Magazine (March 15, 1916)
Photoplay Review (March 16, 1915)
Film Fun (July 1915) an amalgamation of three non-movie titles
Motion Picture Supplement (September 1915) title changed to
Motion Picture Classic (December 1915) title changed to
Classic (September 1922)
Wid's Films and Film Folk (September 9, 1915)
Photo-Play Journal (May 1916)
Photoplay Weekly Mirror (September 30, 1916)
Photoplay World (September 1917)
The California (June 23, 1918)
Shadowland (September 1919) some non-movie content
Screenland (New York) (September 1920)
Filmplay Journal (1921)
Hollywood Informer (1921)
Pantomine (1921)
Photo Drama (1921)
Movie Weekly (February 12, 1921)
Screenland (Seattle) (May 1, 1921)
Filmplay Journal (July 1921)
Movie Melody Magazine (July 1921)
Motion Picture Review (1922?)
Cinema Art (1923)
Movie Monthly (March 1924)
Hollywood (September 20, 1924)
Movie Adventures (October 1924) title changed to

Movie Thrillers (January 1925) title changed to
Movie Magazine (September 1925) title changed to
Pictures (May 1926)
Movie Digest (March 1925)
So This is Paris (March 1925) title changed to
Paris and Hollywood (April 1926) title changed to
Paris and Hollywood Screen Secrets (1928) title changed to
Screen Secrets (April 1928) title changed to
Screen Play Secrets (April 1930) title changed to
Screen Play (October 1931)
Motion Picture Monthly (September 1925)
Hollywood Life (November 1925)
Screen Book (July 1928) title changed to
Screen Life (March 1940)
Screen Romances (June 1929)
New Movie (December 1929)
Passing Show of Today (December 1929)
Cinema (January 1930)
Talking Screen (January 1930)
Modern Screen (November 1930)
Silver Screen (November 1930)
Screen Romances Album (February 1931)
Screen Album (March 1931)
Movie Classic (September 1931)
Movie Mirror (November 1931)
Screen Weekly (September 1932)
Shadowplay (March 1933)
Golden Screen (August 1934)
Screen Star Stories (August 1934)
Popular Screen (September 1934)
Movie Life (November 1937)
Moviepix (February 1938)

Trade Journals

Film Index (Views and Film Index) (April 26, 1906) Absorbed by Moving Picture World, July 1, 1911
Variety (December 16, 1905) Initially a theater magazine which evolved into a movie magazine
Moving Picture World (March 9, 1907) Merged with Exhibitor's Herald to form
Exhibitors's Herald and Moving Picture World (January 7, 1928) title changed to
Exhibitor's Herald World (January 5, 1929) title changed to
Motion Picture Herald (January 1931)
Moving Picture News (May 1908) title changed to
Motion Picture News (October 11, 1913) Absorbed by Moving Picture World, January 3, 1931
Nickleodeon (1909)
Motography (April 1911) Absorbed by Exhibitor's Herald (1918)
Exhibitor's Times (May 17, 1913) Absorbed by Moving Picture News (October 1913)
Moving Picture Publicity (December 1913)
Photoplayer's Weekly (1914)

Photoplay Scenario (May 1914)
Exhibitor's Herald (June 24, 1914) merged with Moving Picture World to form Exhibitor's Herald and Moving Picture World, (January 7, 1928)
Film Daily (June 1922)
Photoplay Weekly Mirror (September 30, 1916)
Exhibitor's Trade Review (December 9, 1916) title changed to
Exhibitor's Daily Review (February 6, 1926)
Cinema News (December 15, 1916)
Affiliated Committees for Better Films Bulletin (1917) title changed to
Film Progress (1924)
Dramatic Mirror of the Stage and Motion Pictures (February 17, 1917)
Camera (April 1918)
Vine Street (November 15, 1918)
It (1920)
Exceptional Photoplays (November 1920)
Screen (1921)
Film News (1923) title changed to
National Ehibitor (August 15, 1927)
Motion Picture Record (1924)
Photoplay Guide to Better Pictures (June 1924)
Film Spectator (June 1926) title changed to
Hollywood Spectator (June 20, 1931)
National Board of Review Magazine (March 1926) A merger of Film Progress, Vine Street and Motion Picture Record
Hollywood Filmograph (1927)
Brevity (July 1927)
Le Cinema (September 1927)
Motion Picture Arts and Sciences (November 1927)
Talking Picture Magazine (October 1929)
Motion Picture Advertising (November 1929)
Hollywood Reporter (1930)
Motion Picture Daily (December 22, 1930) Absorbed Exhibitor's Daily Review
Hollywood Herald (June 8, 1931)
Box Office (January 21, 1932)
Showmen's Round Table (May 27, 1933)
Jones' (1937)
Cinema Arts (June 1937)

In-House Publications

Biograph Bulletin (1902-1912)
Edison Kinetogram (1909)
Bison Magazine (1910)
Essanay News, Essanay Guide (1910)
Selig Polyscope Guide (1910)
Vitagraph Bulletin (1910)
Eclair bulletin (1910-1914)
Film Fancies (Carlton Motion Picture Company) (1910)
Kalem Kalendar (1911-1914)
Vitagraph Exhibitor (1911-1915)

Mutual Film Magazine (1912)
Reel Life (Mutual Films) (1912-1917)
Implet (Carl Laemmle) (January 10, 1912)
Universal Weekly (June 22, 1912) title changed to
Moving Picture Weekly (1915) title changed to
Universal Weekly (1922)
Movies (General Film Company) (1913)
Pathe Fortnightly Bulletin (1913) title changed to
Pathe (April 15, 1915)
Lubin Bulletin (October 27, 1913)
Paramount Progress (1914) title changed to
Picture Progress (June 1915)
The Biograph (September 5, 1914)
Paste, Pot and Shears (Selig) (1915)
Triangle (1915-1917)
Metro Pictures Magazine (September 1915)
Fox Folks (Fox Films) (1916)
Sherry Punch (Sherry Features) (1916)
Mack Sennett Weekly (1917-1919)
Studio Skeleton (Samuel Goldwyn) (1919)
Film Follies (Christie Films) (1919)
Loew's Weekly (December 6, 1920)
Dotted Line (1922-1926)
Distibutor (MGM) (1925-1941)
Movietone Bulletin (June 11, 1928)
Columbia Mirror (November 1934 - October 1941)
MGM Studio News (1935-1940)
MGM Studio Club Club News (1935-1936)
RKO Studio Club News (1935-1956)
Lion's Roar (MGM) 1941-1946

Movie Pulps

Film Stories (1921)
Movie Novel (1929)
Screen Novels Quarterly (ca. 1933)
Romantic Movie Stories (1933)
Sure Fire Screen Stories (1934)
Movie Action (1935)
Saucy Movie Tales (1935)
Stage and Screen Stories (1936)
Movie Love Magazine (1937)
Hollywood Love Romances (1938)
Cowboy Movie Thrillers (1 941)
Movie Love Stories (1941)
Movie Western (1941)
Movie Detective (1942)
Hollywood Detective (1943)

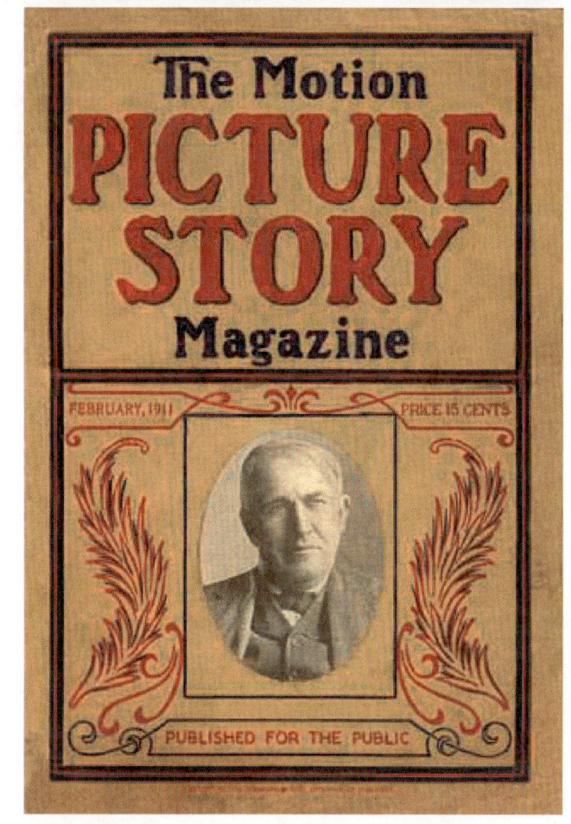

The first movie fan *Motion Picture Story Magazine* February 1911 with the inventor and pioneer Edison on the cover. It shortenened its title to *Motion Picture* with this 1914 issue.

Photoplay is the longest-running and most important of all movie magazines. The back cover of the first issue of *Picture-Play Weekly* points out the economics of the industry in 1915.

The first movies were filmed in West Orange, New Jersey.

The industry's move to California came early and abruptly.

Wid's Films and Film Folk was one of the first magazines to deal with all movies produced at the time. Prior to this, the major periodicals were dominated by Motion Picture Patents Company (MPPC), which went to great lengths to freeze out independent filmmakers such as Carl Laemmle. To the ultimate benefit of all, largely due to federal anti-trust legislation, the feud ended in 1915.

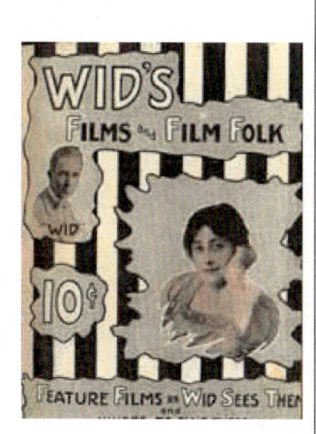

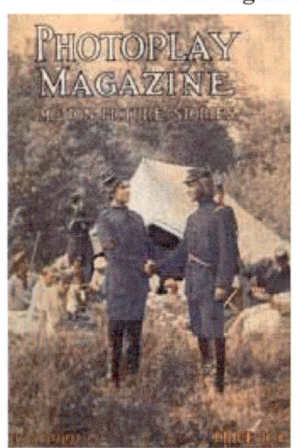

109   The Great American Magazine: Movies

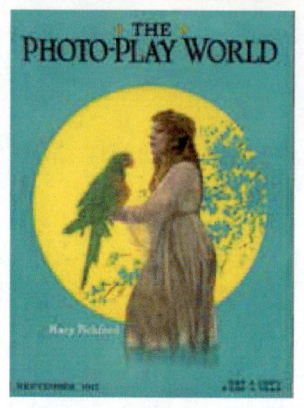

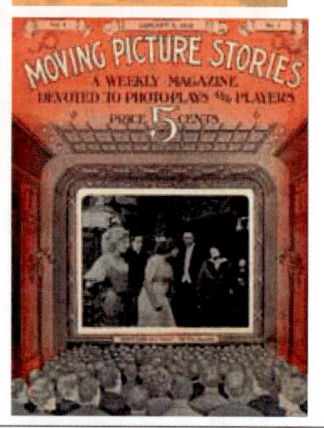

More examples of fan magazines
started before 1920.
All are rare, many extremely so.

The Great American Magazine: Movies

The Great American Magazine: Movies

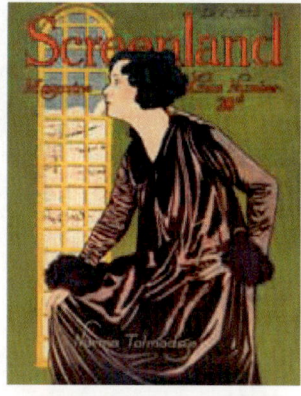

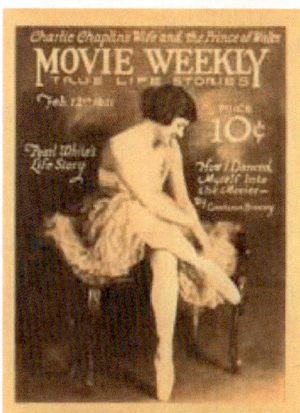

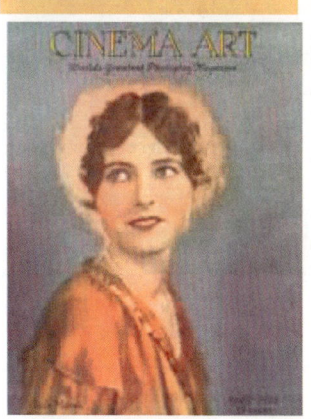

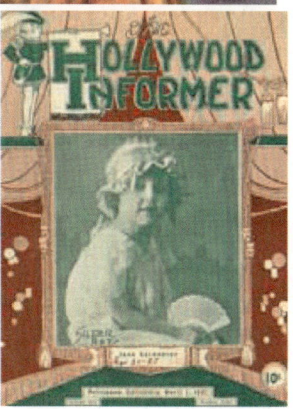

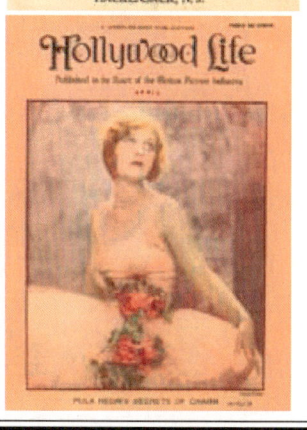

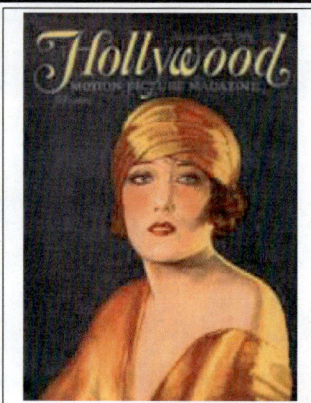

"I'm ready for my close-up Mr. DeVille!"
New stars, new fan magazines; some gossipy, some elegant and slick, all fueling the growing popularity of the cinema in the roaring twenties and in the thirties; a brief respite from the worries of the great depression.
Motion Picture Mail was a weekly supplement to a newspaper.
Movie Adventures/ Movie Thrillers, prior to its title change to *Movie Monthly* (note the wonderful, menacing image of Lon Chaney) is completely unrecorded.
The artwork of *Shadowplay*, the first issue featuring the original blonde bombshell, Jean Harlow, is a particular favorite.

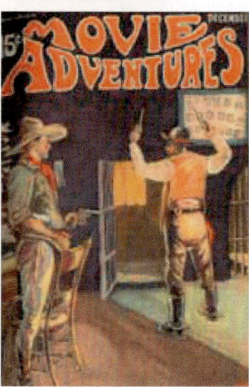

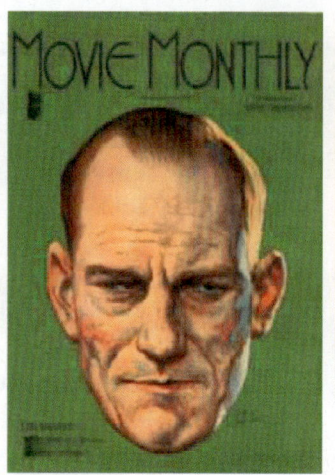

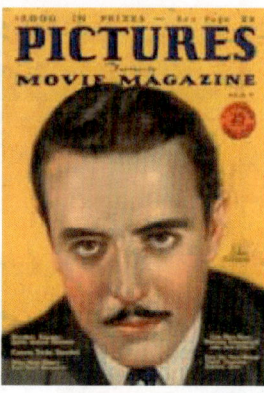

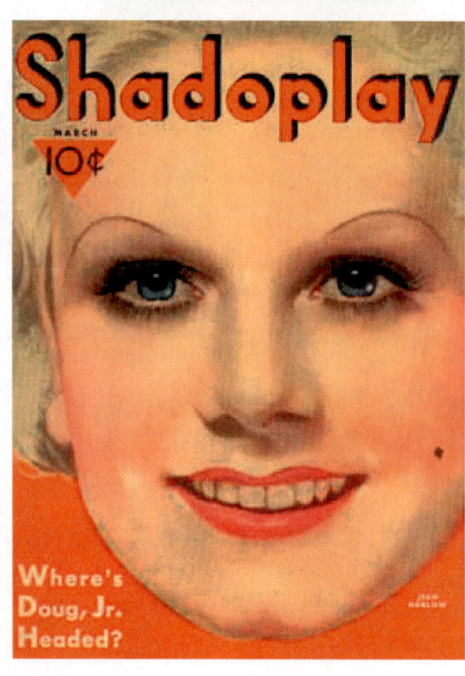

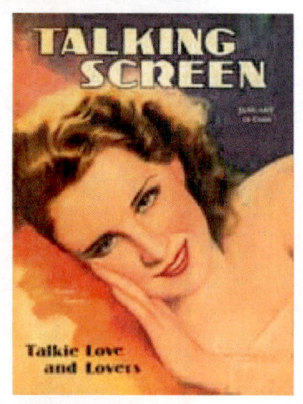

The Great American Magazine: Movies   112

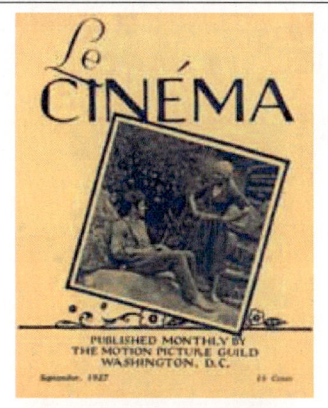

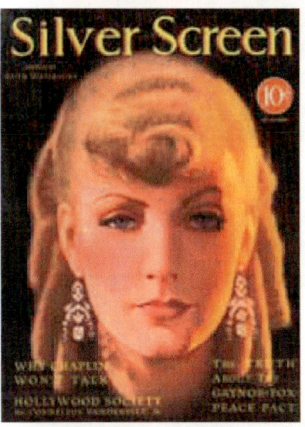

A potpourri of titles from the twenties and thirties. Garbo, Dietrich, Crawford, Wow!

113   The Great American Magazine: Movies

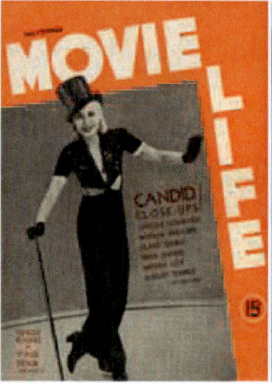

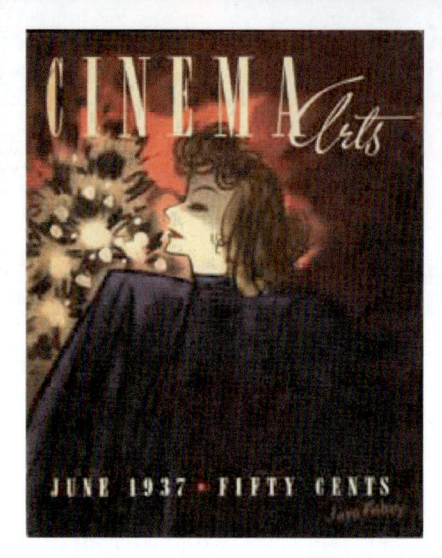

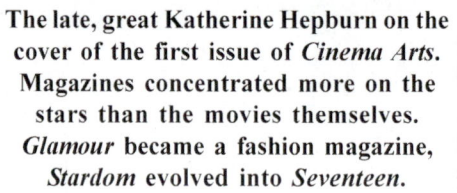

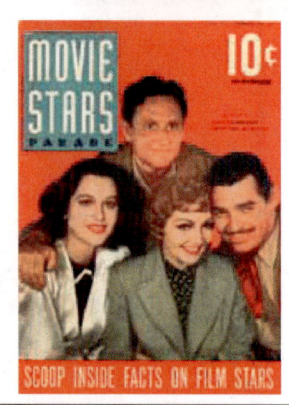

The late, great Katherine Hepburn on the cover of the first issue of *Cinema Arts*. Magazines concentrated more on the stars than the movies themselves. *Glamour* became a fashion magazine, *Stardom* evolved into *Seventeen*.

The Great American Magazine: Movies

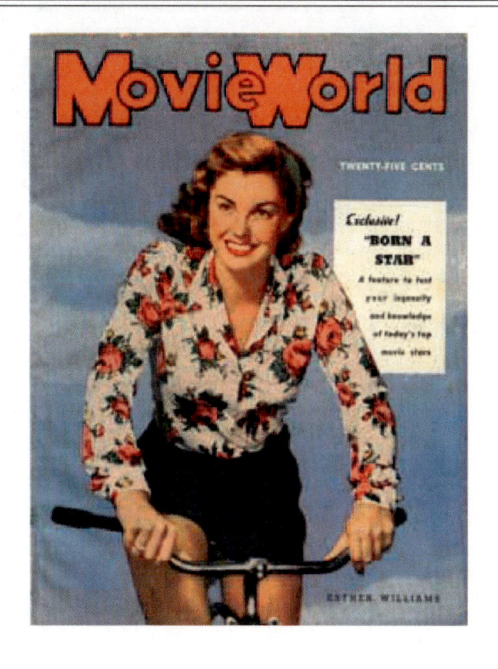

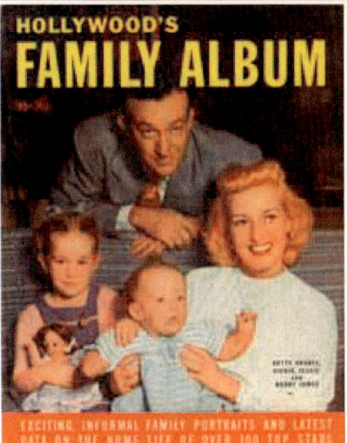

The forties and fifties.
Almost too many new magazines to keep up with.
National Velvet all grown up on the first issue of *Filmland*.
The athletic star Esther Williams,
Bo Derek's dad and the ill-fated Natalie Wood

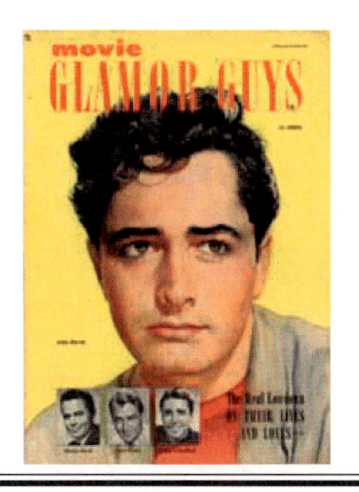

115   The Great American Magazine: Movies

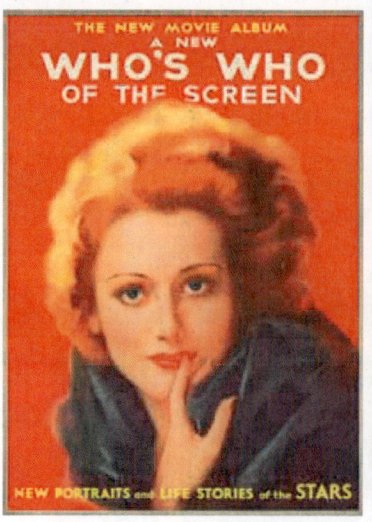

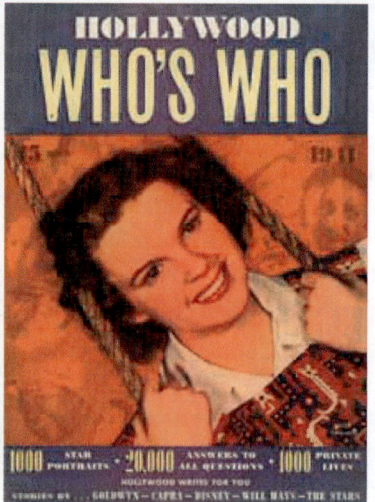

A recurrring theme: teens, thirties and forties!
A very rare, albeit stereotyped, image of an African-American, Hattie McDaniel,
sneaks onto the cover on the right. We've come a long way.

Onward into the 21st Century.
Movie fan magazines are stronger and more
ubiquitous than ever.

The Great American Magazine: Movies   116

Trade Journals appeared very soon after the genesis of the movie art form. *Film Index* was the first movie-oriented periodical, beginning in 1905. *Variety* began as a theatre journal and slowly incorporated movies as they expanded to occupy a greater portion of the entertainment industry. Many trade journals went through convoluted mergers, evolving into the most prominent and long-lasting title, *Motion Picture Herald*, in the early 1930's.

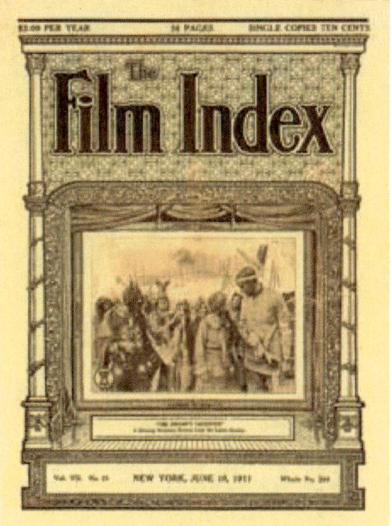

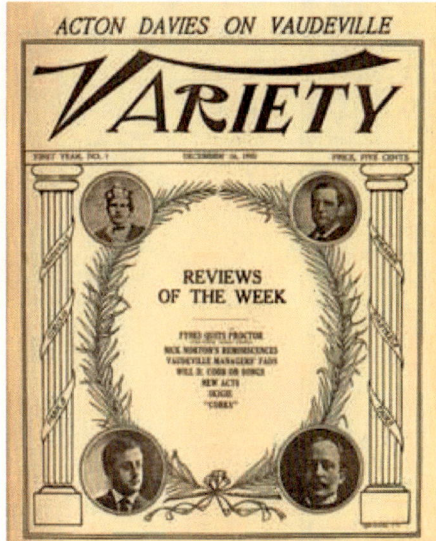

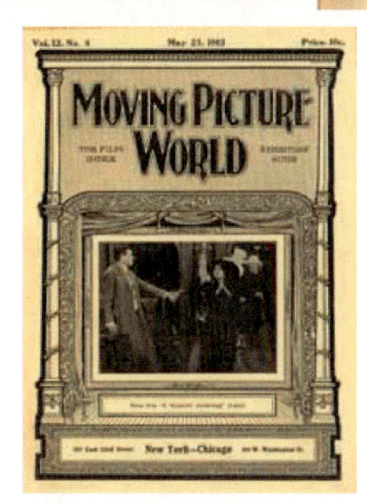

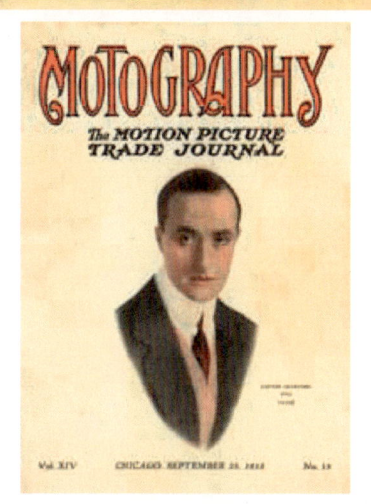

Pulps are fiction magazines named for the cheap paper they used. Their fragile and ephemeral nature make them quite scarce and collectible. Pulps were a predominant source of printed American popular culture in the first half of the twentieth century. Themes from movies, a fertile visual source, were often employed, many reprinting screenplays. Thanks to recent bibliographies by Gunnison et al. and Cottrill, the scope of this important genre of periodicals has come into better focus. All are scarce, but *Film Stories*, published by the Street and Smith and *Screen Novel Quarterly* are particularly rare.

117   The Great American Magazine: Movies

There were sixteen pulps with movie themes issued between 1921 and 1947. These are the first issues of eight of them.

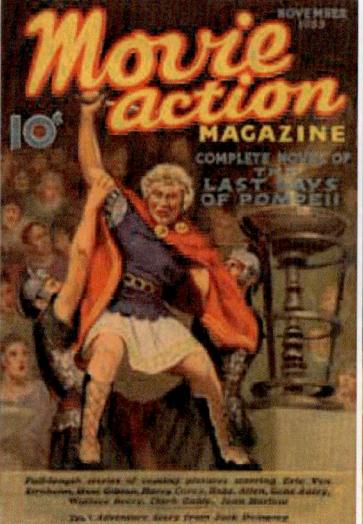

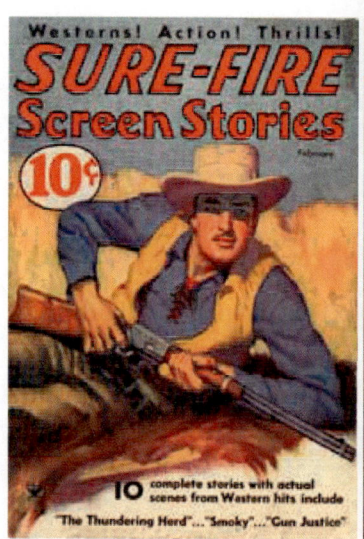

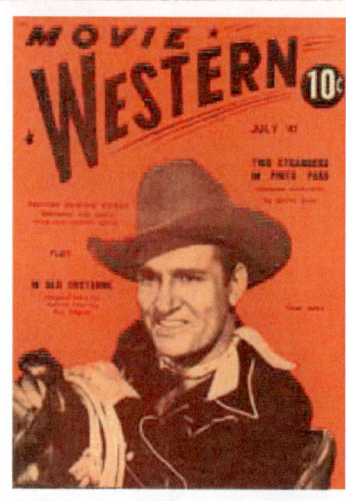

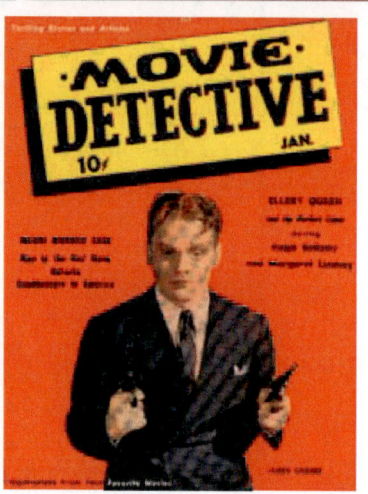

The Great American Magazine: Movies

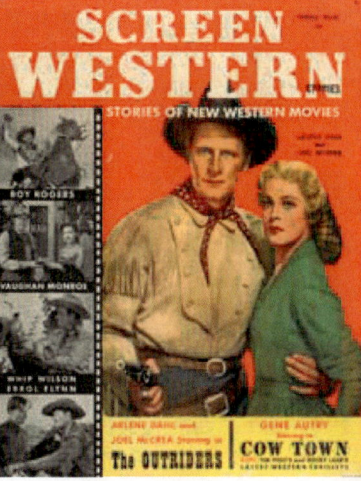

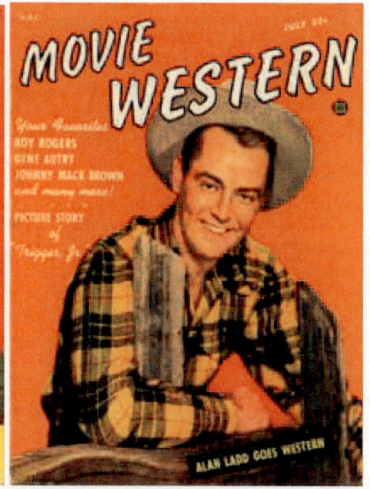

From the very beginning of movies, the western has captured the public's interest.
Jackie Coogan, known to many as Uncle Fester from "The Adams Family", began as "The Kid", the first child star.
The association of film and music has always been prominent, first as a supplement to the viewing of silent films and then as a more integral part of the movies themselves.

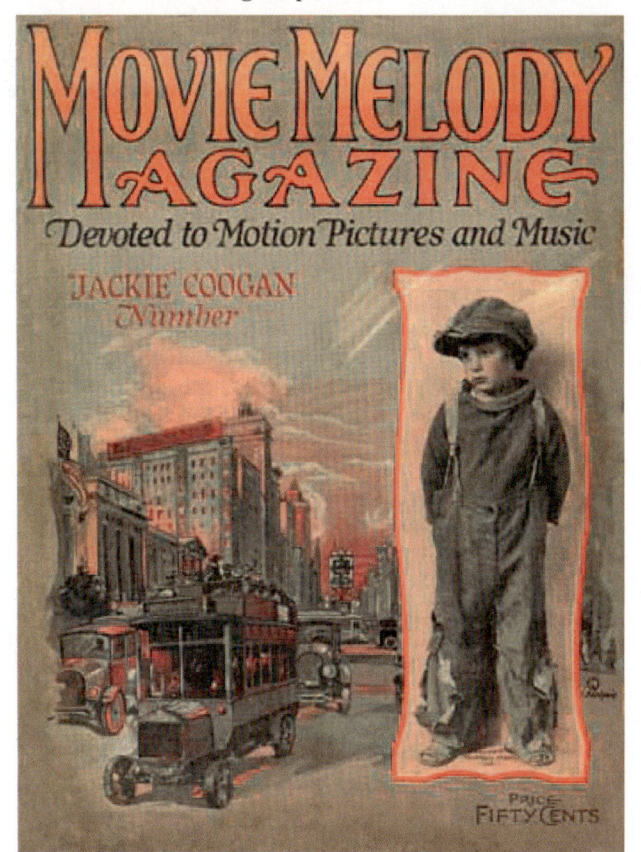

119   The Great American Magazine: Movies

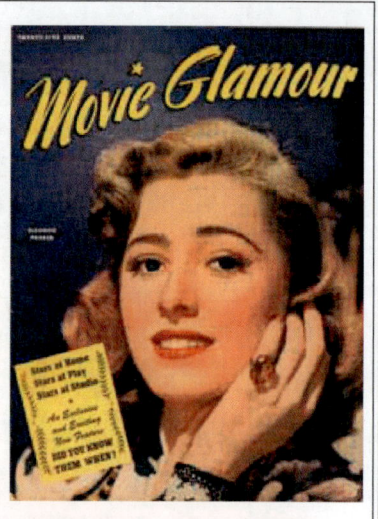

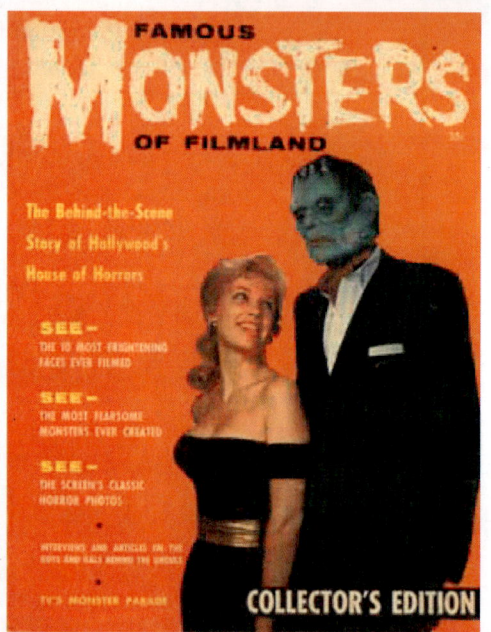

Romance, gossip, glamor, and, since Forest Ackerman's pioneering and highly collected *Famous Monsters of Filmland*, horror; all important sub-categories.

Movie magazines have always been a vehicle for great illustrators such as Rolf Armstrong (above) and Enoch Bolles.

The Great American Magazine: Movies

In 1915, the publishers of *Judge*, one of the most important humor magazines of the day, merged three of its less successful magazines into *Film Fun*, the first movie theme humor periodical, with many of the early covers prominently featuring the cinema's first superstar, Charlie Chaplin. The formula hit paydirt and the magazine went on to have quite a successful run, employing a combination of humor and cheesecake. Pictured above are the first and second issues, both quite rare.
Left: A very scarce Judge publication featuring the truly tragic movie clown, Roscoe (Fatty) Arbuckle.

Sex and humor have always sold magazines, those with a movie theme are no exception.

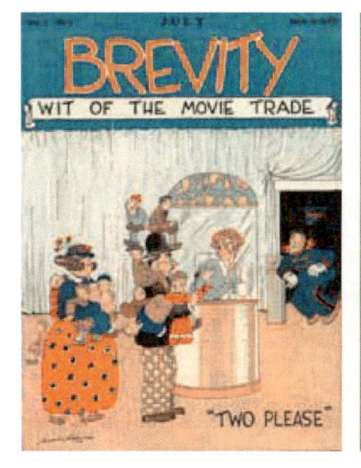

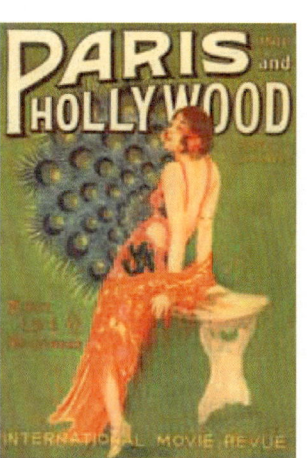

121   The Great American Magazine: Movies

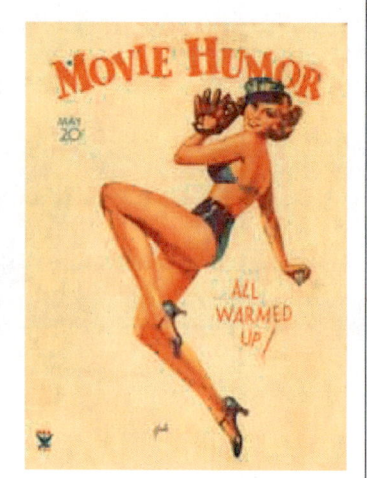

The first issues of a plethora of risque Movie cheesecake magazines from the thirties.

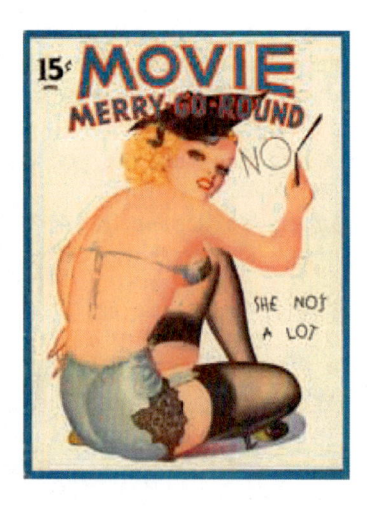

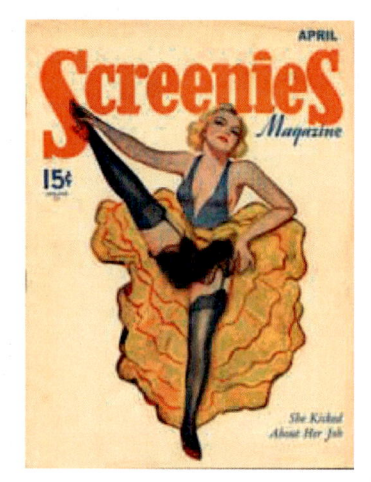

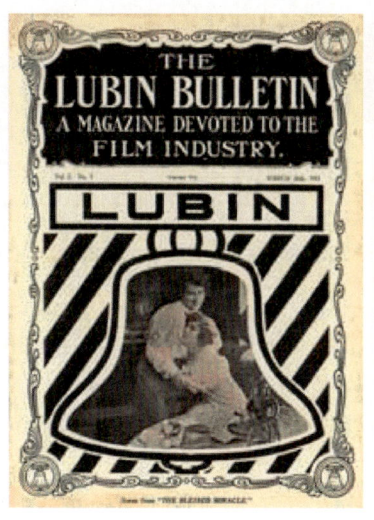

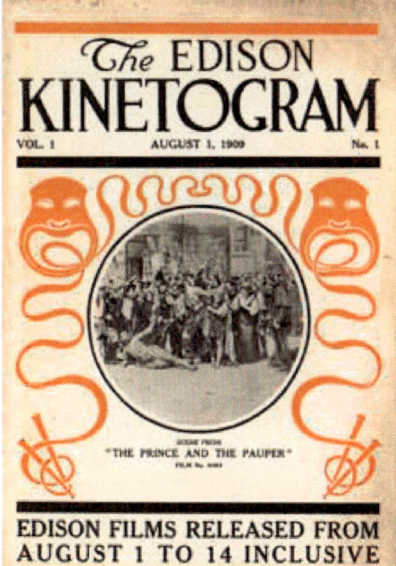

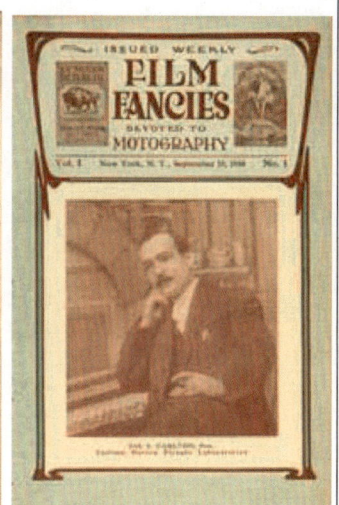

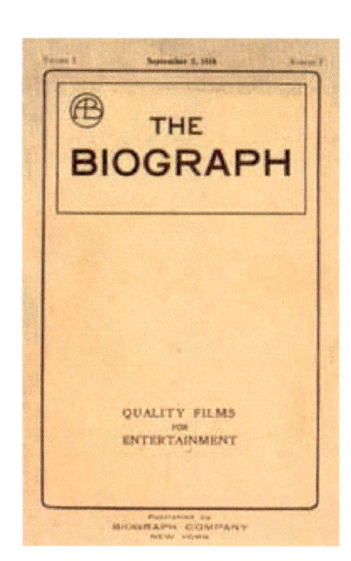

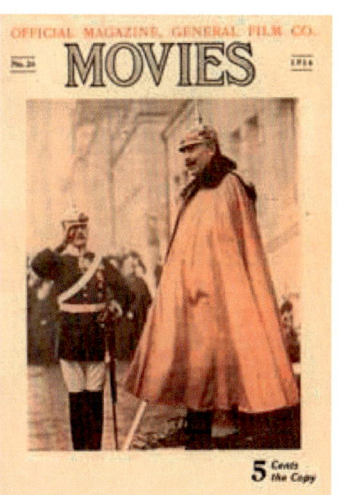

These are early and rare examples of magazines published by studios to publicise their recent films. Since many of original films are long since lost, they are invaluable repositories of film history.
Edison Kinetogram is among the very earliest, published in 1909.
The first *Paramount Magazine* featured America's (and Douglas Fairbanks') sweetheart, Mary Pickford.

The tradition of studio-published magazines lasted through the mid-forties, with MGM's *Lion's Roar*, with its still familiar logo, being the last of the breed.

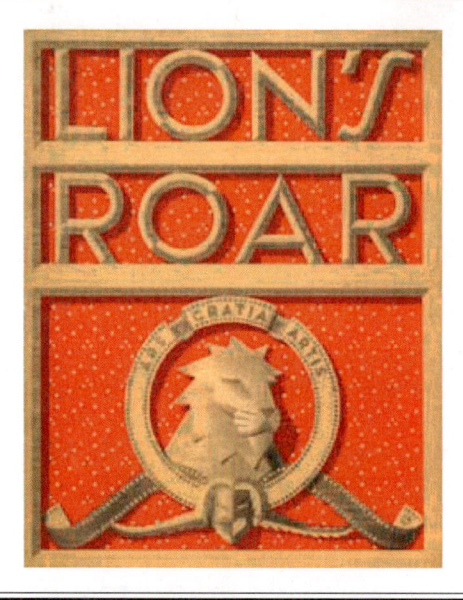

The Great American Magazine: Movies   124

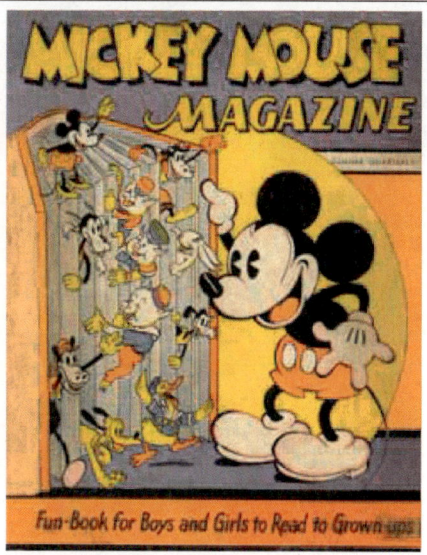

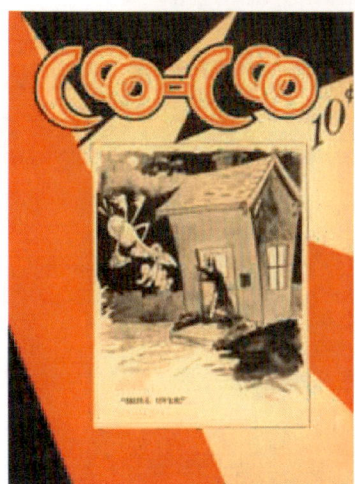

Walt Disney's Mickey Mouse has been the theme for numerous magazines and comics. The earliest was used by local dairies to advertise their products. *Coo-Coo* is a very rare humor magazine illustrated by Disney artist Carl Barks, most remembered as the creator of Donald Duck.

During World War II, Disney studios created a magazine *Dispatch From Disney*, intended for distribution to all Disney employees in the Armed Forces. The cover illustration and feature article is devoted to "Der Feuhrer's Face", the academy award-winning and still suppressed, now politically incorrect Donald Duck cartoon feature.

Included within each issue was a risque pinup, created by Disney artists, which today would not likely be approved by censors for distibution!

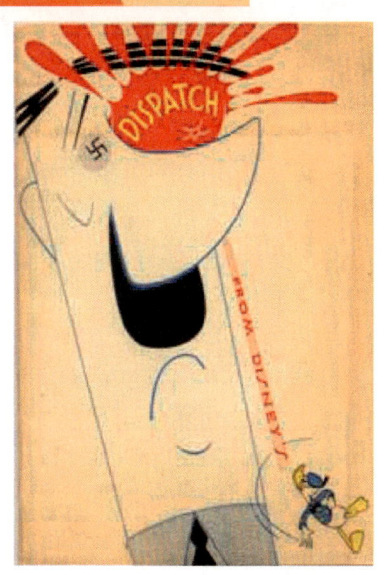

125   The Great American Magazine: Movies

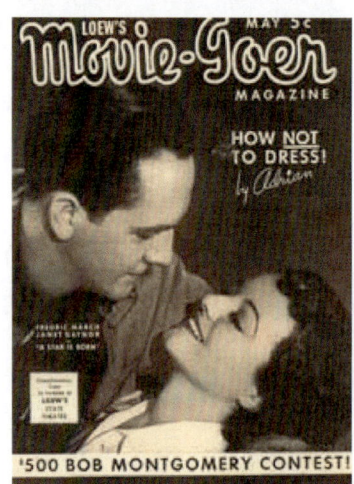

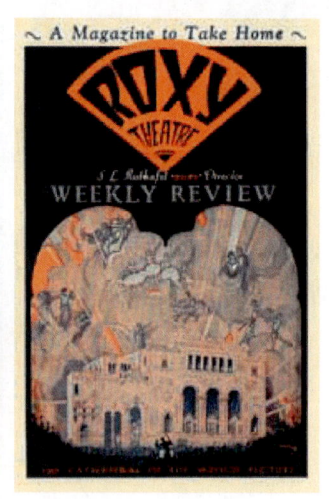

These magazines were distributed,
often without charge, by theatre chains
to their patrons.

The Great American Magazine: Movies

Marilyn Monroe, arguably the number one female cultural icon of the twentieth century, had a short-lived and truly meteoric career. She began quite modestly, first appearing in magazines as a dark-haired Norma Jean Dougherty in 1946. Within a few years she would appear on hundreds of magazine covers. There is considerable visual literature devoted to Marilyn, the most comprehensive being a series of books by Clark Kidder and a volume published by Rizzoli. Here is a potpourri of her appearances, many from her earliest photos by Andre de Dienes, with a smattering of later appearances.

The unobtrusive first commercial appearance of the 18 year old
Norma Jean on the cover of the
Douglas Aircraft trade magazine.

Below: Two very rare foreign magazine appearances in 1946, one just prior to and another shortly after her American solo debut as a cover model.
Photo by Andre de Diene.

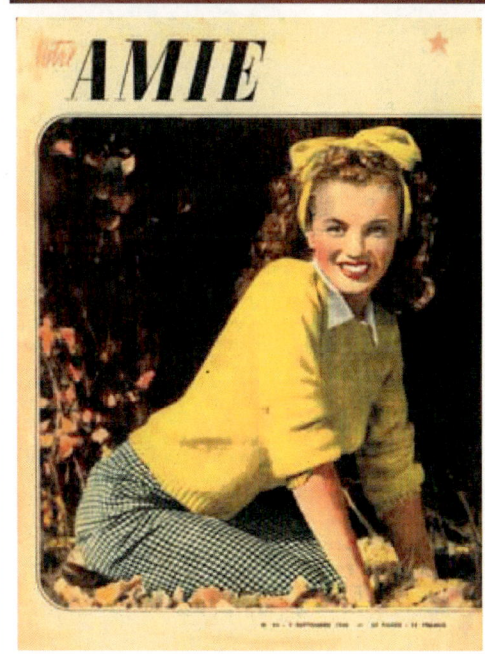

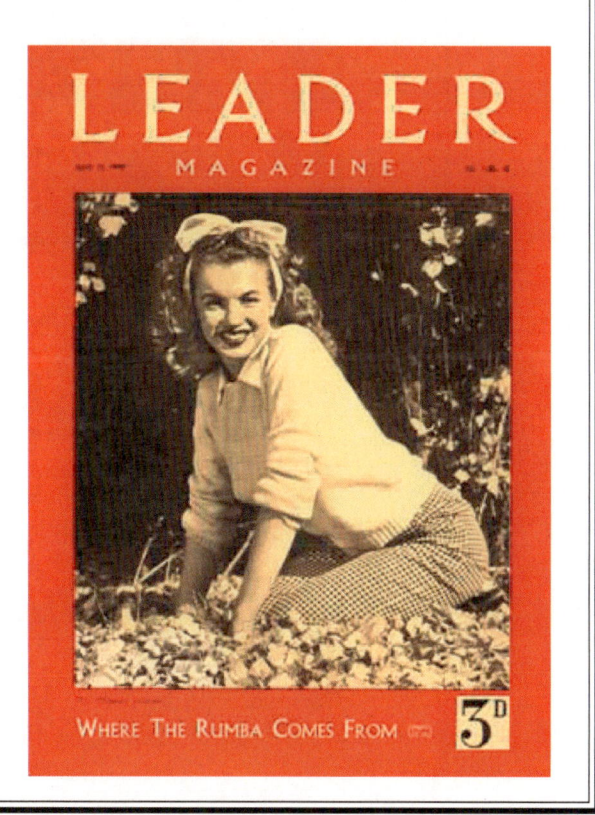

127   The Great American Magazine: Movies

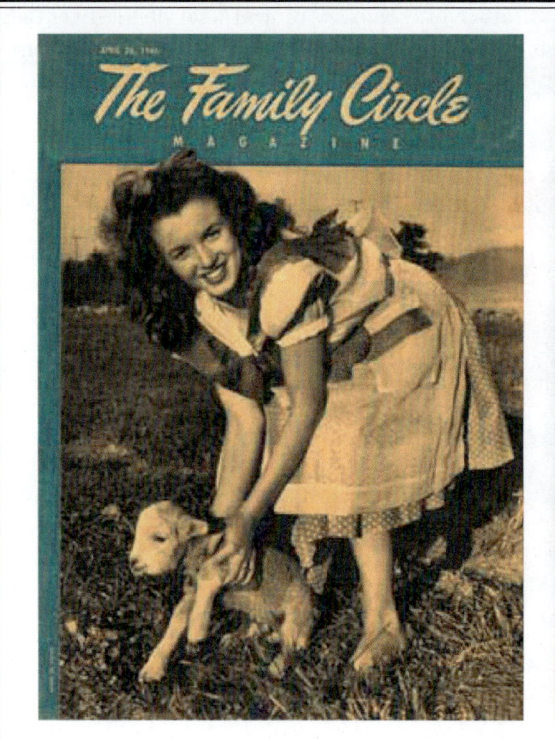

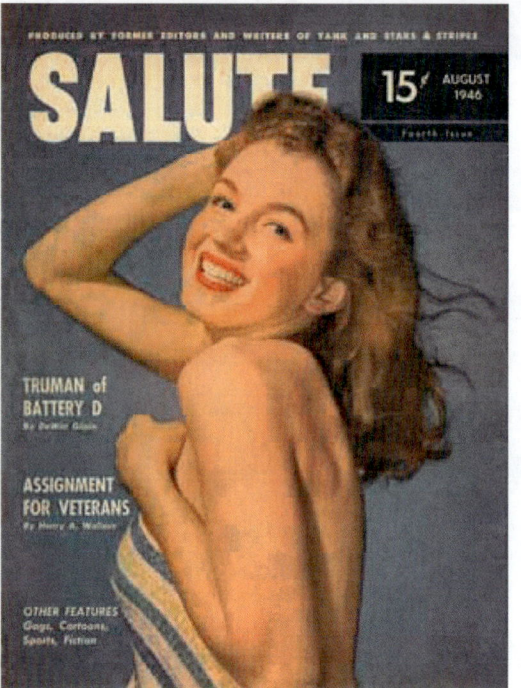

A modest first appearance in April 1946, followed by her first cheesecake a few month's later.

Vivacious 19-year-old Norma Jean Daugherty was working in an aircraft factory when she was asked to pose for official War Department pictures. She has been modeling ever since. Norma Jean likes the outdoor life and cooking for her Coast Guard husband. Photograph for Pageant by Andre de Dienes.

The Great American Magazine: Movies

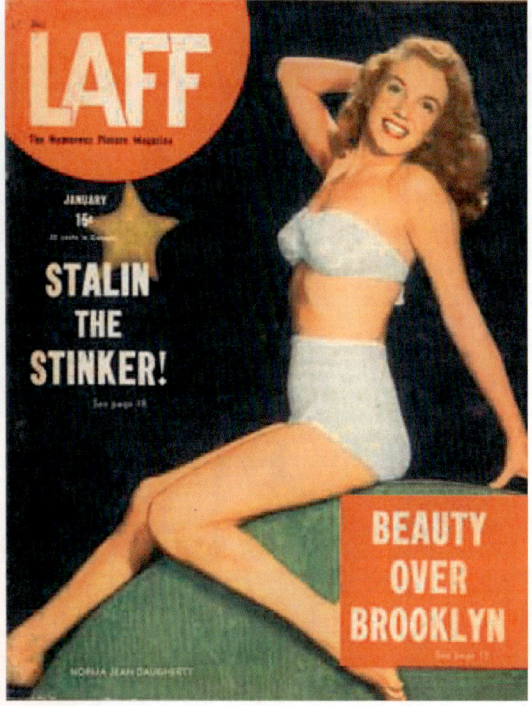

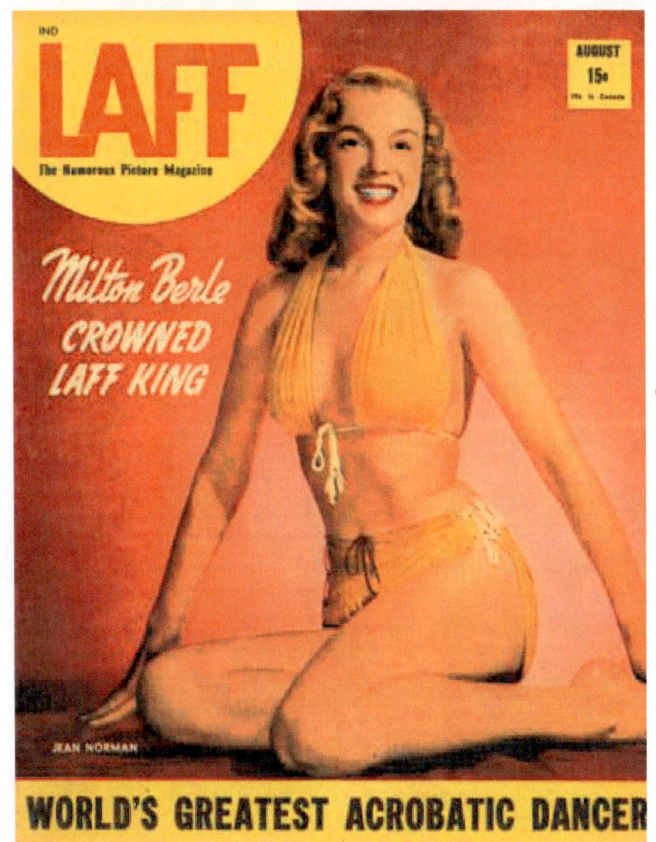

More early cheesecake.
The only two magazine covers with her
original name on the cover and one with
a virtually unknown
transitional name!

129   The Great American Magazine: Movies

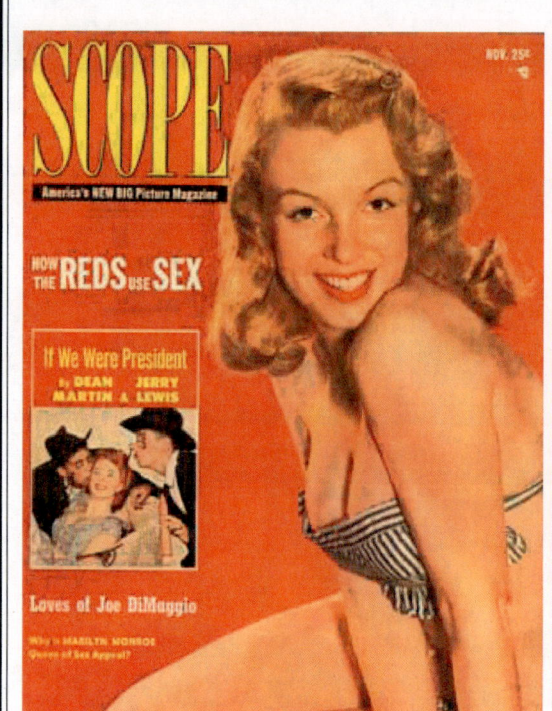

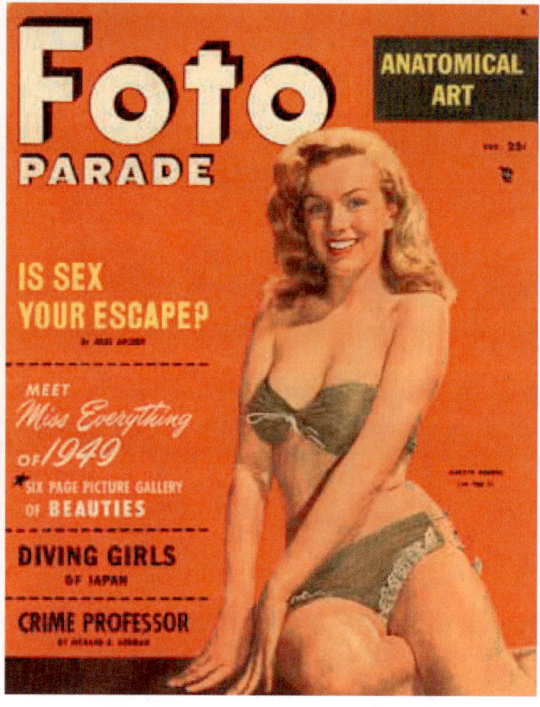

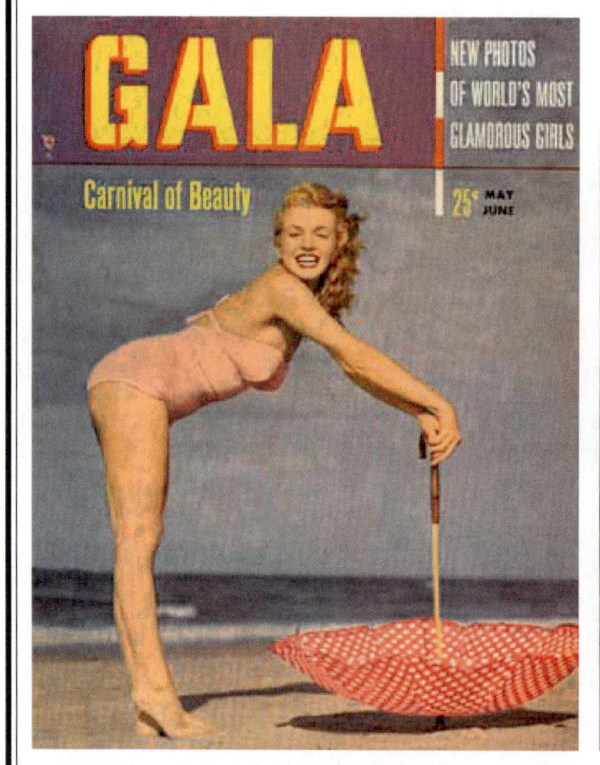

Two magazine covers and a more matronly catalog cover while still a minor starlet and another after her fame skyrocketed.

The Great American Magazine: Movies

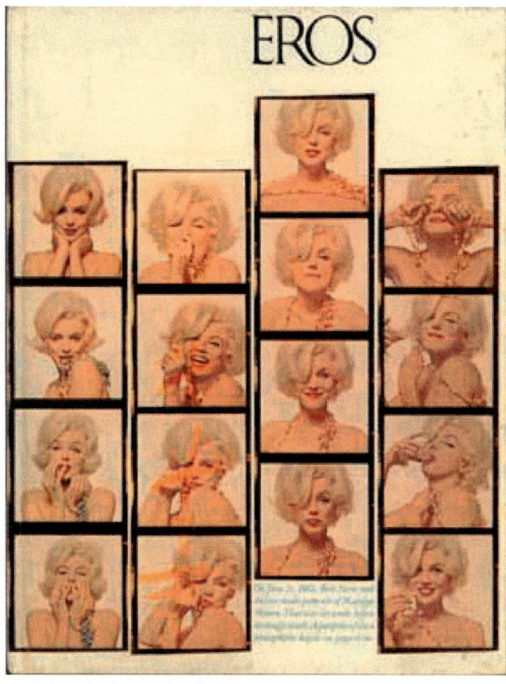

MM was *Playboy's* first cover model and centerfold in December 1953. Only nine years later, a posthumous appearance in Ralph Ginsberg's soon to be banned *Eros*, from her last photo shoot with Bert Stern. Quite a contrast from the innocent milkmaid of 1946!

In 1943, Howard Hawks was looking for a fresh new face to star in his latest movie. The alluring beauty of the cover model of this issue of *Harper's Bazaar* impressed his wife. Hence the discovery of the elegant Lauren Bacall.

The year prior to appearing in his first movie, The Painted Desert, in 1931, Clark Gable appeared on the cover of *The Wasp*, a continuation of the San Francisco based, formerly satiric humor magazine. This is very likely his first magazine cover appearance.

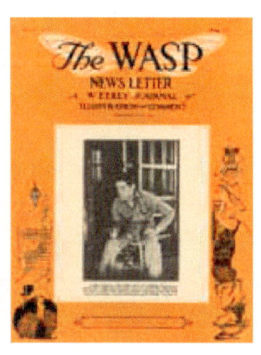

131   The Great American Magazine: Movies

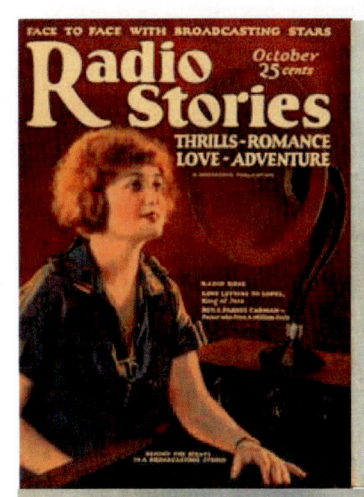

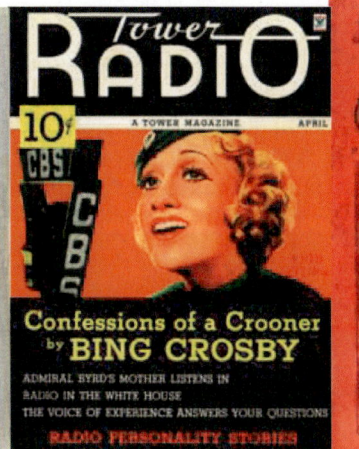

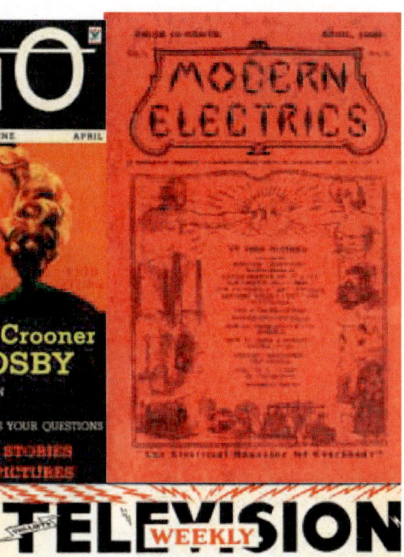

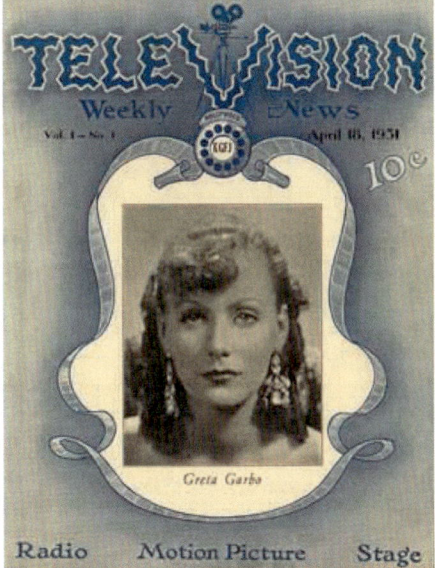

RADIO
AND
TELEVISION
MAGAZINES

STEVEN LOMAZOW, M.D.

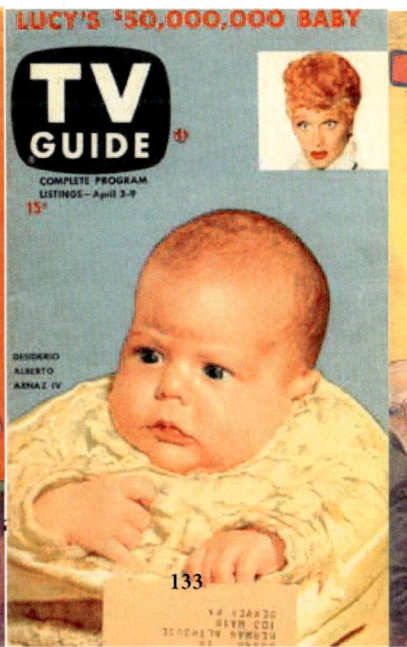

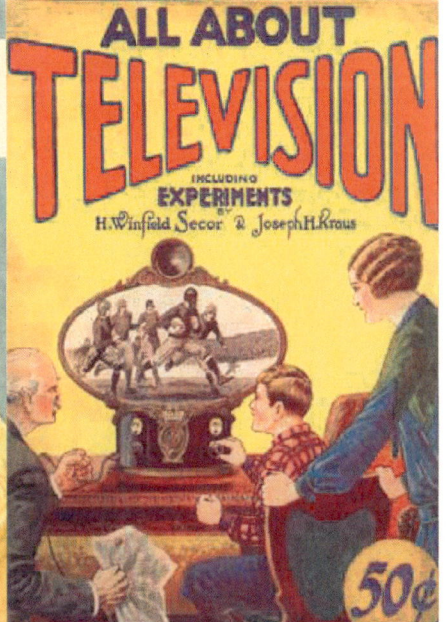

133

The father of "wireless" was Gugliemo Marconi. An early radio magazine bearing his name, *Marconigraph,* started in Britain in 1911. An American edition began in 1912, changing its title to *Wireless Age* in 1913. Another key personality was Hugo Gernsback, who started the first radio magazine, *Modern Electrics,* in 1908 where he introduced his novel, "Ralph 124C 41+", in twelve installments in 1911 and 1912. "Ralph" is not great literature by any means, nor is it the first story to deal with scientific fiction (a term coined by Gernsback). It is, though, an important indication of Gernback's incredible sense of what the future held in store.

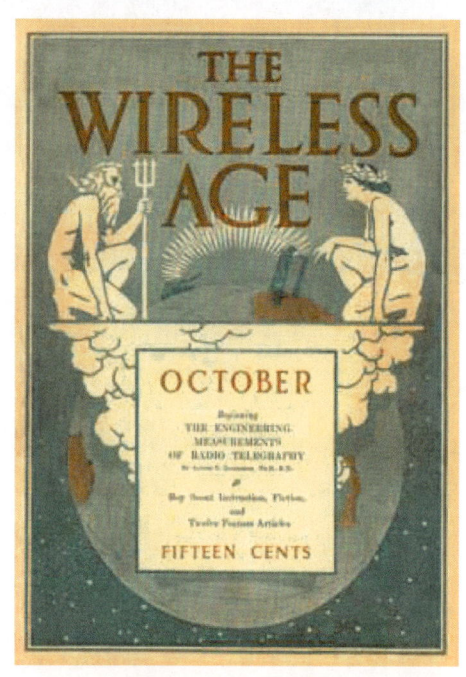

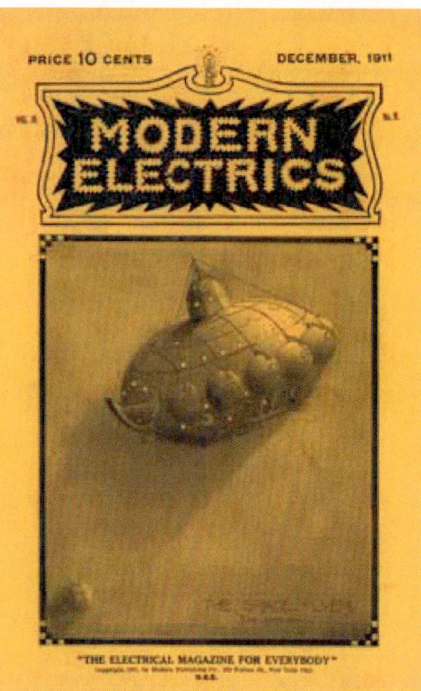

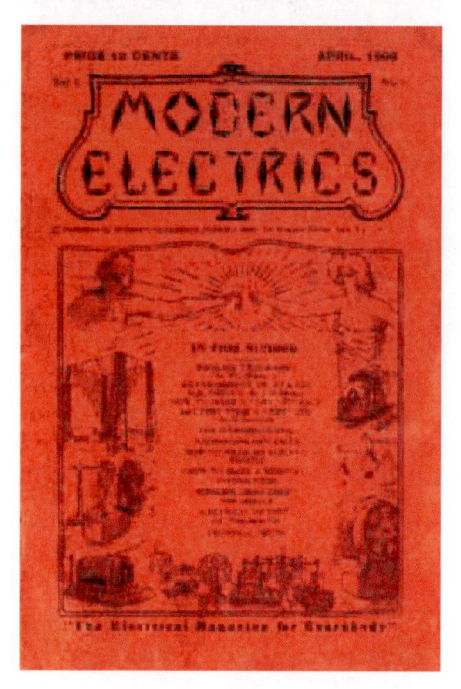

The very rare first issues of *Modern Electrics* and *Wireless Age.* The two earliest magazines devoted to radio.

One of the twelve monthly installments of the original appearance of Hugo Gernsback's futuristic classic "Ralph 124C 41+". Each cover features an illustration from the story.

The Great American Magazine: Radio and Television

Most early radio literature focused on hobbyists called radio amateurs or "hams". Amateur Radio's pioneer organization was the The American Radio Relay League, founded by Hiram Percy Maxim, and its journal, *QST*, first issued in December 1915, is the first and still the foremost publication in its field.

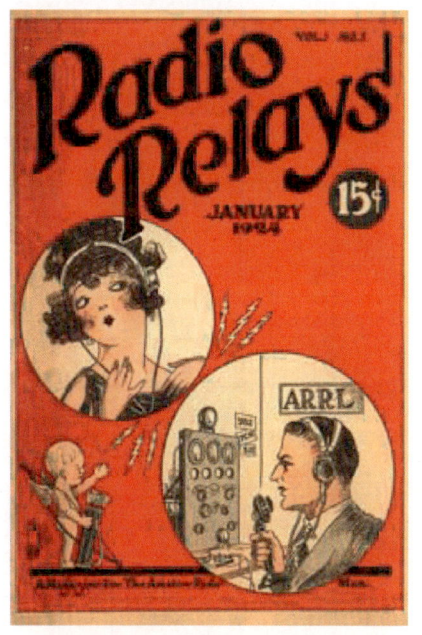

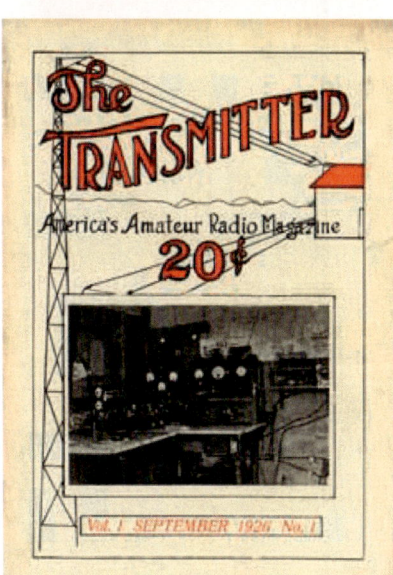

The first issue of *QST* and other rare and early Amateur Radio Journals.

135   The Great American Magazine: Radio and Television

Commercial radio broadcasting was made practical by Lee de Forest's Audion tube and initially backed by Westinghouse, a leading radio manufacturer, in an effort to increase sales. Dr. Frank Conrad, a Pittsburgh area radio amateur, made the first broadcast (a term he himself coined) on November 2, 1920, over Pittsburgh station KDKA, in conjunction with the national presidential election. KDKA was a huge hit and within four years there were more than 600 radio stations across the country.

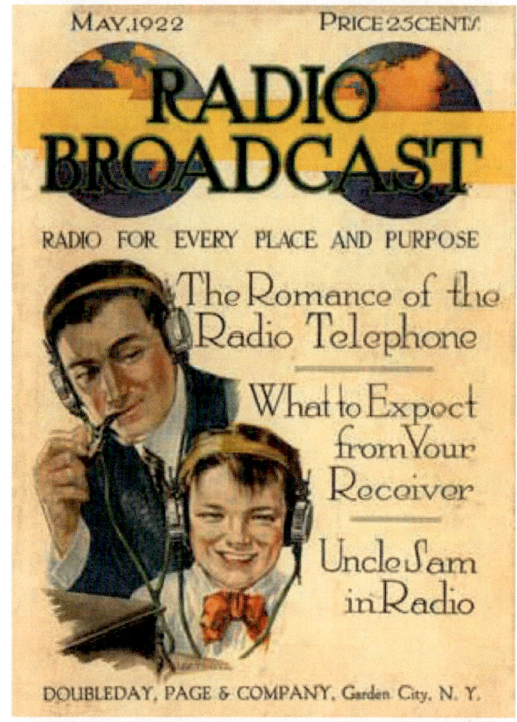

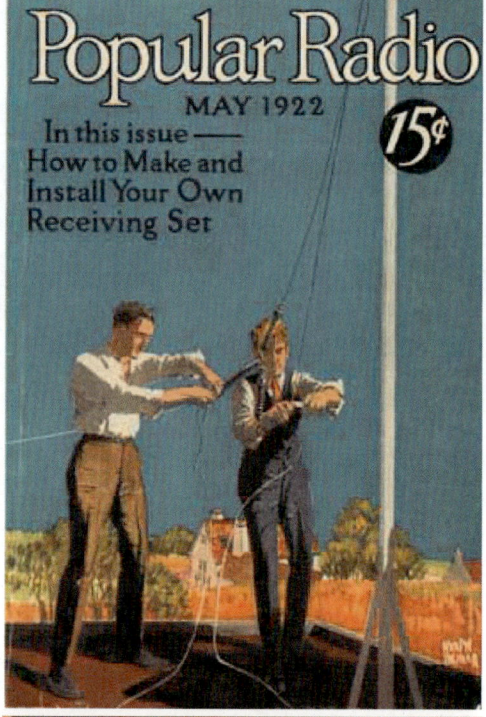

The Great American Magazine: Radio and Television

Tuning in to commercial stations and short wave broadcasts around the world was a popular pastime and hobby. Magazines devoted to all aspects of Radio appeared to support the interest, some more technical than others, many of them published by Hugo Gernback.

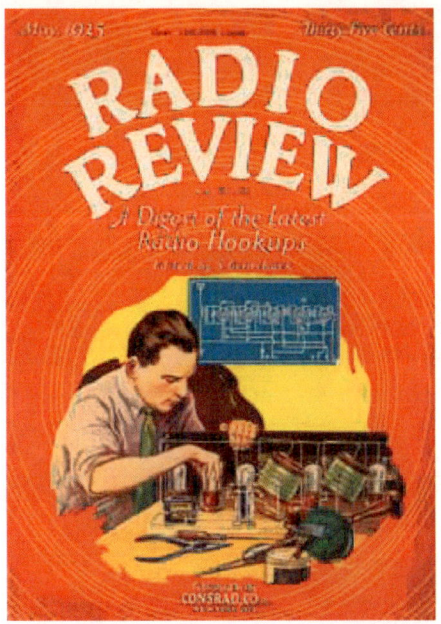

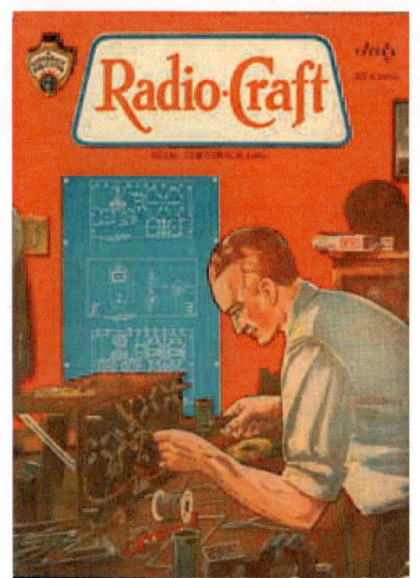

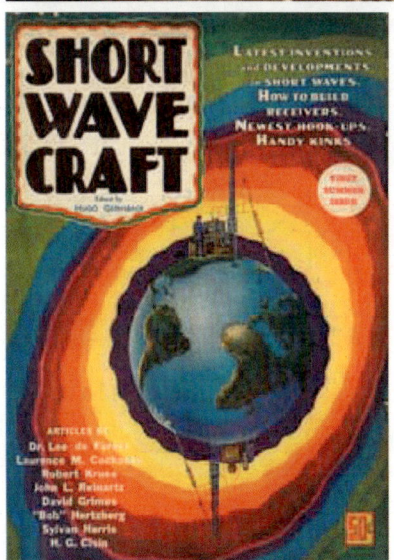

137 The Great American Magazine: Radio and Television

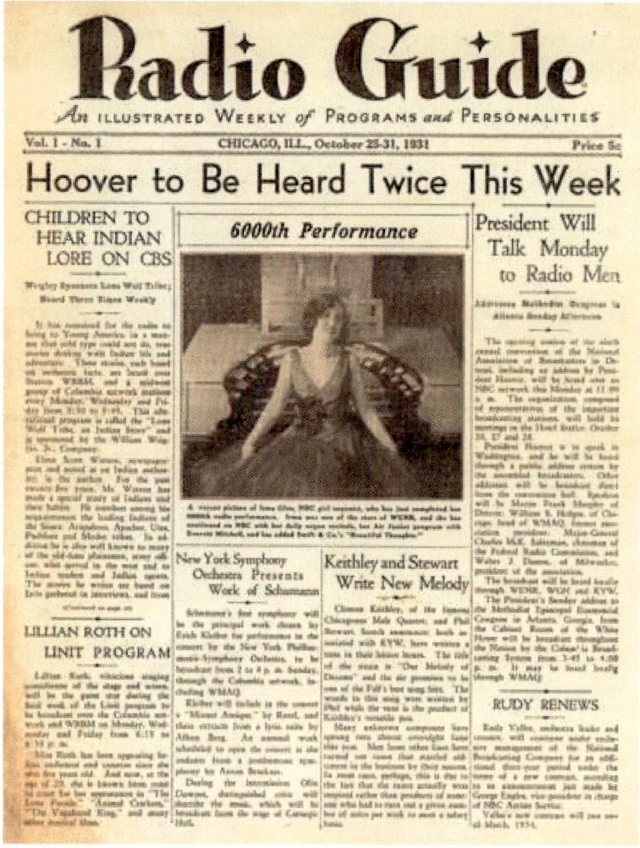

The increased listenership created a demand for programming guides.

Radio Guide was the most prominent and long-standing. As with movies earlier and television later, the periodical press was a rich source of supplementary information, both reflecting and enhancing the value of the medium.

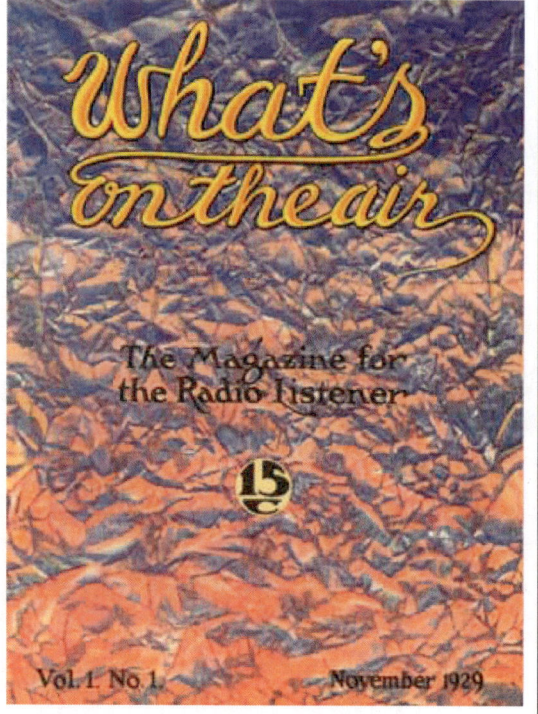

The Great American Magazine: Radio and Television

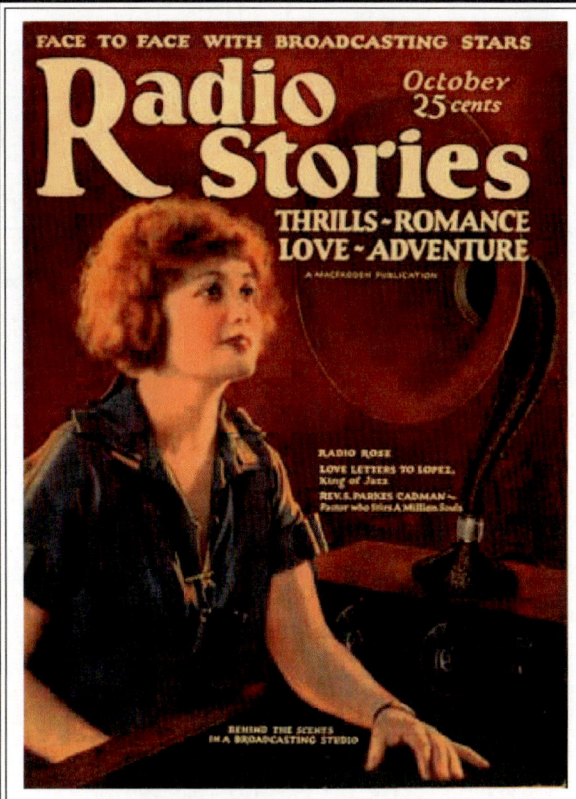

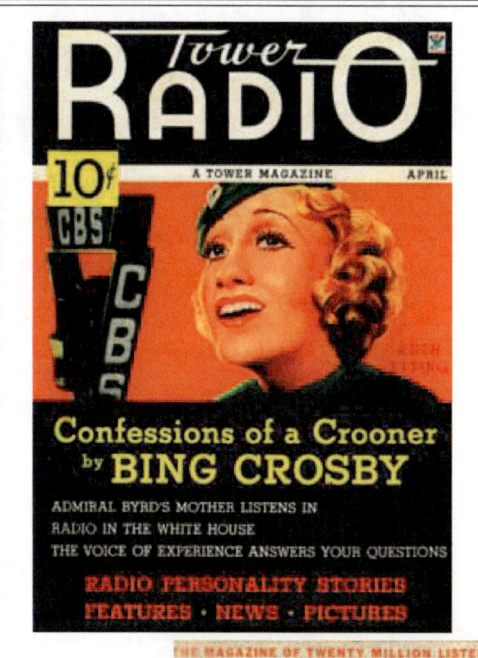

Radio Stories came closest to a radio-themed pulp magazine.

Radio did not escape the public's insatiable appetite for gossipy information about the lives of the stars. Fan magazines began to appear.

Major Bowe's Amateur Hour, the nineteen-thirties' version of Starsearch, was so popular that it issued its own magazine.

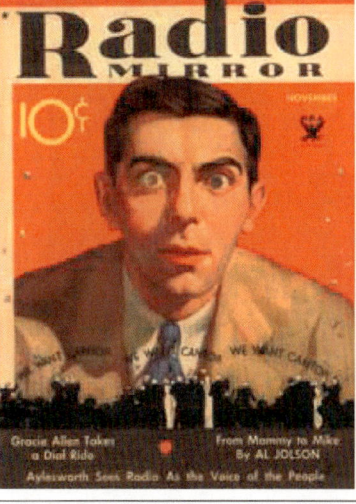

139 The Great American Magazine: Radio and Television

Some radio magazines were designed to appeal to a more rural audience.

During World War II, radio was an important source of news. President Roosevelt made very effective use of it through "fireside chats" and frequent national addresses.

The Great American Magazine: Radio and Television

Dinah Shore made a successful transition to television, which, by the mid-fifties, had replaced radio as America's number one household entertainment medium. As the popularity of radio diminished, the magazines disappeared.

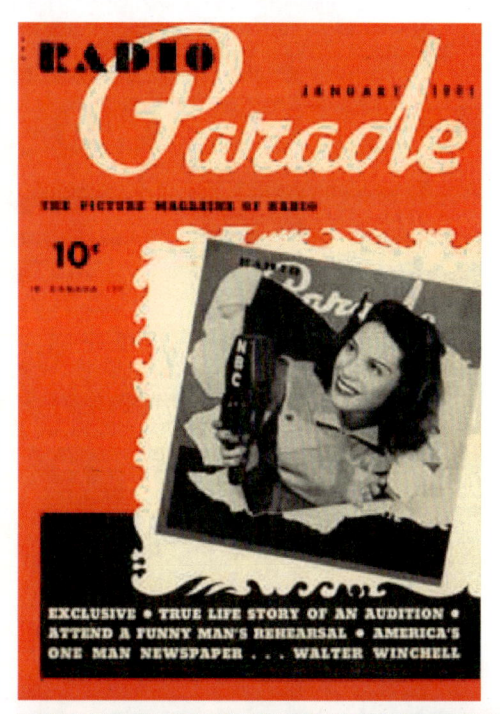

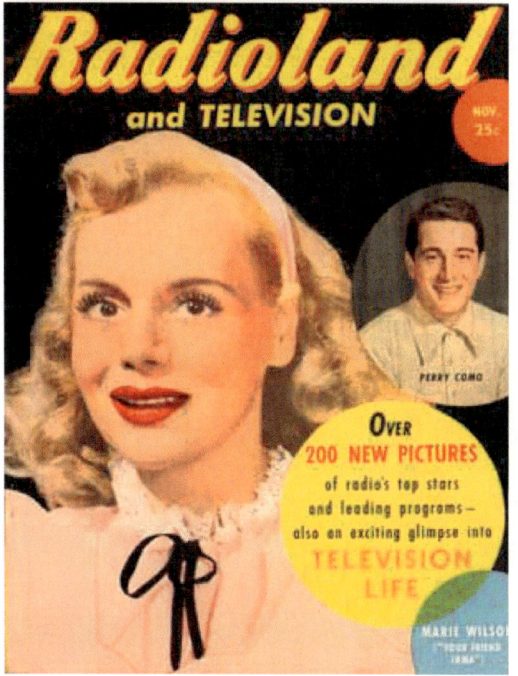

The Great American Magazine: Radio and Television

Through the twenty-first century, Amateur Radio continues to be an area of avid hobby interest and public service. Aside from *QST*, *CQ, 73* and *Ham Radio* are the most long-standing, well-established journals in the field. A commerical operator's radio magazine, also entitled *CQ* (which is radio jargon means "I would like to make contact") appeared in 1931. The radio amateur version started in 1945.

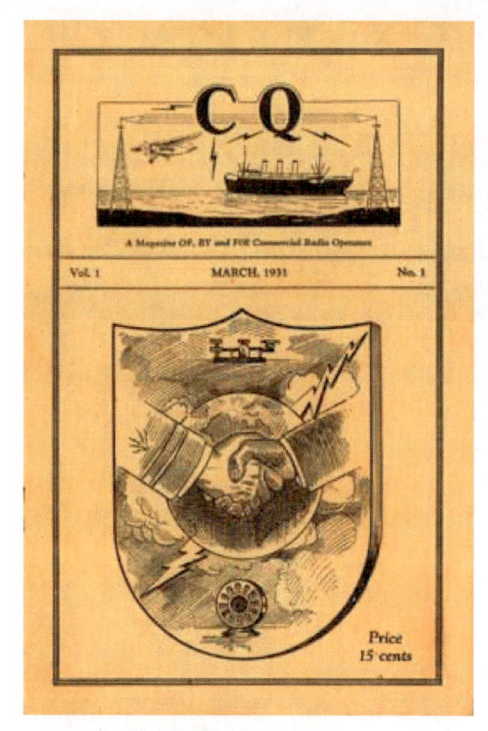

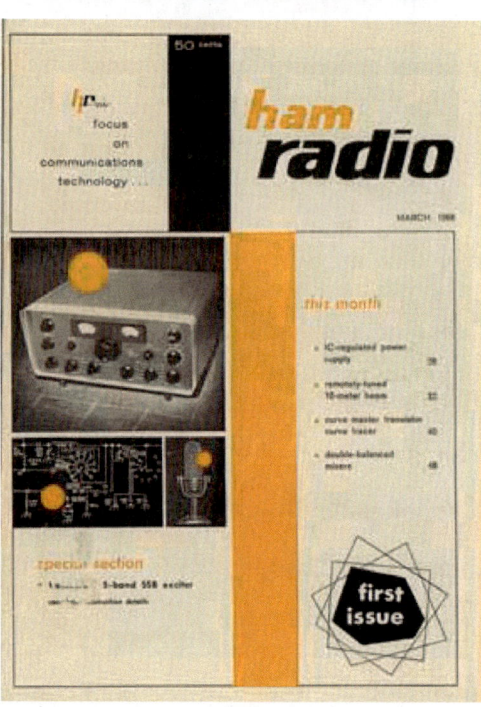

The Great American Magazine: Radio and Television   142

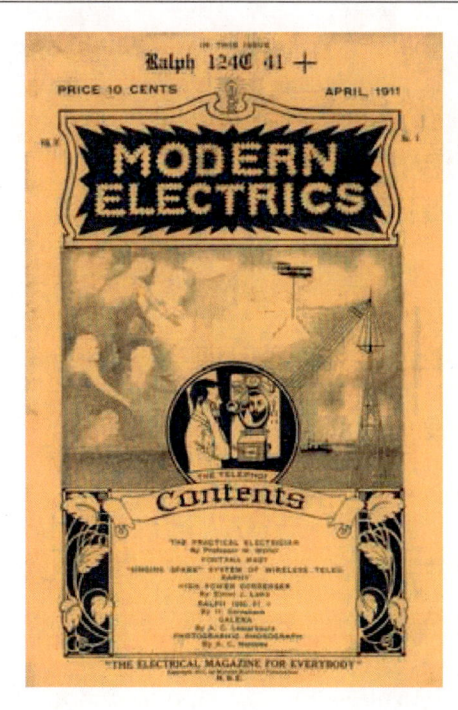

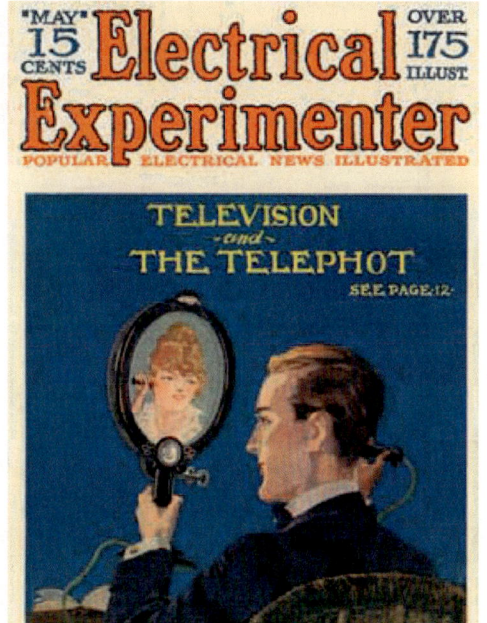

Well before Television became a practical reality, Hugo Gernsback, the imaginative futurist and popularizer of the terms "television" and "science fiction" wrote stories and published articles about it in his magazines *Modern Electrics*, in 1909, and *Electrical Experimenter*, in 1918. Magazines specifically devoted to television began with Gernsback's *All About Television* in the summer of 1927. WRNY was Gernsbach's TV broadcast station.

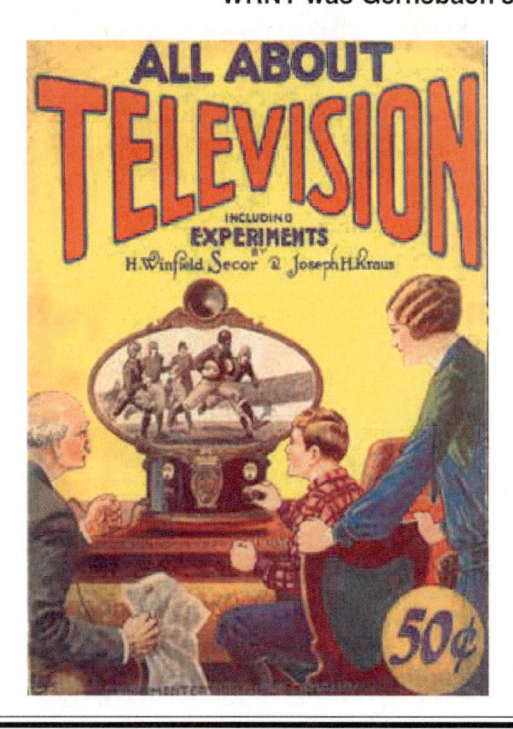

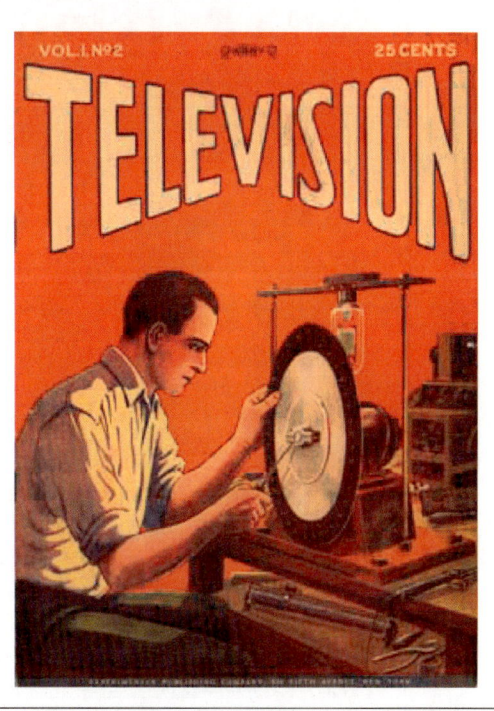

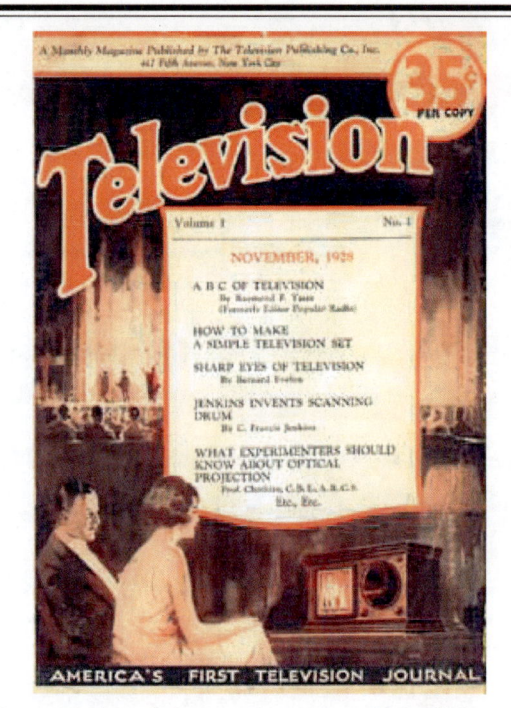

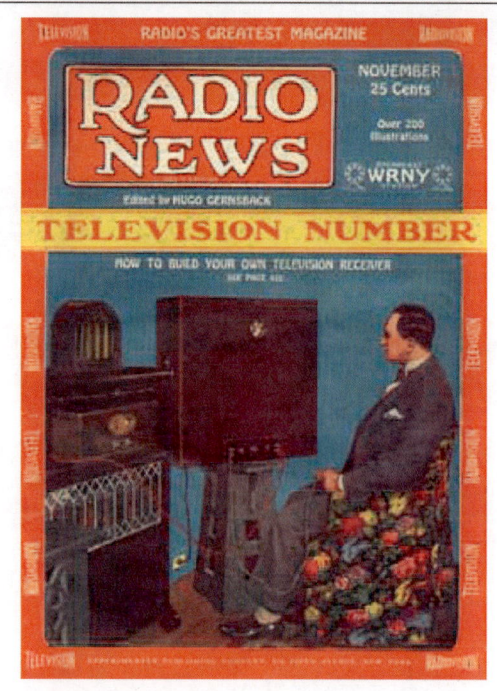

Despite the claim on the cover, *Television* was not America's first TV magazine. It was published concurrently in Britain. *Radio News* featured a television issue in 1928. The omnipresent Gernsback began publishing *Television News* in 1931. In April 1931, the exquisitely rare *Weekly Television News* became the first weekly magazine principally devoted to television and included a list of all presently operating TV stations.

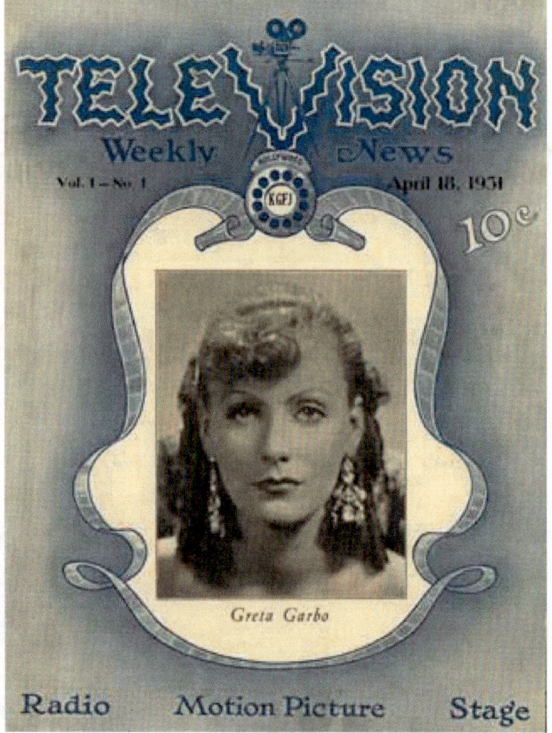

The Great American Magazine: Radio and Television

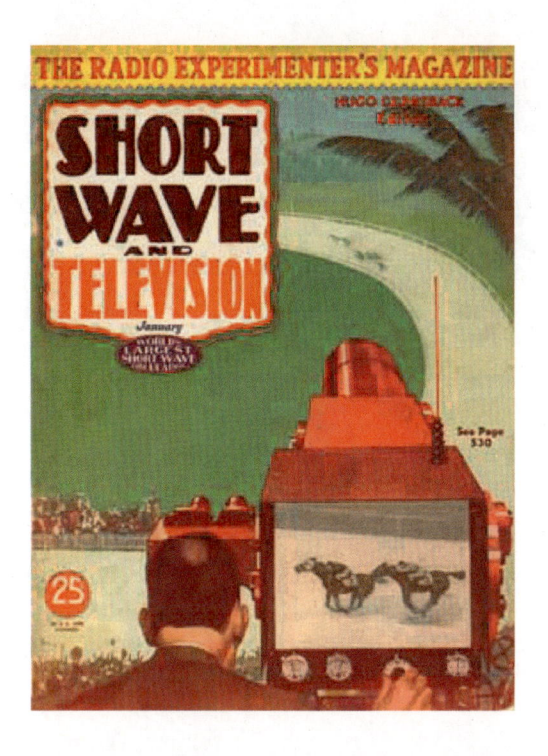

Many of Hugo Gernsback's publications in the 1930's continued to pique the public's interest in this new and exciting visual medium.

After a marked improvement in technology, exhibitions at the 1939 World's Fair in New York City created great excitement about the commercial possibilities of television. World War II derailed the momentum, but in the immediate post-war period it was regained.

The earliest programming schedules were sent by mail from broadcasting stations to the buyers of TV sets.

In 1948, beginning with Phillips's *Television Weekly*, programming magazines began to appear. The first of the familiar digest-sized publications was Chicago's *TV Forecast*, soon joined by Walter Annenberg's *Local Televiser*, later *TV Digest*, in Philadelphia and *Television Guide*, later *TV Guide*, in New York. Other regional editions and offshoots appeared until the mid-fifties. In April 1953, Annenberg unified the market into national *TV Guide*, which continues today as the pre-eminent weekly television magazine.

The first weekly programming guide

The Great American Magazine: Radio and Television

The first digest-sized programming guide, Chicago, 1948.

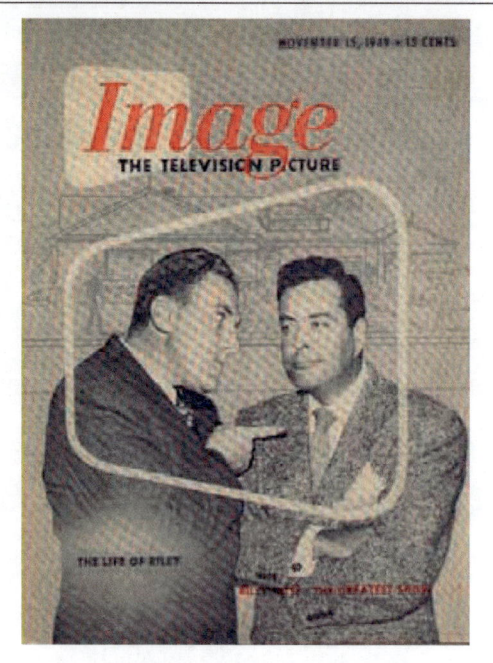

The first issue of a rare and early Los Angeles programming guide. Jackie Gleason played Riley before William Bendix.

An early issue of Walter Annenberg's *Local Televisor*, the first issue of *TV Digest* after the name change and other collectible "pre-national" issues.

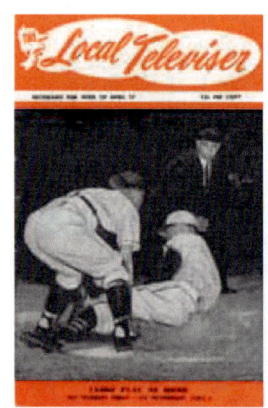

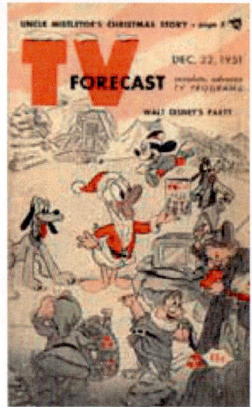

The Great American Magazine: Radio and Television   146

The first local New York *TV Guide*, 1948

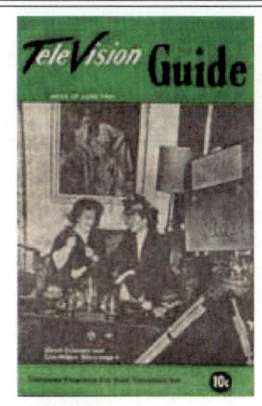

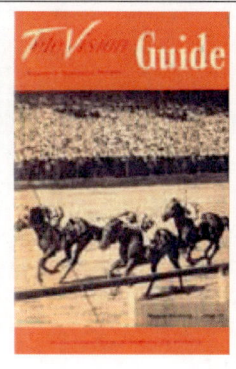

Local issues of New York *TV Guide*, especially early issues, were rarely saved. A complete file is not known to exist.

Among the most collectible programming guide issues are those with science fiction, sports and juvenile themed (Disney, Howdy Doody) covers.
Fall preview and anniversary issues are also important for the wealth of important source material they contain.

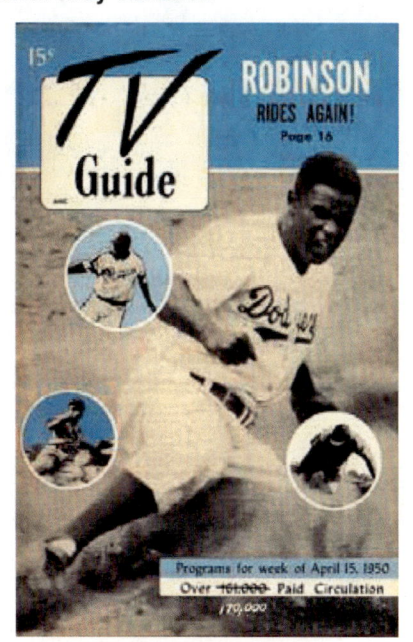

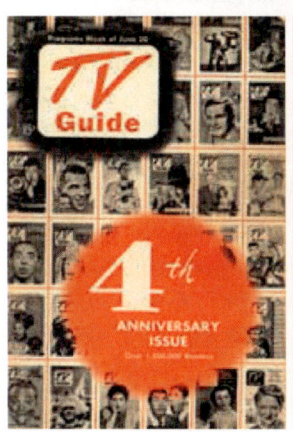

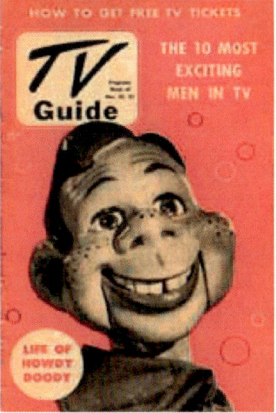

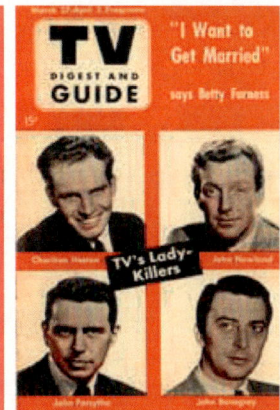

The last "pre-national" issue prior to the merger

147   The Great American Magazine: Radio and Television

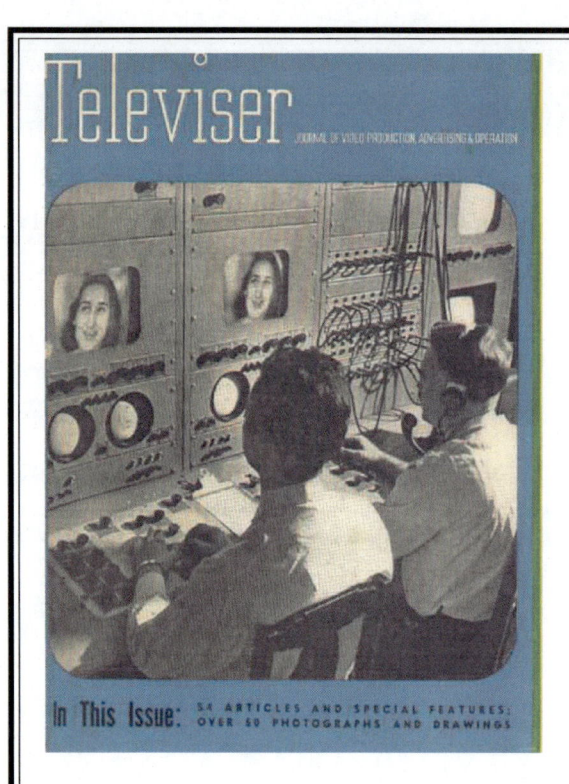

Journal's like *Televiser* showed the technical state of
the television art in the mid-forties.
There were relatively few television trade journals.

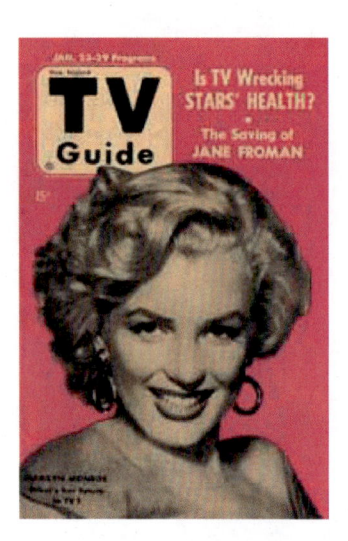

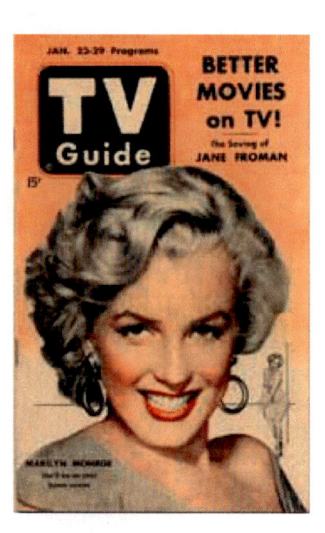

Marilyn Monroe was never a major TV personality but
her image on the cover definitely sold magazines!
Here are some rare and highly collected appearances on
pre-national issues.

The Great American Magazine: Radio and Television

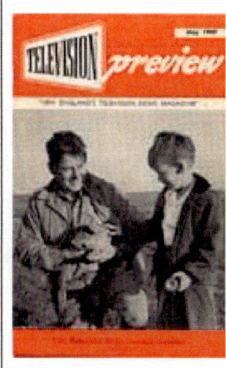

A potpourri of of local programming guides, weekly newspaper supplements and digest-sized fan magazines. All are rarely encountered.

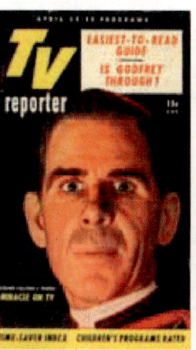

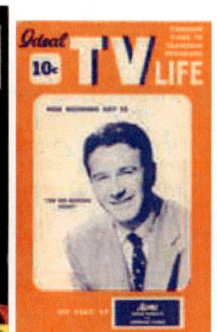

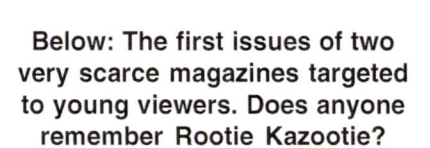

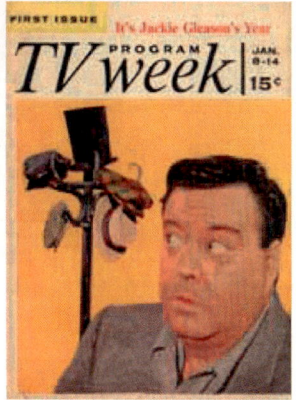

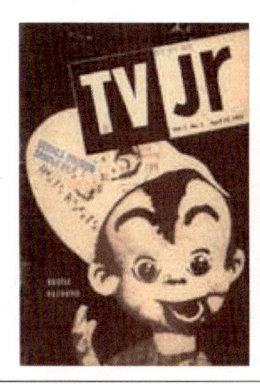

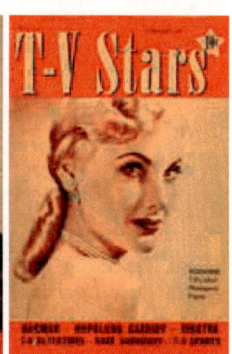

Below: The first issues of two very scarce magazines targeted to young viewers. Does anyone remember Rootie Kazootie?

149 The Great American Magazine: Radio and Television

In the late forties and early fifties as the medium became more practical and affordable, programming increased and the stars were showcased on a wide variety of fan magazines, some of which combined TV with movies.

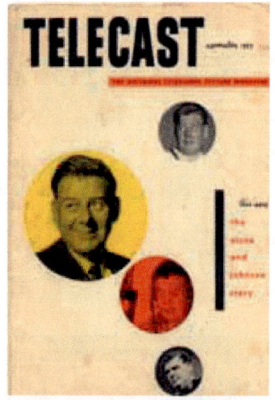

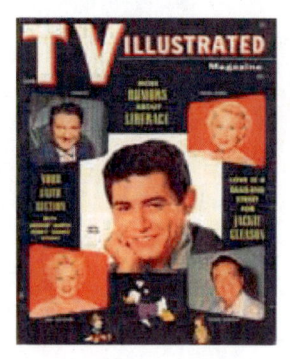

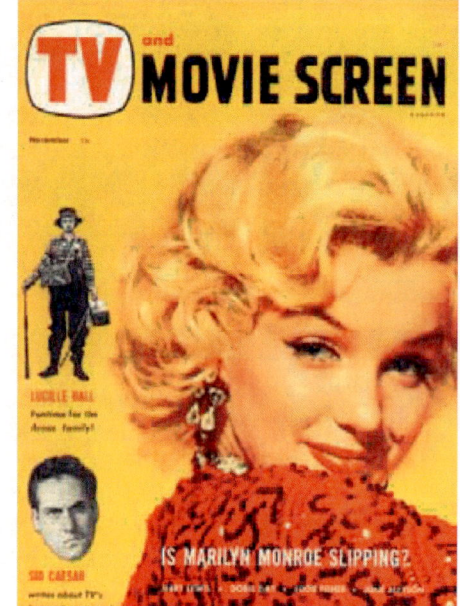

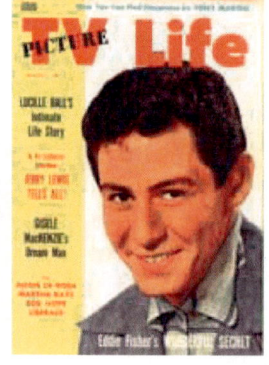

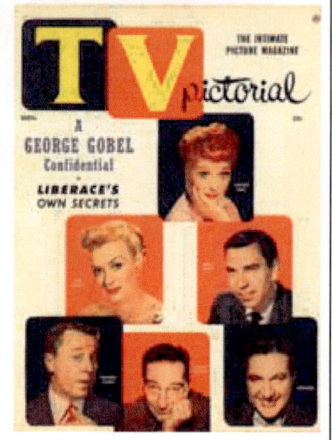

On her popular TV variety program, the vivacious Dinah Shore urged viewers to "see the USA in your Chevrolet".

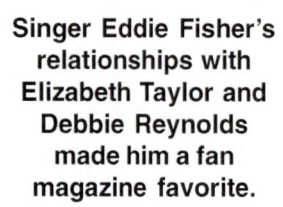

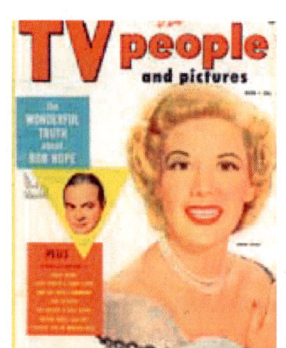

Singer Eddie Fisher's relationships with Elizabeth Taylor and Debbie Reynolds made him a fan magazine favorite.

The Great American Magazine: Radio and Television

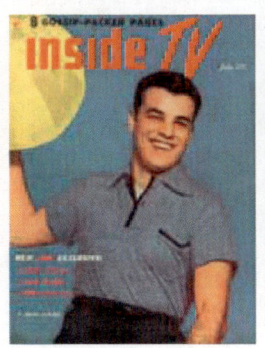

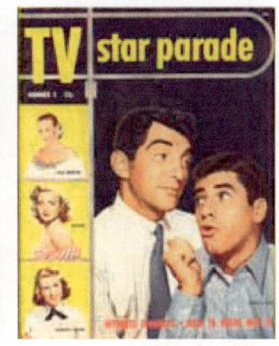

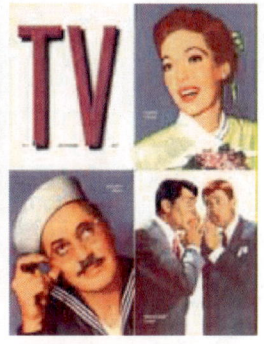

Many stars made the transition from radio and the movies. Others, like Arthur Godfrey, made their reputation solely as TV stars.

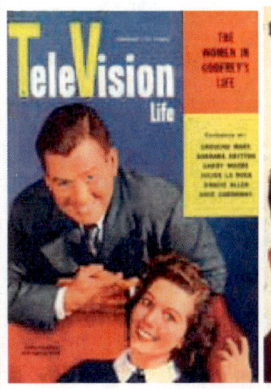

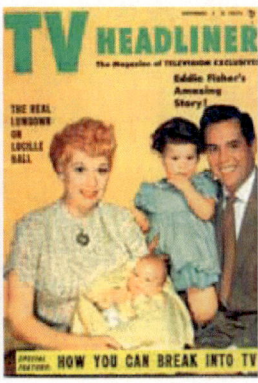

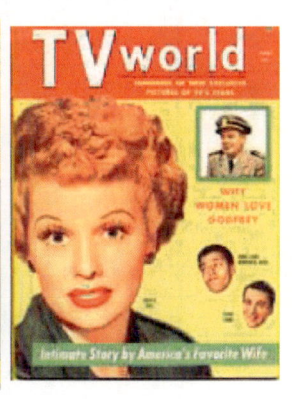

Lucille Ball was the undisputed queen of television in the 1950's. She still holds the record for the most *TV Guide* cover appearances.

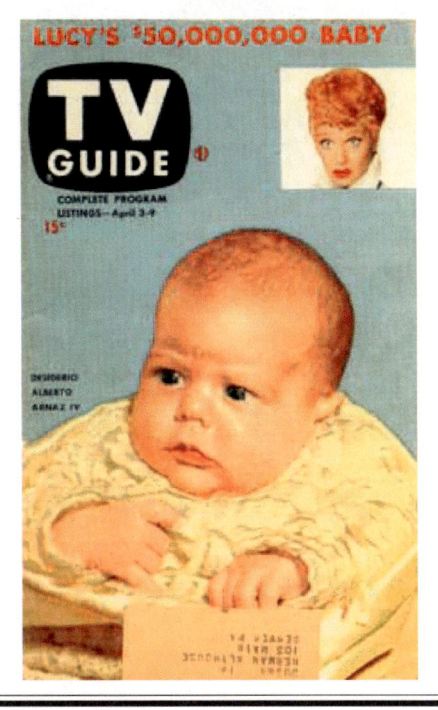

The first national *TV Guide* and a few of the most collectible from the first year of publication. Individual issues of the amalgamated national publication are readily available.

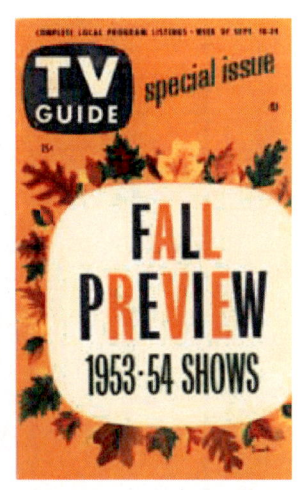

151   The Great American Magazine: Radio and Television

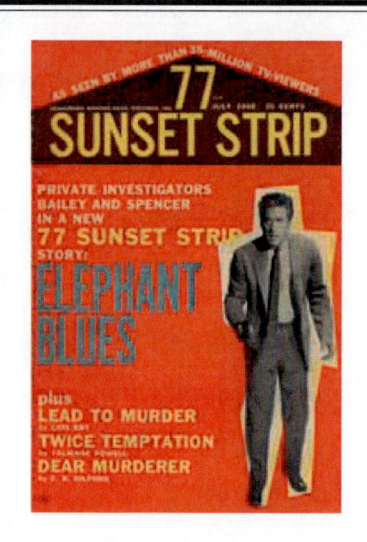

As the market expanded some programs had their own magazines, including *77 Sunset Strip*, *Bonanza*, *Laugh-in* and *All in the Family*.

Here are some first issues of more recent TV magazines. New ones are constantly appearing.

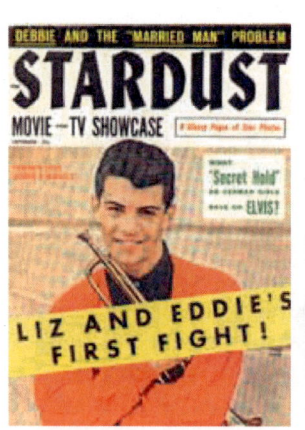

Soap Opera Digest continues to be a supermarket check-out aisle favorite.

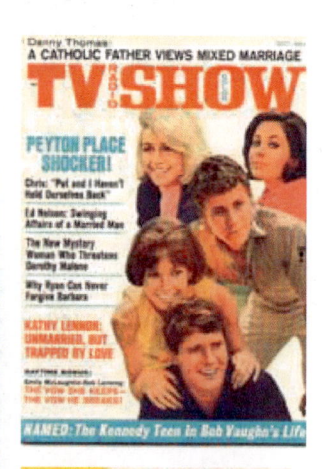

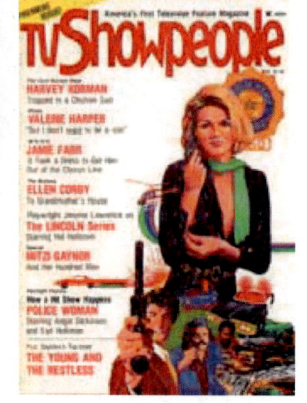

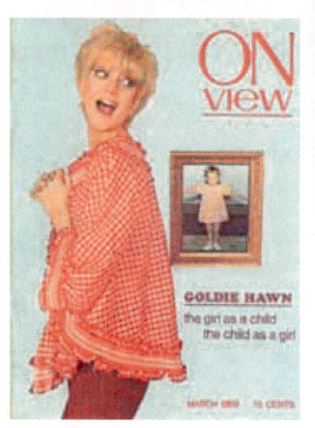

The Great American Magazine: Radio and Television   152

America at War: A Magazine History

Prepared for the New York Military Affairs Symposium
New York, New York. January 6, 2012
By Steven Lomazow, M.D.

Beginnings

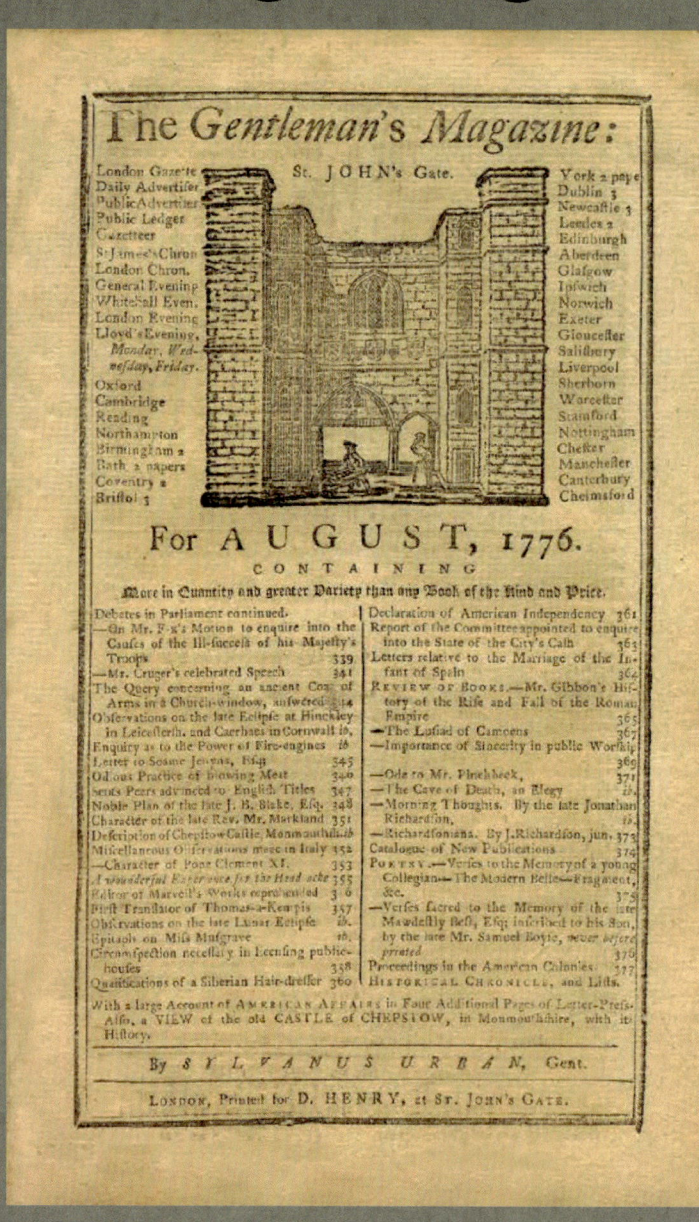

The word "magazine" in the context of a periodical comes from a military origin. It was first used by Edward Cave (pseudonym Sylvanus Urban) in 1731 for his *Gentleman's Magazine* of London, as it was intended as a "storehouse" of information, as the magazine of a ship.

First American Magazines

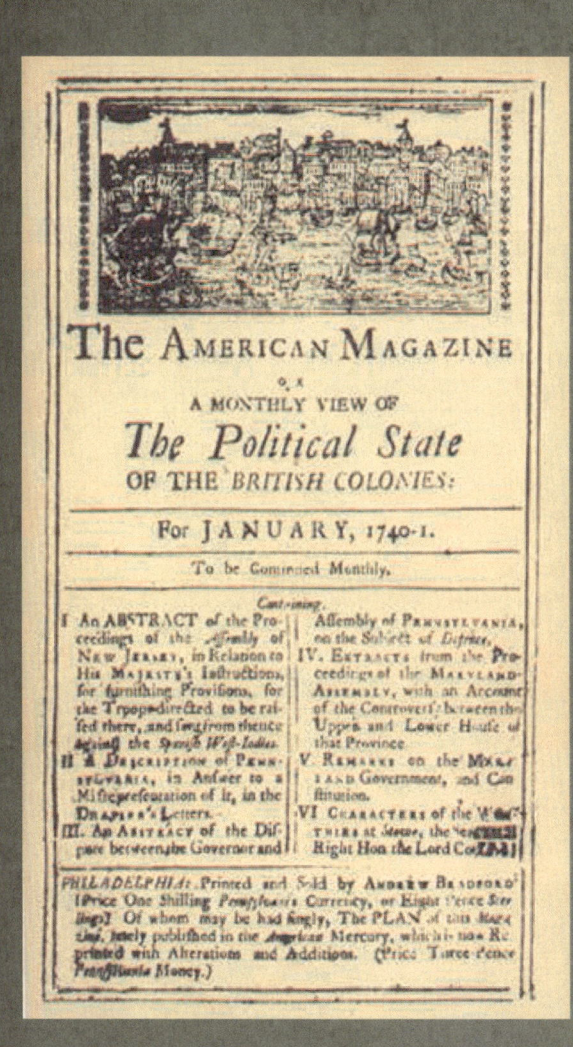

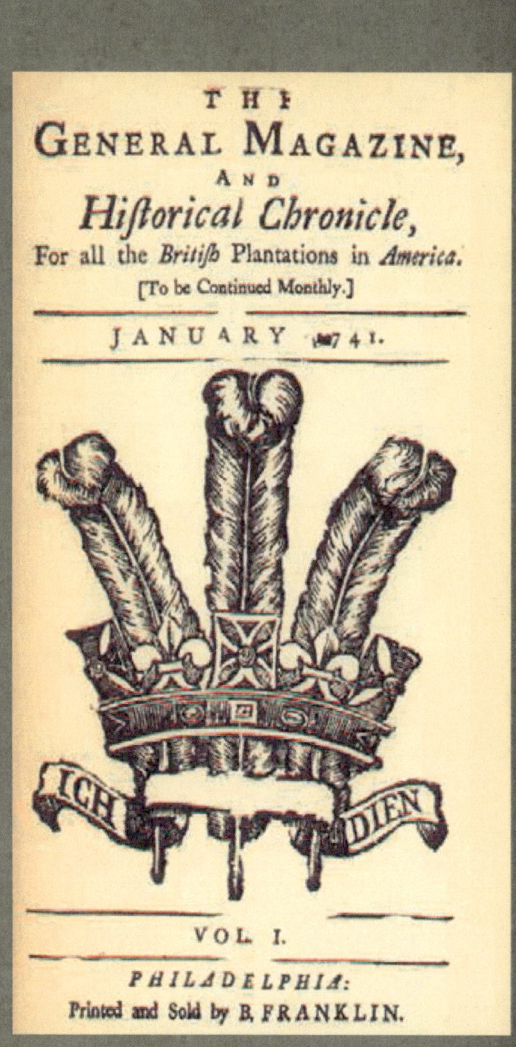

The first two exquisitely rare American magazines appeared in 1741. The idea came from Benjamin Franklin, who was beaten to press by three days by Andrew Bradford.

An Army of New Englanders under the command of Col. William Pepperell supported by an English Fleet under Commander Peter Warren attacked the fortress of Louisburg on April 30th 1745 and finally captured it on June 17th, a great British Victory which endangered the French position in North America. The fortifications were handed back to France in 1748 in the treaty of Aix-La-Chapelle.

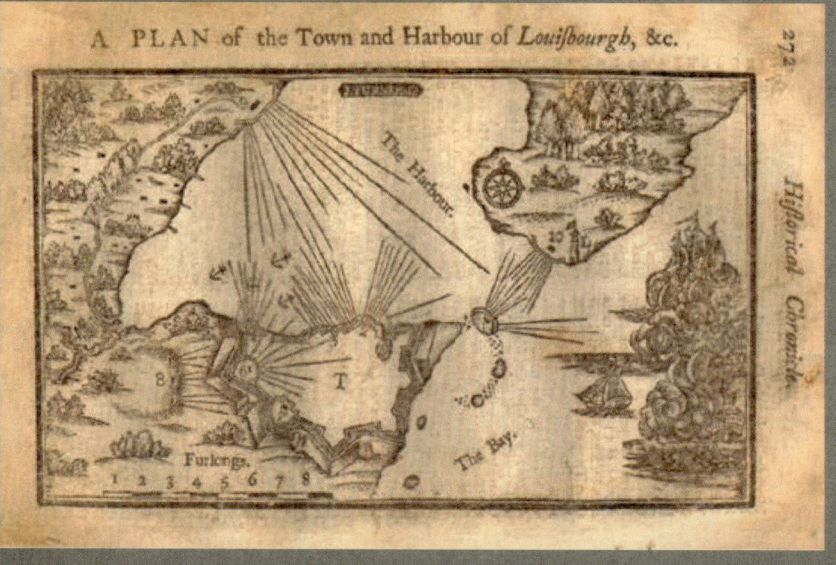

The fi st engraved plate in a American magazine

The Great American Magazine: America at War

French and Indian War

The only magazine published in the American colonies during the French and Indian War featured the first American political cartoon.

"Praevalebit Aequior" or, the more equitable will prevail

The motto amplifies the importance of the Native American in tipping the balance of the war. The Frenchman offers a tomahawk and a purse of money while the Englishman holds out a bible and roll of cloth.

This political cartoon editorializes that if Native Americans made the proper moral decision, that the British would prevail.

Revolutionary War

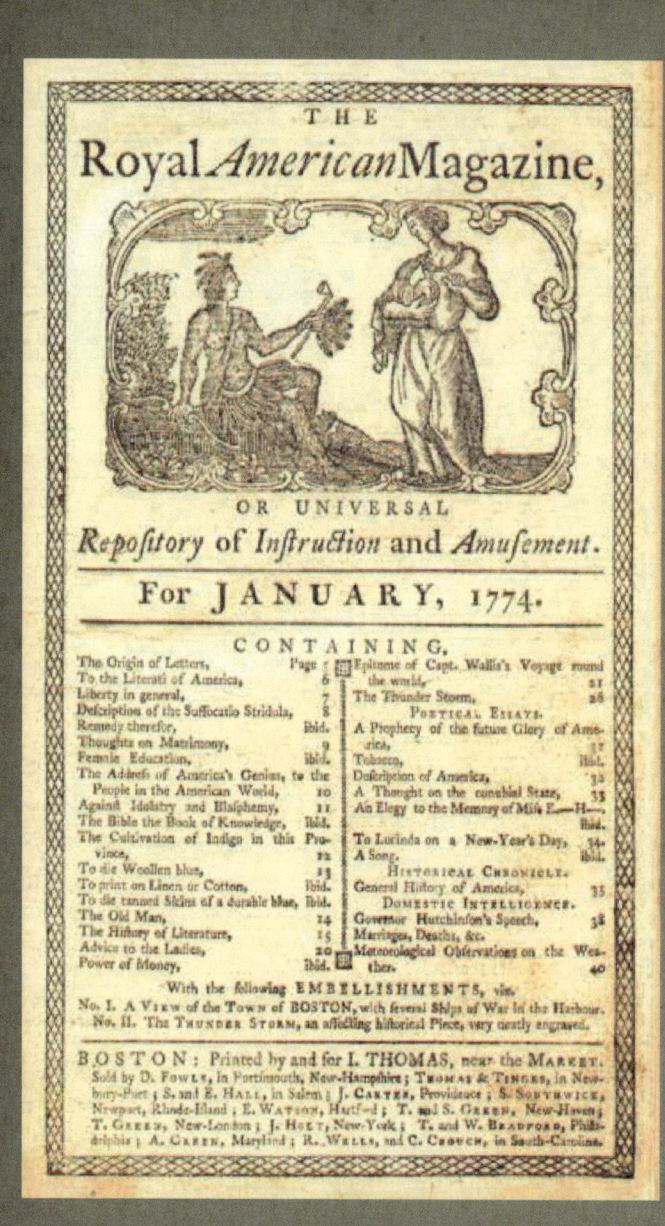

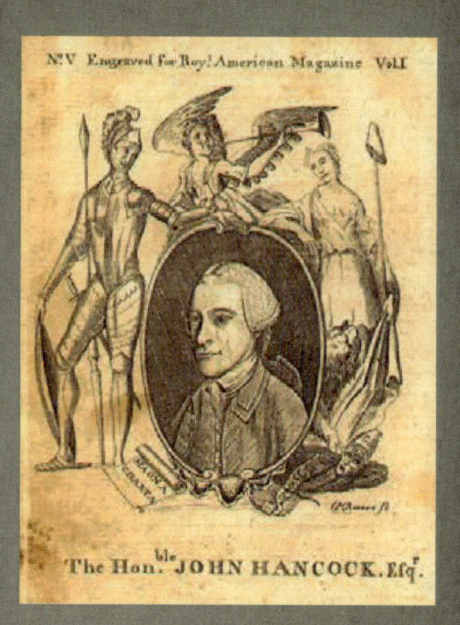

While the legend of Paul Revere's ride was created by Longfellow's 1861 poem in *Atlantic Monthly*. Revere's engravings in *Royal American Magazine* did much to incite colonial revolutionary passion.

The Great American Magazine: America at War

Thomas Paine's *Pennsylvania Magazine* was the only magazine printed in 1775 and 1776 The June 1776 issue contains the first printed notice of independence. The Declaration appeared in the last issue in July.

Phillis Wheatley's Ode to George Washington

Pennsylvania Magazine

April 1776

The following LETTER and VERSES, were written by the famous Phillis Wheatley, the African Poetess, and presented to his Excellency Gen. Washington.

SIR,

I Have taken the freedom to address your Excellency in the enclosed poem, and entreat your acceptance, though I am not insensible of its inaccuracies. Your being appointed by the Grand Continental Congress to be Generalissimo of the armies of North America, together with the fame of your virtues, excite sensations not easy to suppress. Your generosity, therefore, I presume, will pardon the attempt. Wishing your Excellency all possible success in the great cause you are so generously engaged in. I am,

Your Excellency's most obedient humble servant,

Providence, Oct. 26, 1775.
His Excellency Gen. Washington.
PHILLIS WHEATLEY.

Celestial choir! enthron'd in realms of light,
Columbia's scenes of glorious toils I write.
While freedom's cause her anxious breast alarms,
She flashes dreadful in refulgent arms.
See mother earth her offspring's fate bemoan,
And nations gaze at scenes before unknown!
See the bright beams of heaven's revolving light
Involved in sorrows and the veil of night!

The goddess comes, she moves divinely fair,
Olive and laurel binds her golden hair:
Wherever shines this native of the skies,
Unnumber'd charms and recent graces rise.

Muse! bow propitious while my pen relates
How pour her armies through a thousand gates:
As when Eolus heaven's fair face deforms,
Enwrapp'd in tempest and a night of storms;
Astonish'd ocean feels the wild uproar,
The refluent surges beat the sounding shore;
Or thick as leaves in Autumn's golden reign,
Such, and so many, moves the warrior's train.
In bright array they seek the work of war,
Where high unfurl'd the ensign waves in air.
Shall I to Washington their praise recite?
Enough thou know'st them in the fields of fight.
Thee, first in place and honours,—we demand
The grace and glory of thy martial band.
Fam'd for thy valour, for thy virtues more,
Hear every tongue thy guardian aid implore!

One century scarce perform'd its destin'd round,
When Gallic powers Columbia's fury found;
And so may you, whoever dares disgrace
The land of freedom's heaven-defended race!
Fix'd are the eyes of nations on the scales,
For in their hopes Columbia's arm prevails.
Anon Britannia droops the pensive head,
While round increase the rising hills of dead.
Ah! cruel blindness to Columbia's state!
Lament thy thirst of boundless power too late.

Proceed, great chief, with virtue on thy side,
Thy ev'ry action let the goddess guide.
A crown, a mansion, and a throne that shine,
With gold unfading, WASHINGTON! be thine.

The first literary work published by an African American

Boston Magazine
1783-1786

This is how most American's found out what these iconic men looked like!

The Monthly Military Repository

The first American Magazine devoted to the military, 1796

War of 1812

The first periodical published in America devoted to contemporary reports of a war.

The first printed image of the White House appeared in the British *Lady's Magazine*

DEFENCE OF FORT M'HENRY.

[These lines have been already published in several of our newspapers; they may still, however, be new to many of our readers. Besides, we think that their merit entitles them to preservation in some more permanent form than the columns of a daily paper. The annexed song was composed under the following circumstances.—A gentleman had left Baltimore, in a flag of truce for the purpose of getting released from the British fleet a friend of his who had been captured at Marlborough. He went as far as the mouth of the Patuxent, and was not permitted to return lest the intended attack on Baltimore should be disclosed. He was, therefore, brought up the bay to the mouth of the Patapsco, where the flag vessel was kept under the guns of a frigate, and he was compelled to witness the bombardment of Fort M'Henry, which the Admiral had boasted that he would carry in a few hours, and that the city must fall. He watched the flag at the fort through the whole day with an anxiety that can be better felt than described, until the night prevented him from seeing it. In the night he watched the bombshells, and at early dawn his eye was again greeted by the proudly-waving flag of his country.]

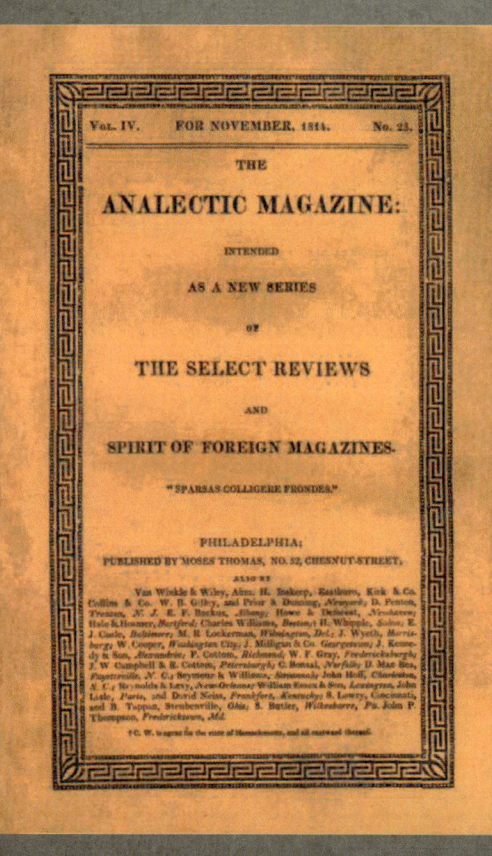

The first national appearance of what was to become "The Star Spangled Banner" published in *Analectic Magazine* in November 1814

POETRY.

DEFENCE OF FORT M‘HENRY.

[These lines have been already published in several of our newspapers; they may still, however, be new to many of our readers. Besides, we think that their merit entitles them to preservation in some more permanent form than the columns of a daily paper. The annexed song was composed under the following circumstances.—A gentleman had left Baltimore, in a flag of truce for the purpose of getting released from the British fleet a friend of his who had been captured at Marlborough. He went as far as the mouth of the Patuxent, and was not permitted to return lest the intended attack on Baltimore should be disclosed. He was, therefore, brought up the bay to the mouth of the Patapsco, where the flag vessel was kept under the guns of a frigate, and he was compelled to witness the bombardment of Fort M‘Henry, which the Admiral had boasted that he would carry in a few hours, and that the city must fall. He watched the flag at the fort through the whole day with an anxiety that can be better felt than described, until the night prevented him from seeing it. In the night he watched the bomb-shells, and at early dawn his eye was again greeted by the proudly-waving flag of his country.]

Tune—ANACREON IN HEAVEN.

O! say can you see, by the dawn's early light,
  What so proudly we hail'd at the twilight's last gleaming,
Whose broad stripes and bright stars through the perilous fight,
  O'er the ramparts we watch'd, were so gallantly streaming?
    And the rockets' red glare, the bombs bursting in air,
    Gave proof through the night that our flag was still there—
      O! say, does that star-spangled banner yet wave
      O'er the land of the free, and the home of the brave?

On the shore, dimly seen through the mists of the deep,
  Where the foe's haughty host in dread silence reposes,
What is that which the breeze o'er the towering steep,
  As it fitfully blows, half conceals, half discloses?
    Now it catches the gleam of the morning's first beam,
    In full glory reflected now shines on the stream—
      'Tis the star-spangled banner, O! long may it wave
      O'er the land of the free, and the home of the brave.

And where is that band who so vauntingly swore
  That the havock of war and the battle's confusion
A home and a country should leave us no more?
  Their blood has wash'd out their foul foot-steps' pollution.

VOL. IV. New Series.

The Mexican War

The most comprehensive magazine accounts of the Mexican War were published in this New York humor magazine. It featured the serialization of "Authentic Anecdotes of Old Zack" (Taylor) By Herman Melville.

The Great American Magazine: America at War

The Civil War

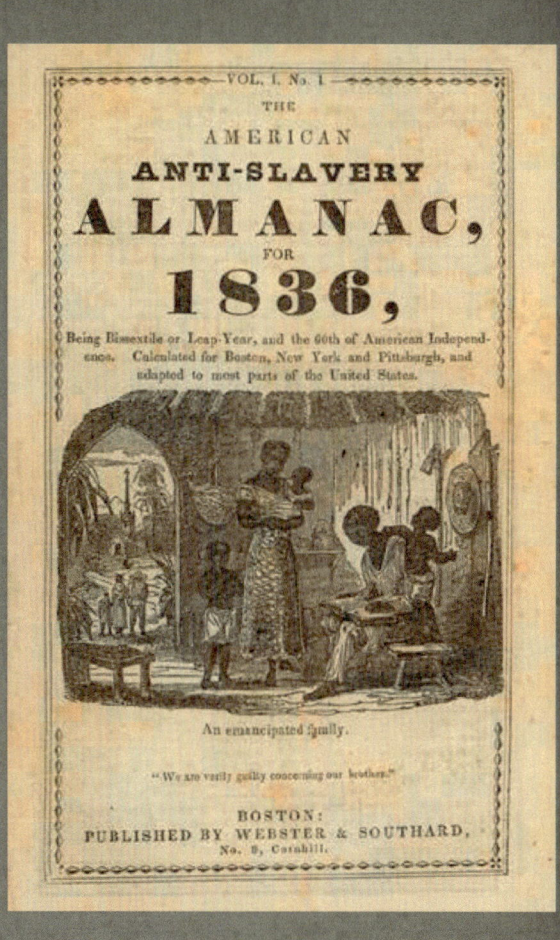

The magazine roots of anti-slavery sentiment
extend back to the 1830's

THE ABOLITIONIST:

OR RECORD OF THE

NEW-ENGLAND ANTI-SLAVERY SOCIETY.

VOL. I.] JANUARY, 1833. [NO. I.

EDITED BY A COMMITTEE.

CONTENTS.

Introductory Remarks	1	Census of 1830	10
New-England Anti-Slavery Society	2	Why and Because	"
American Colonization Society	3	Plain Questions to Plain Men	11
Eloquent Extract	"	Letter to George Washington	"
Prayer for Deliverance	4	A Negro's Soliloquy	14
Safety of Immediate Emancipation	"	Poetry—Song of the Angel—	
Letters from James Cropper	6	The Child's Evening Hymn—	
Letter to Thomas Clarkson	8	The Slave's Appeal	16

BOSTON:
PRINTED BY GARRISON AND KNAPP, AGENTS FOR PRINTING AND PUBLISHING THE ABOLITIONIST—TO WHOM SUBSCRIPTIONS ARE TO BE PAID, AND ALL LETTERS DIRECTED, RELATING TO THE WORK.

Postage, less than 100 miles, one cent—any greater distance, one cent and a half.

THE COLONIZATIONIST

AND

JOURNAL OF FREEDOM.

No. I.

CONTENTS.

BOSTON:
PUBLISHED BY GEORGE W. LIGHT & Co.
Lyceum Press, 3 Cornhill.

APRIL, 1833.

The Great American Magazine: America at War 172

William Lloyd Garrison's *Liberator* was the most important abolitionist periodical

Rare and important periodicals published by African-Americans Frederick Douglass and the nearly forgotten Martin Robinson Delaney

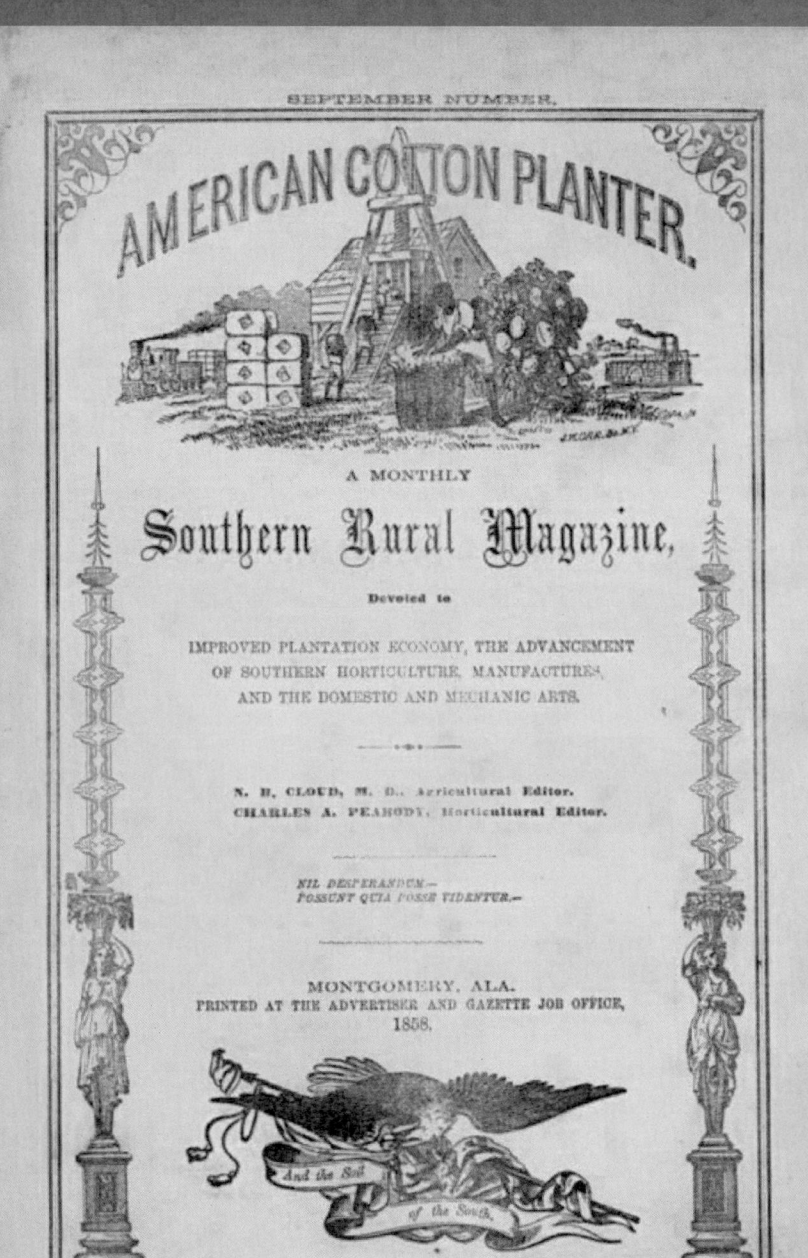

The motto of this 1858 Alabama Magazine speaks volumes

Uncle Tom's Cabin

The serialization of Harriet Beecher Stowe's classic in this abolitionist periodical was one of the most important factors to incite the Civil War

Union Magazines

The two most widely circulated periodicals in the North were *Harper's Weekly* and Frank Leslie's *Illustrated Newspaper*. The engraving of a beardless Lincoln, taken from a Matthew Brady photo did much to promote Lincoln's image. Winslow Homer's 1862 image of sharpshooter is his most important of the era.

177 The Great American Magazine: America at War

Frank Leslie's Illustrated Newspaper published the best contemporary images of the Lincoln assassination

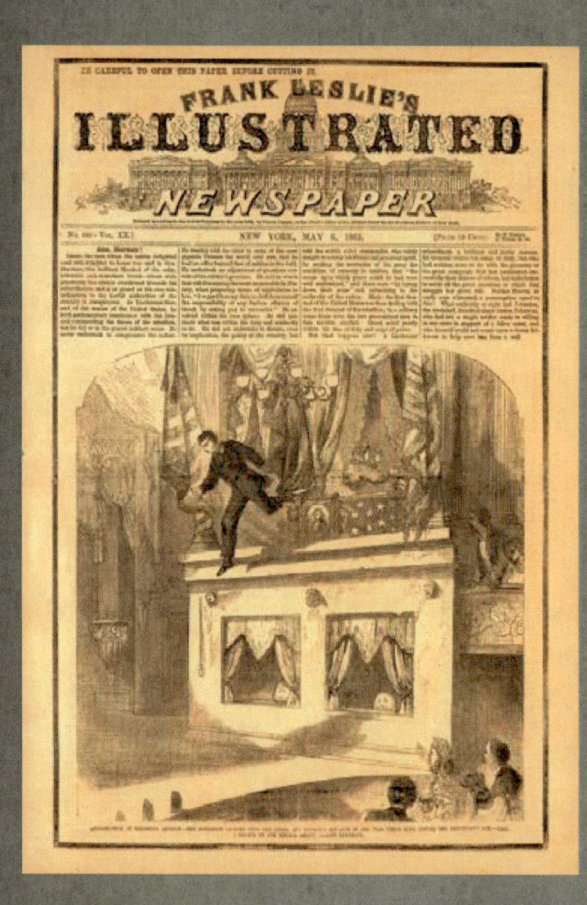

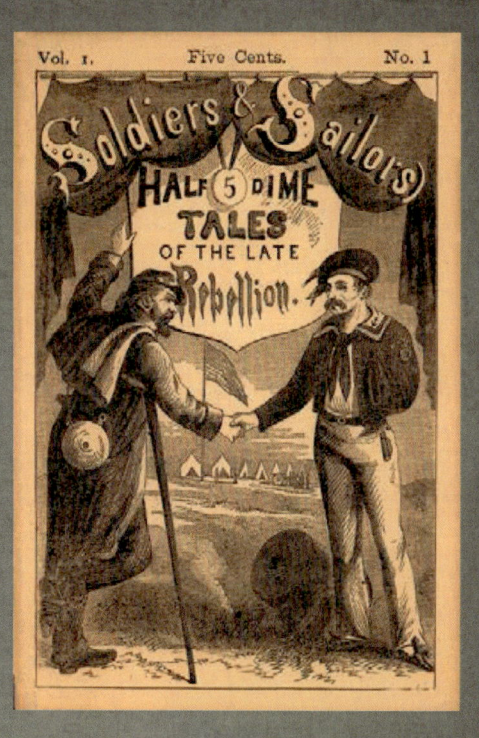

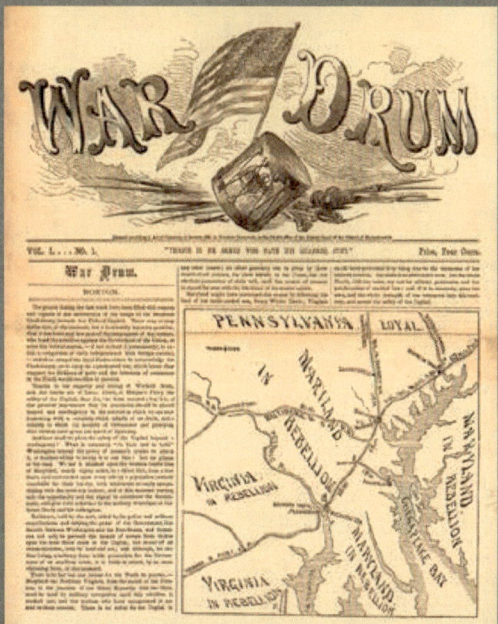

There is a nearly countless panoply of Union magazines, including short-lived publications associated with "sanitary fairs", akin to today's Red Cross. Dime Novels and Story papers romanticized the massive carnage during and after the war.

The Great American Magazine: America at War

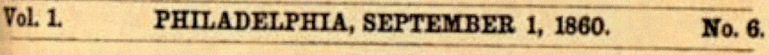

There was even an astrological publication that featured Lincoln's horoscope in 1860 and correctly forewarned of his assassination in April 1865!

Confederate Magazines

Confederate publications are far scarcer due to lack of raw materials. General Lee's account of the Pennsylvania campaign is featured on the first page of this official journal.

Southern Illustrated News

The *Southern Illustrated News* was the Confederate equivalent of *Harper's Weekly*, though issues are considerably scarcer and more valuable to collectors

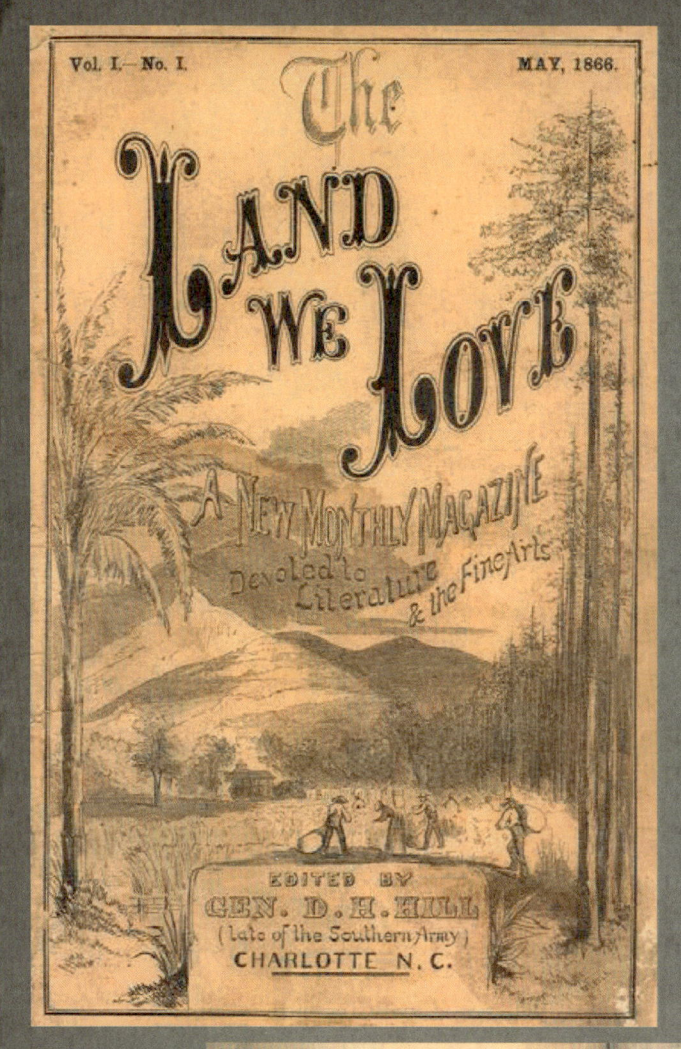

This magazine was founded in 1866 by the brother of General A.P. Hill

Copperhead Magazines

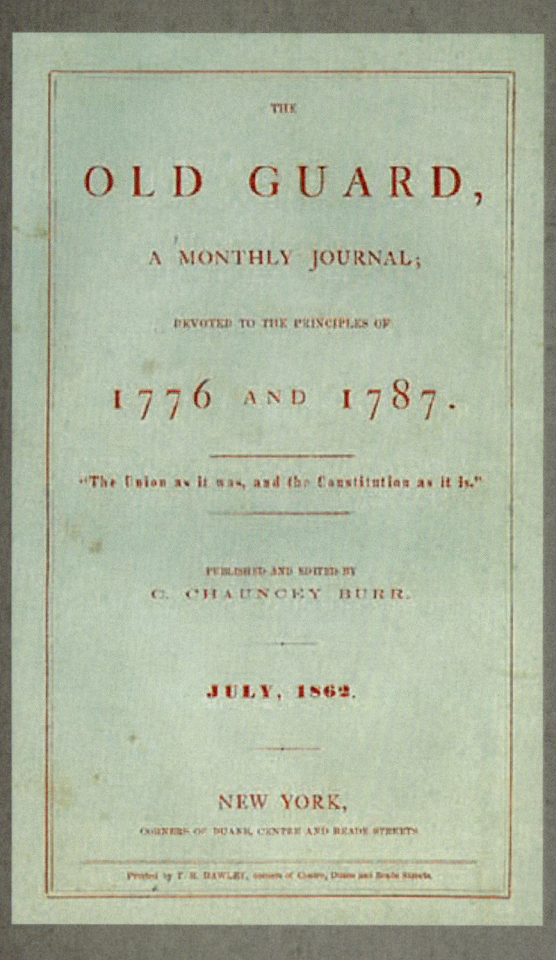

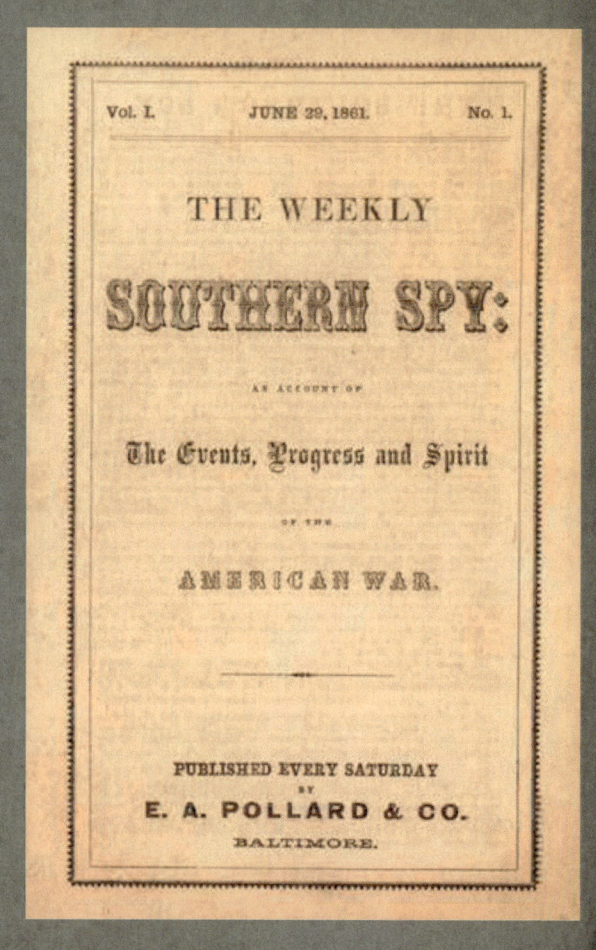

"Copperhead" magazines were printed in the North by those with Southern sympathies. *The Old* Guard is the most common.

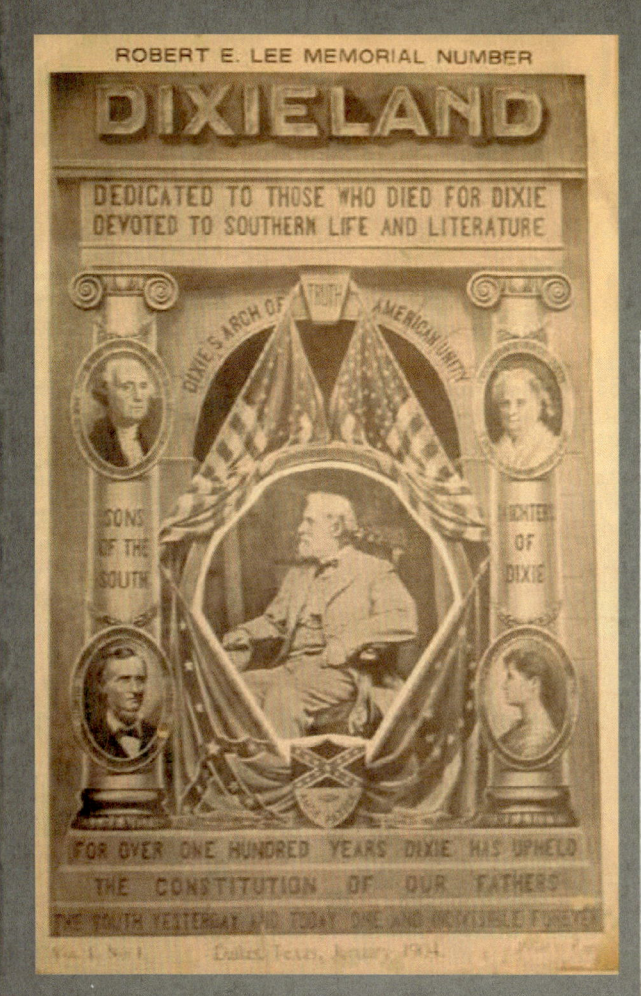

For many years after the war, periodicals reflected ongoing Southern sympathies

While in the north, military publishing focused on the veteran

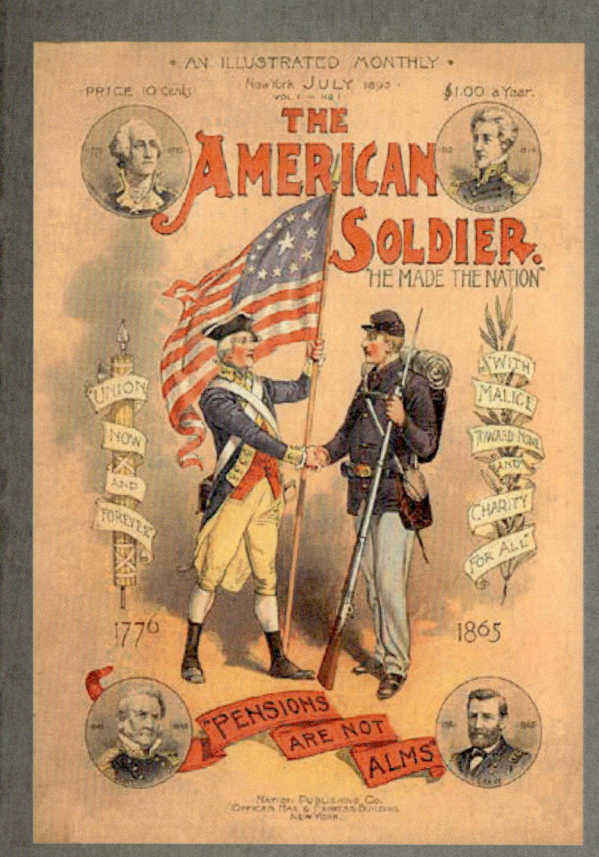

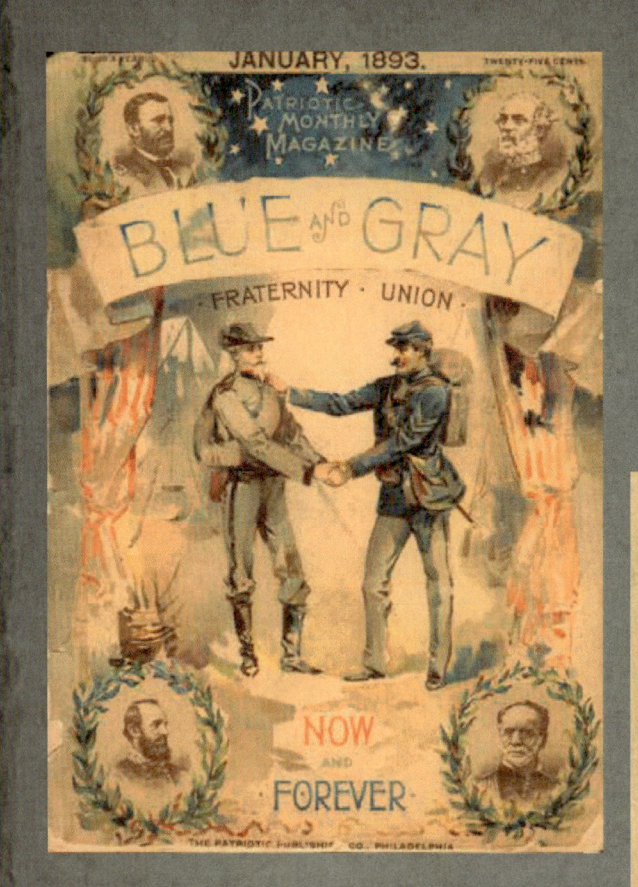

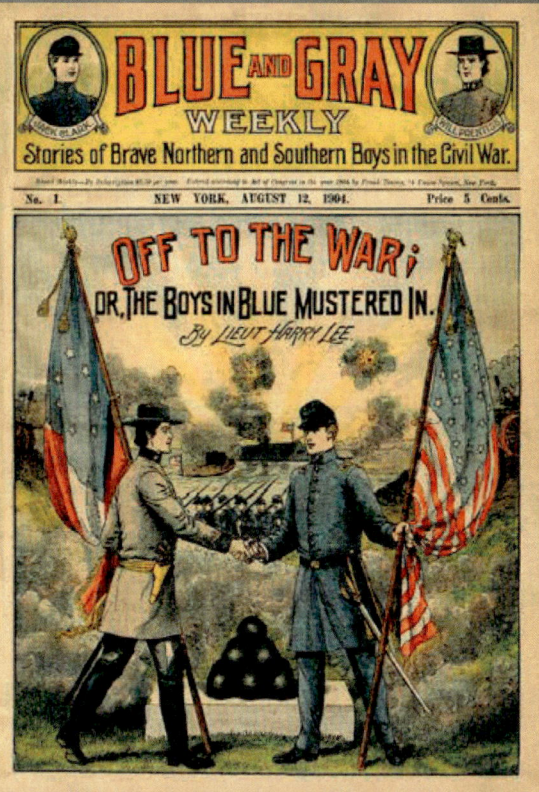

Eventually a spirit of reconciliation predominated.

The Spanish American War

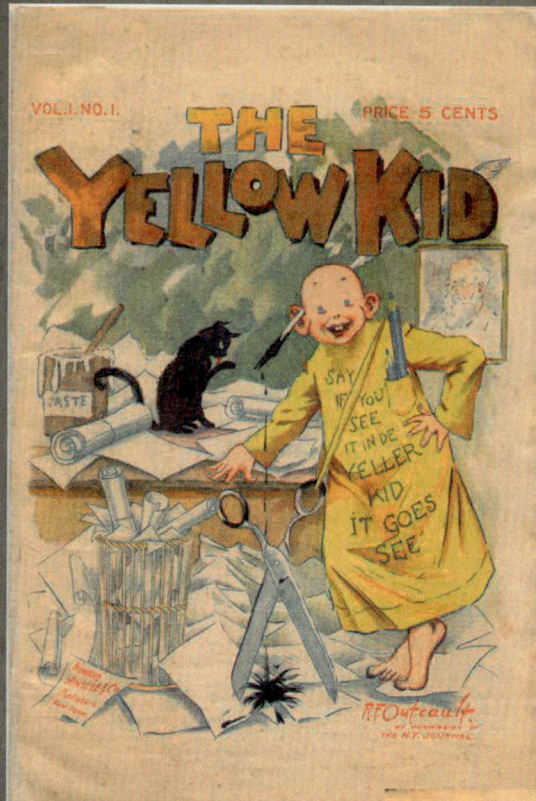

The Spanish American War was greatly influenced by journalists, especially William Randolph Hearst and Joseph Pulitzer whose competition over R.F. Outcault's cartoon character, The Yellow Kid, and blatant sensationalism spurred the term **Yellow Journalism**

"You furnish the pictures,
I'll furnish the war!"
A telegram allegedly sent by
William Randolph Hearst to
Frederic Remington.

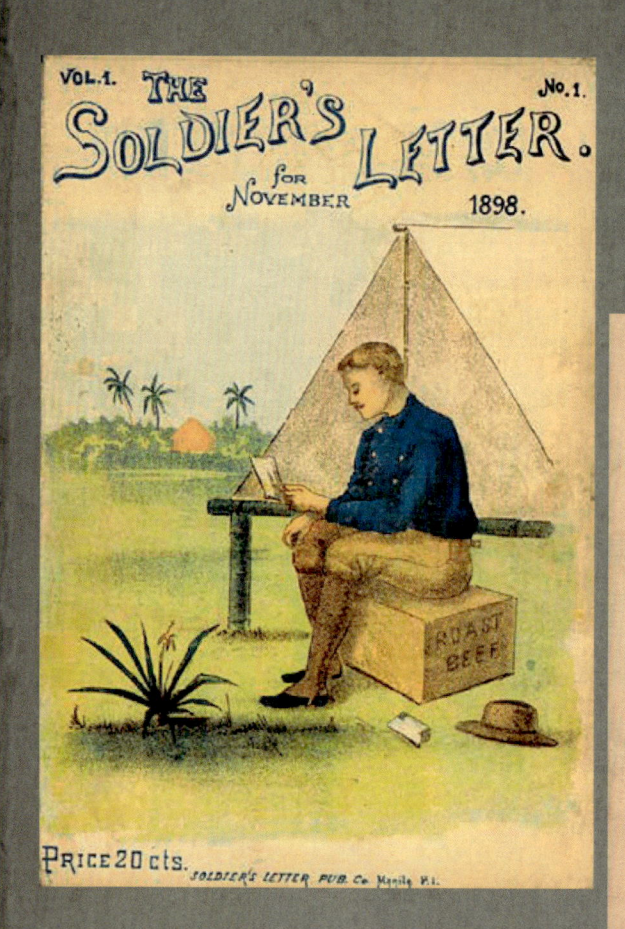

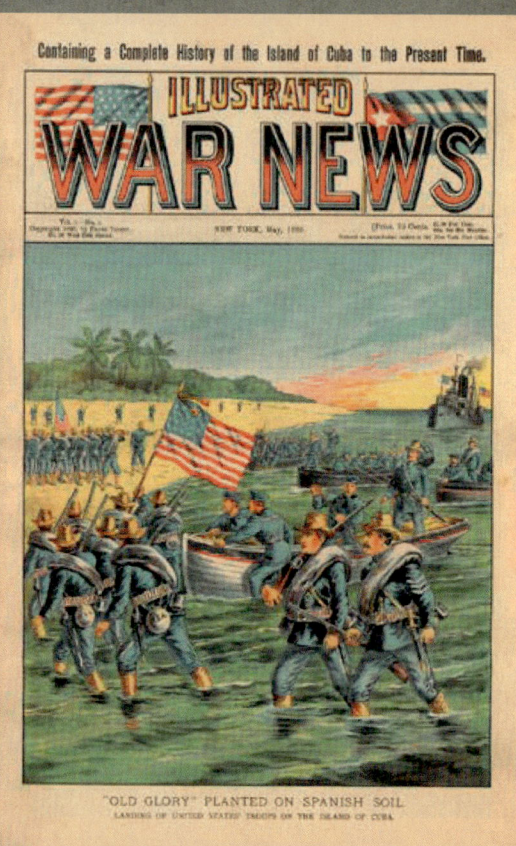

In the golden age of American illustration, magazines were graphically beautiful. *The Soldier's Letter*, issued by American forces in the Philippines, was the first to be published overseas.

The Great American Magazine: America at War

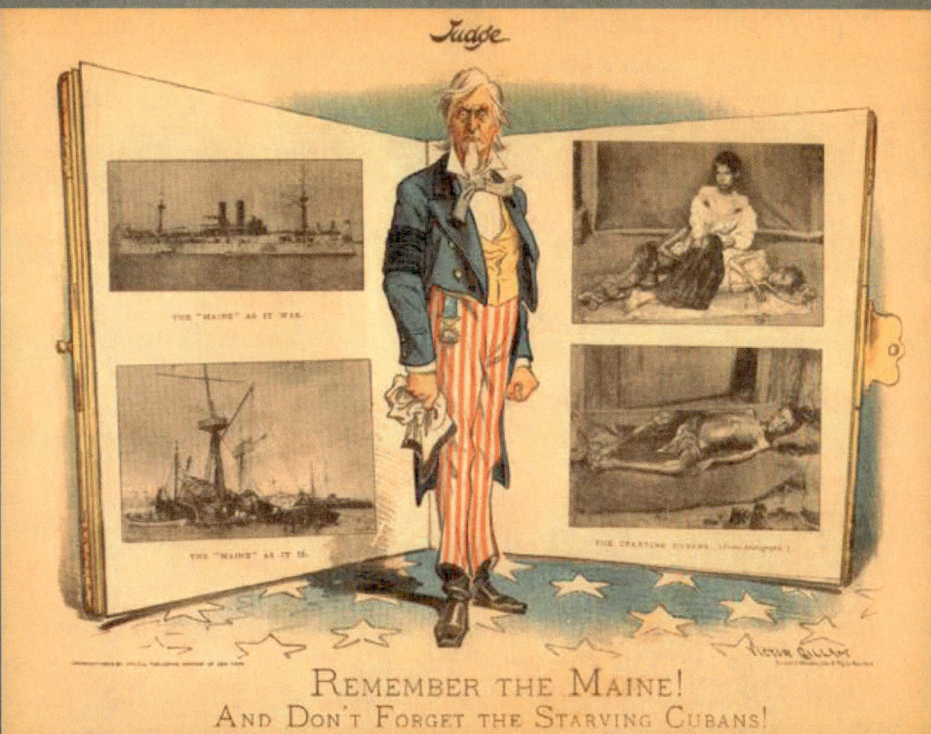

World War One

James Montgomery Flagg's iconic image of Uncle Sam, the most famous American image of the war, was adapted from a 1914 British poster of Lord Kitchener. It appeared twice on the cover of *Leslie's Illustrated Weekly Newspaper*, the second with the caption "I Want You". The famous poster was released after the magazine.

There are dozens of First World War magazine images, including those issued for the AEF in France.

The Great American Magazine: America at War

The Great American Magazine: America at War   194

Not all were pro-British!

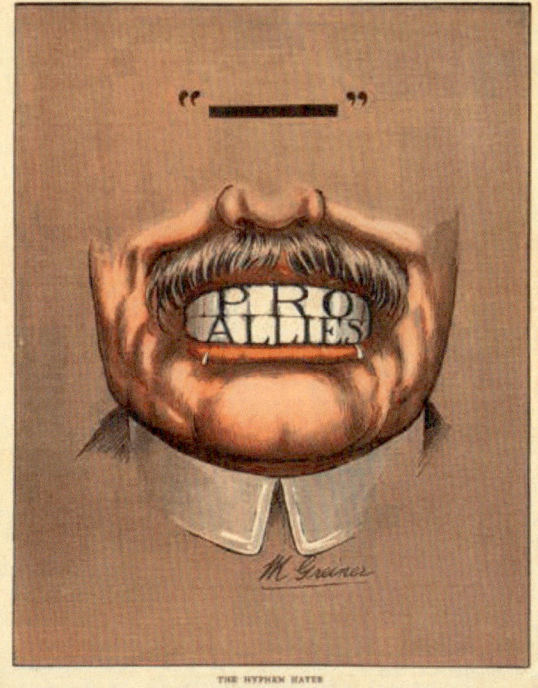

George Harvey's *War Weekly* was the most important and comprehensive title

Pulp Magazines

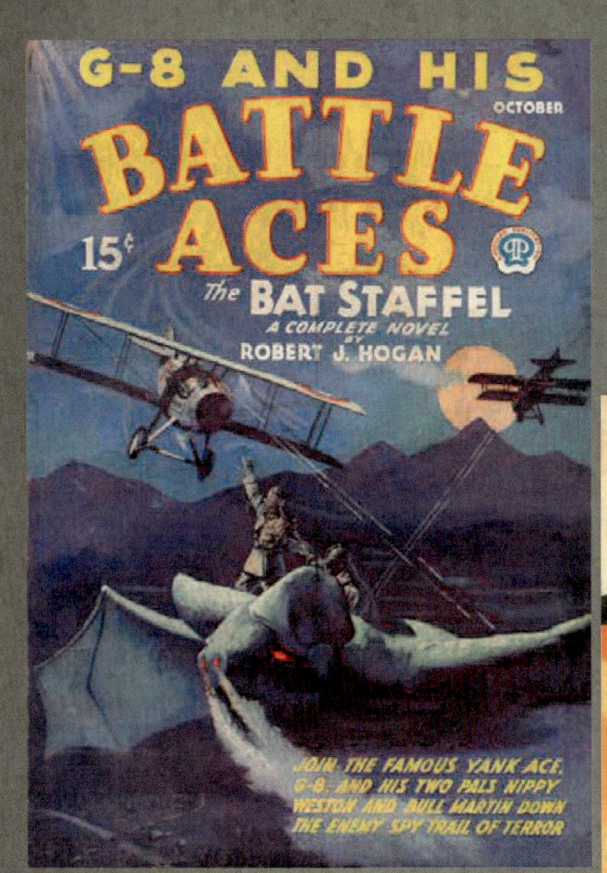

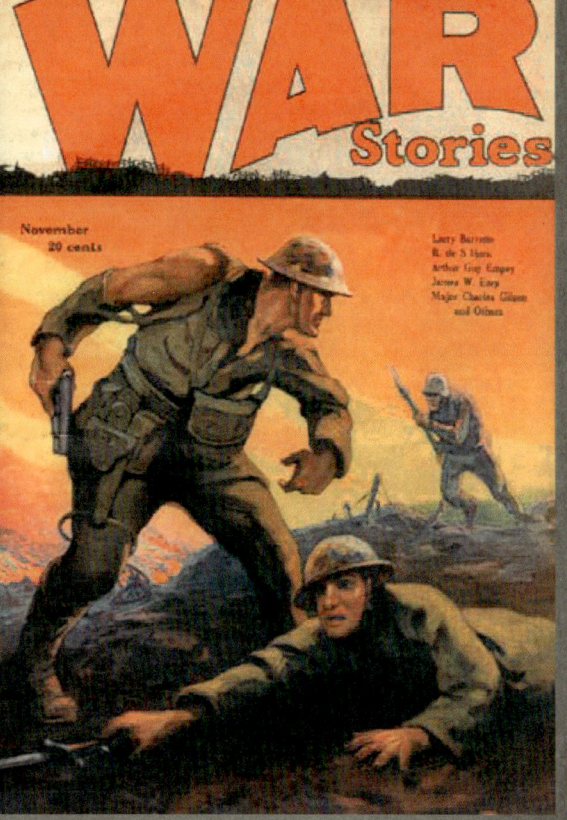

The Great American Magazine: America at War 198

AIR STORIES
BY
REAL AIRMEN
FLYING
ACES
20¢
OCT.
GANGSTERS OF THE AIR
by EUSTACE L. ADAMS
THE PILOT
WHO FOUND
HIMSELF
THE
DEATH DIVE
by ACE WILLIAMS
A Bookfull of Air Thrills

MARCH
AIRPLANE
STORIES
25¢
30¢ IN CANADA
Knights of the Thunder
by John Gerard
The Blizzard Buster
by David Kent
and other Thrilling Stories of Air Action

The Great American Magazine: America at War   200

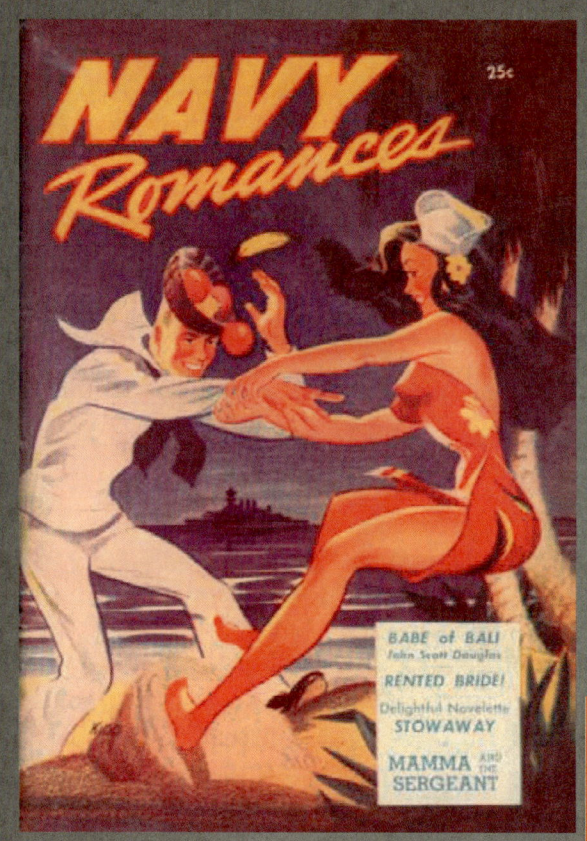

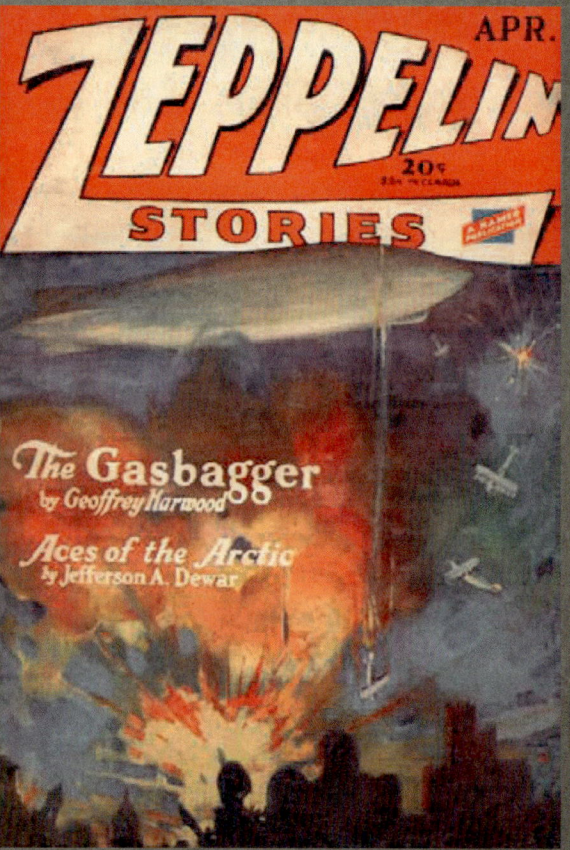

World War Two

Magazines heralded the upcoming conflict beginning in the early thirties

201 The Great American Magazine: America at War

United We Stand July 1942

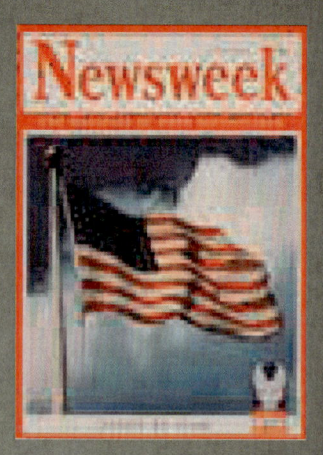

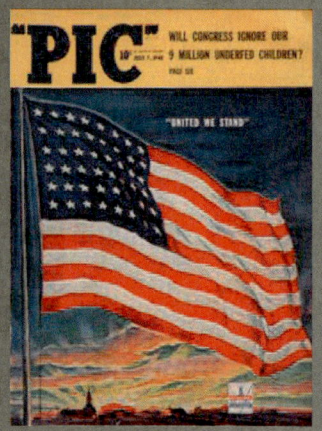

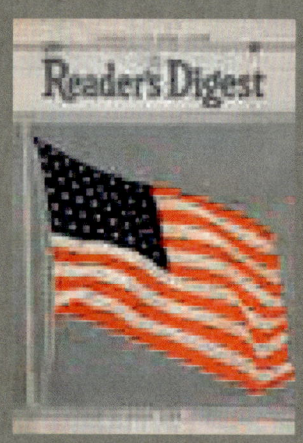

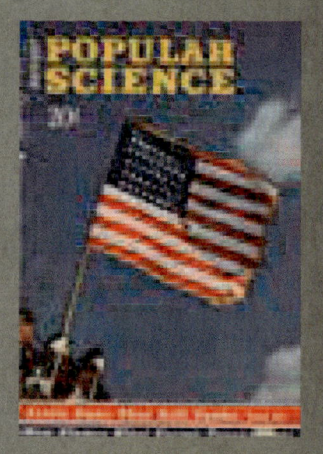

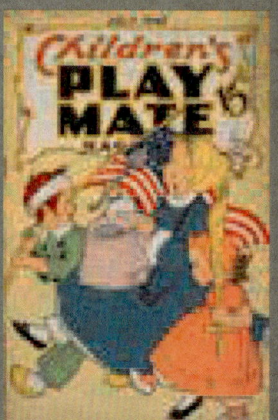

As a sign of unity and resolve, in July 1942, every magazine included a flag

203 The Great American Magazine: America at War

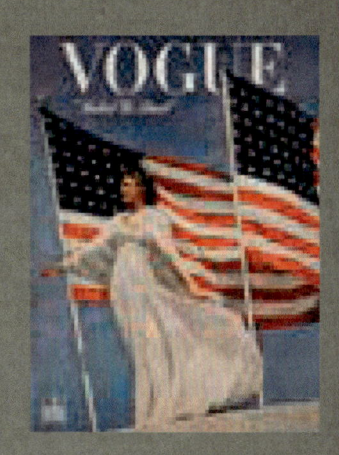

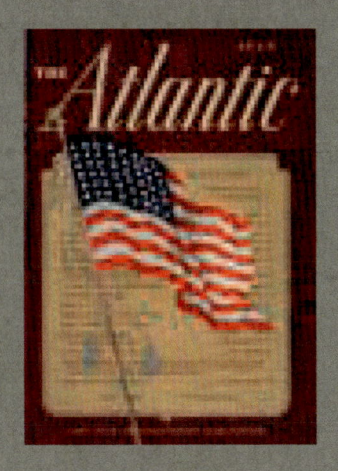

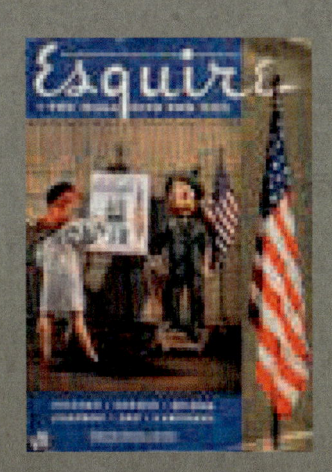

The Great American Magazine: America at War   204

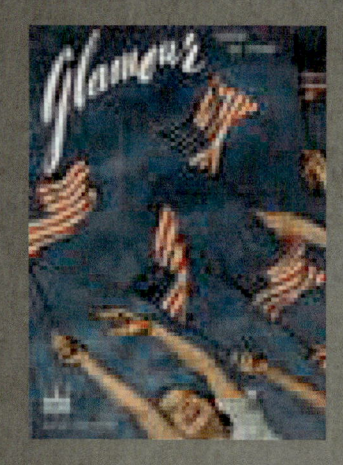

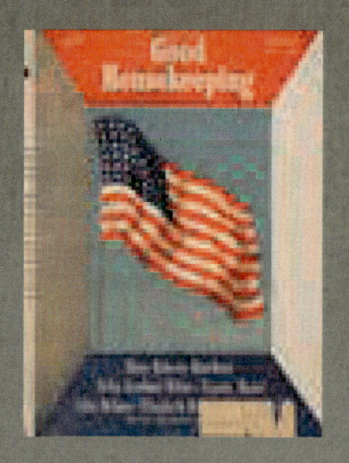

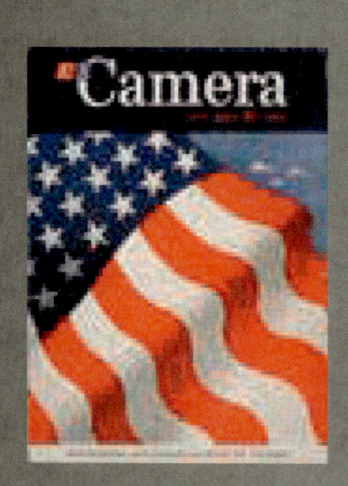

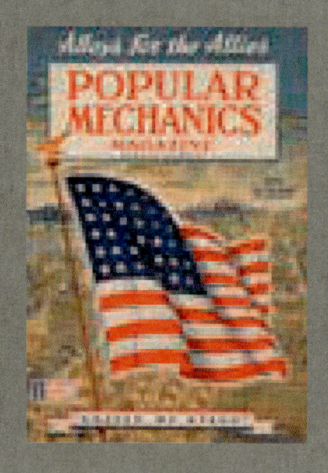

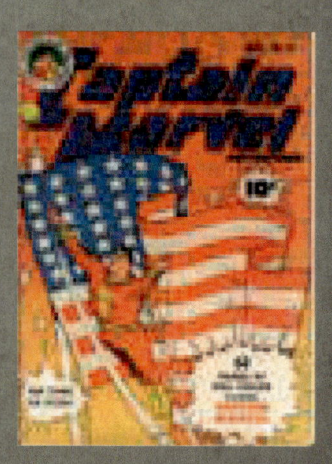

The massive war effort produced a cornucopia of war images

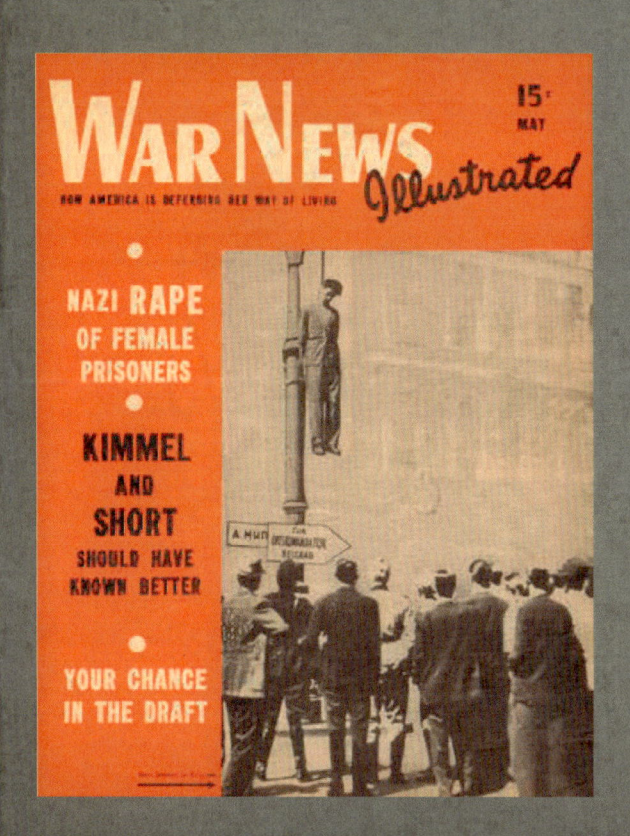

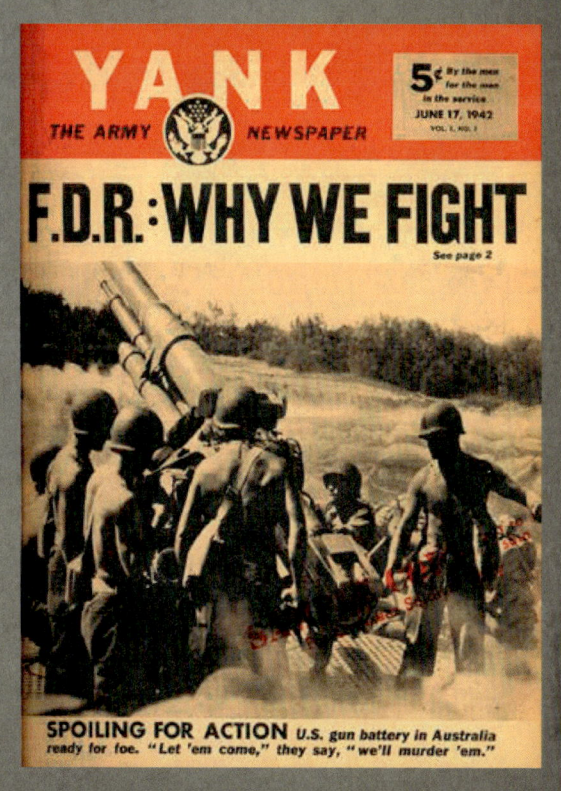

The Great American Magazine: America at War

Der GAG Bag

"Mein Chump"

15¢ Or 15 Days in a Concentration Camp

Including this parody of Hitler as Edgar Bergen

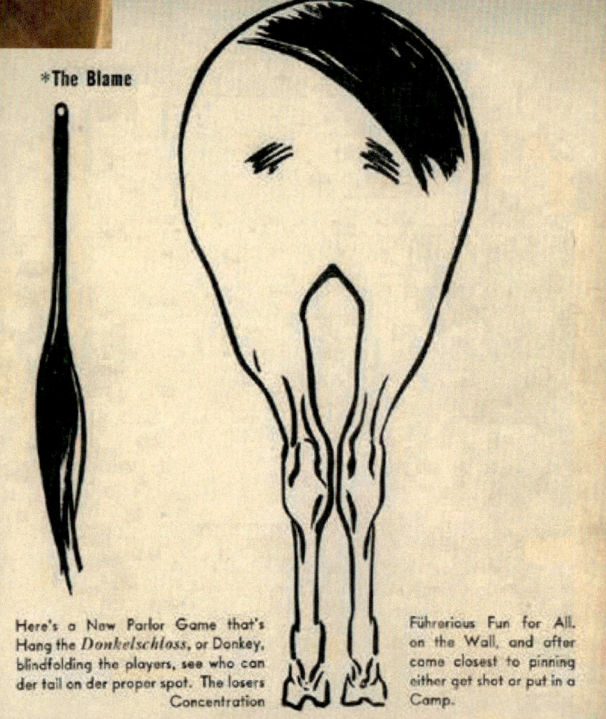

*The Blame

Here's a New Parlor Game that's Fuhrerious Fun for All. Hang the *Donkelschloss*, or Donkey, on the Wall, and after blindfolding the players, see who can come closest to pinning der tail on der proper spot. The losers either get shot or put in a Concentration Camp.

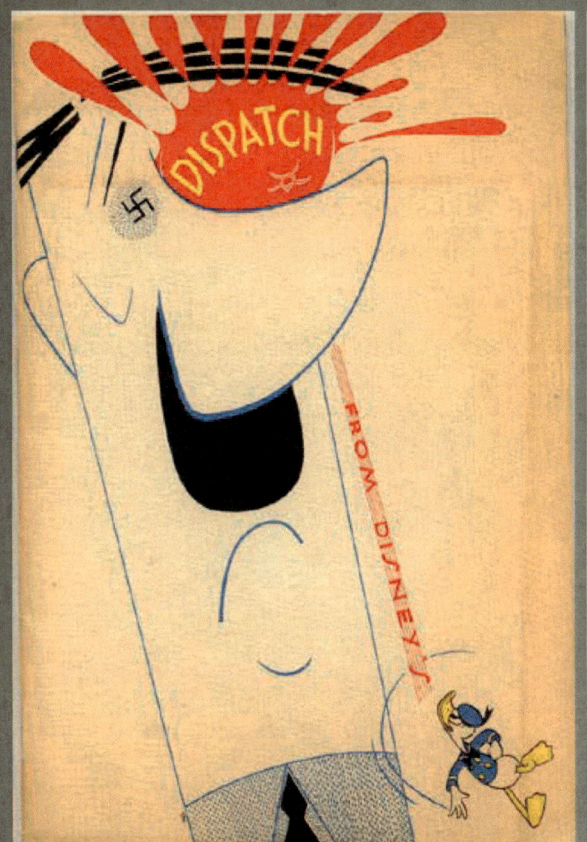

And this from Disney Studios that was sent to all of its former employees overseas, including a racy (and controversial) centerfold pinup. The cover theme is from the Disney cartoon "Der Fuehrer's Face", that won an Oscar and was later banned.

The generation's greatest illustrator, Norman Rockwell, pitched in with many covers for the Saturday Evening Post, the most memorable of "Rosie the Riveter", adapted from a drawing by Michaelangelo. He also created a series of paintings of "Willie Gillis" his prototypical American GI, here seen on "pony editions" intended for soldiers overseas.

The most famous image to come out of the war was Joe Rosenthal's iconic photo of the second flag raising at Iwo Jima. The crude wire photo first appeared on a military newspaper and was shortly reproduced on a national magazine.

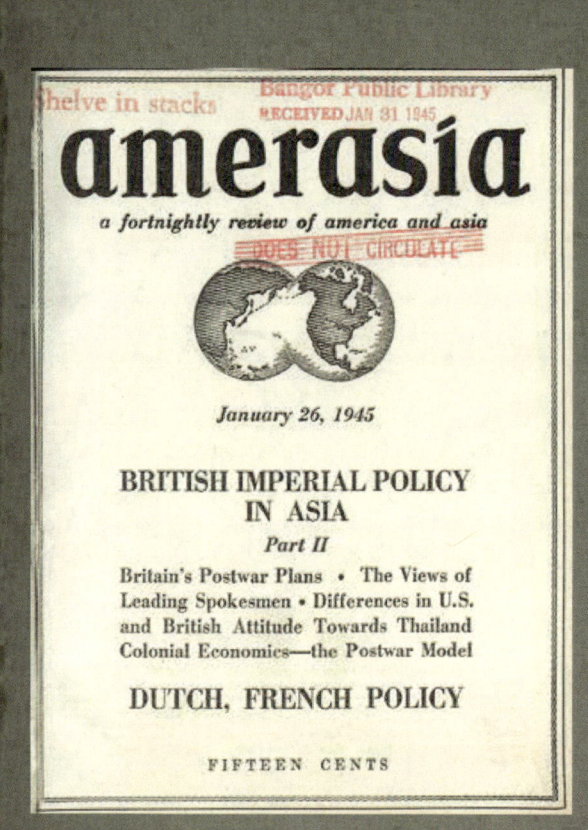

Wikileaks notwithstanding, the publishing of top secret State Department documents in Amerasia magazine created a firestorm that was later to fuel the red-baiting of Senator Joseph McCarthy. Henry Luce's LIFE magazine provided the best record of ongoing WW2 photojournalism, including this one from VJ day.

Korea

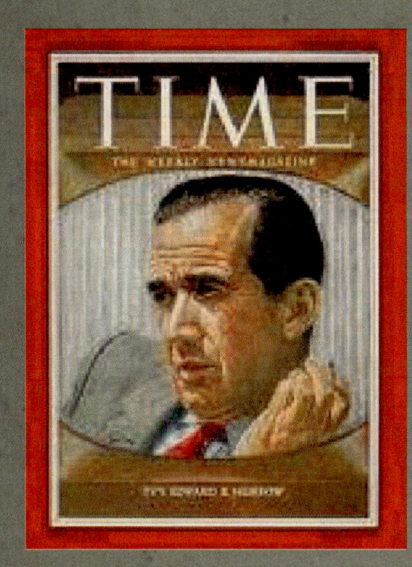

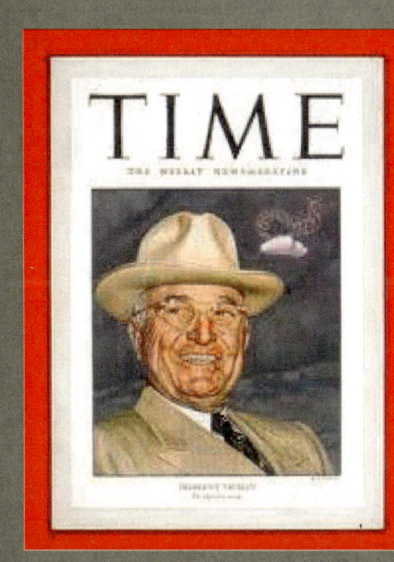

Quite remarkably, there are no iconic images from the Korean War. The cover of Time Magazine featured the personalities of this turbulent era

The Cold War

In 1956, a cultural exchange program provided an opportunity for America and the Soviet Union to put their best foot forward.

Vietnam

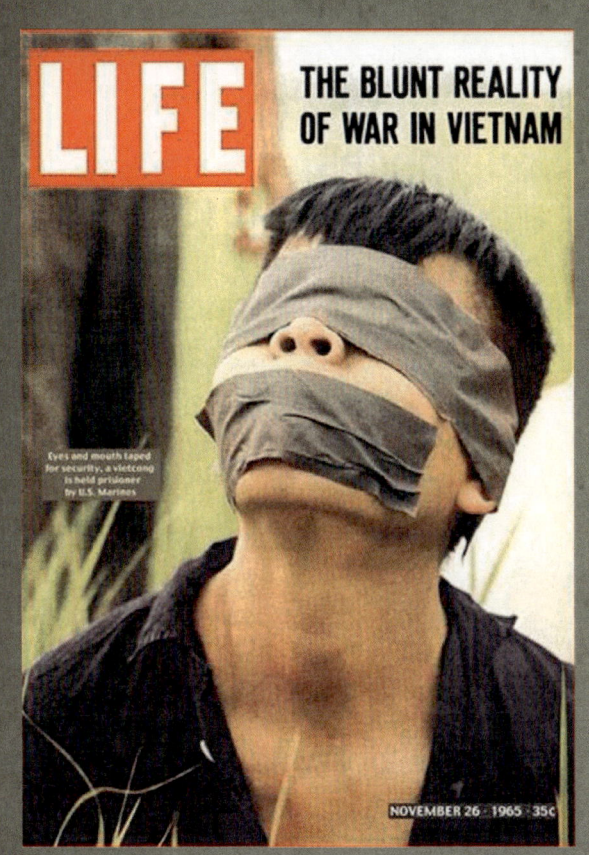

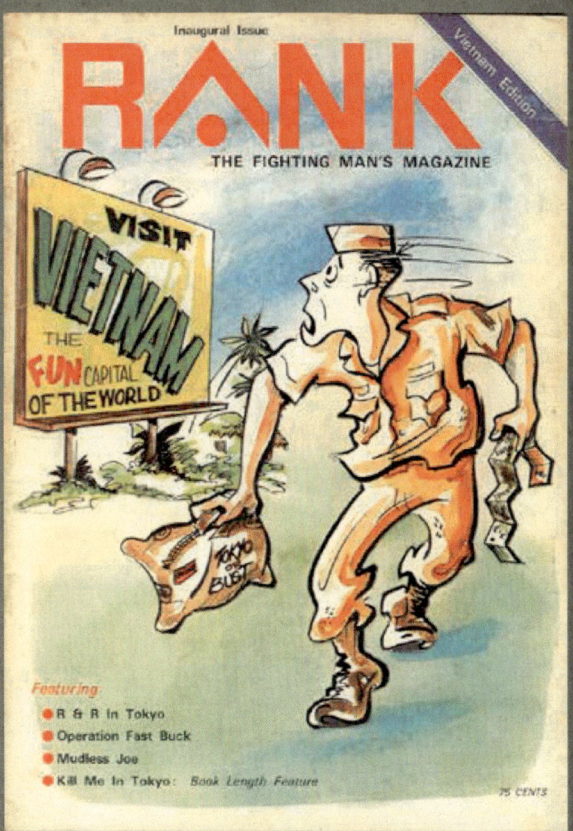

The War in Vietnam was reported with distinctly greater candor than any previous conflict. *Rank* was published in Vietnam predominantly as a Tokyo tour guide for soldiers on liberty.

LIFE — Changed War Convulsion in Politics

"...I shall not seek and I will not accept the nomination of my party for another term as your President."

APRIL 12 · 1968 · 35¢

These two magazines have the same issue date. The first was pulled after the even more monumental tragedy of the assassination of Martin Luther King.

LIFE — WEEK OF SHOCK
- Vietnam: Burst of Hope
- Convulsion in U.S. Politics
- EXCLUSIVE PICTURES The Murder in Memphis

Martin Luther King
1929 – 1968

APRIL 12 · 1968 · 35¢

The Great American Magazine: America at War

Likewise, this Orangutan cover was rapidly changed when a shocking and dramatic photo of a legless child was received.

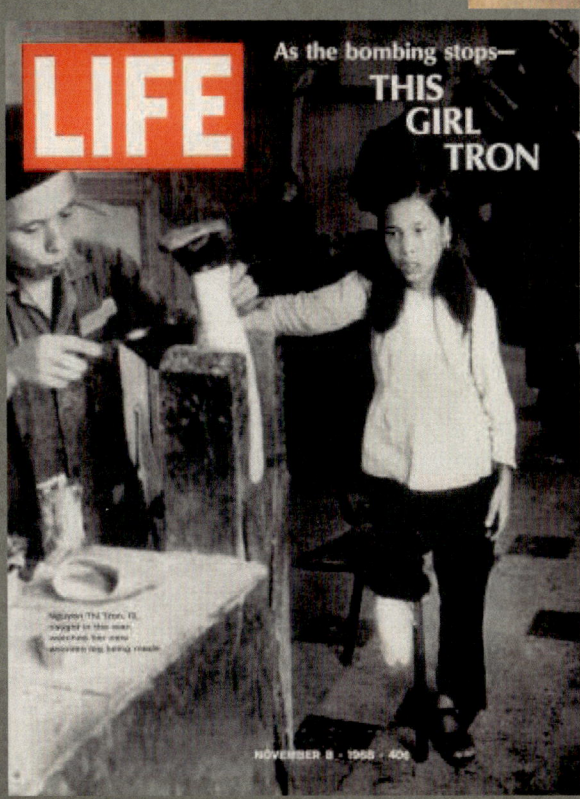

215   The Great American Magazine: America at War

Made in the USA
Columbia, SC
11 April 2019